COMMUNICATING OUT OF A CRISIS

Communicating Out of a Crisis

Michael Bland

MACMILLAN
Business

First published 1998 by
MACMILLAN PRESS LTD
Houndmills, Basingstoke, Hampshire RG21 6XS
and London
Companies and representatives
throughout the world

ISBN 0–333–72097–0

A catalogue record for this book is available from the British Library.

10   9   8   7   6   5   4   3   2   1
07   06   05   04   03   02   01   00   99   98

Copy-edited and typeset by Povey–Edmondson
Tavistock and Rochdale, England

Printed and bound in Great Britain by
Antony Rowe Ltd
Chippenham, Wiltshire

The Moving Finger writes; and, having writ,
Moves on: nor all thy Piety nor Wit
Shall lure it back to cancel half a Line,
Nor all thy Tears wash out a Word of it.

The Rubaiyat of Omar Khayyam
(trans. Edward Fitzgerald)

Contents

CASE STUDIES

List of Figures

Acknowledgements

In addition to the contributors of sections and case studies for this book, the author would like to thank the following people for their help:

Jonathan Church, Susan Croft (Hill & Knowlton), Carol Felton (Courtaulds), Hilary Gallagher (Courtaulds), Natasha Gould (Leeds Metropolitan University), Matt Huber (RMC), Dr Peter M. Sandman (Rutgers University), John Stonborough (John Stonborough & Co.).

The author and publishers wish to thank the following for their kind permission to reproduce copyright material:

Chapman & Hall: *Crisis Management in the Food Industry* by Colin Doeg, 1995
Blackwell Publishers: 'The Role of the Internet' in *Business Ethics*, Jan 1997
News International Syndication for the use of the *Sun* montage

Every effort has been made to contact all the copyright-holders, but if any have been inadvertently omitted the publishers will be pleased to make the necessary arrangement at the earliest opportunity.

List of Contributors

Joseph L. Badaracco Jr   John Shad Professor of Business Ethics, Harvard Business School

Colin Doeg   a former journalist, now a public relations consultant

Colin Duncan   Director of Public Affairs, British Nuclear Fuels plc

Christopher Flint   Group Security Adviser, Cadbury Schweppes plc

Kate Graham   handled the PR response to the Piper Alpha disaster and now provides consultancy and management training in media response and lectures widely in crisis management

Matthew J. Harrington   Executive Vice President/General Manager of a leading PR company, Edelman Worldwide, based in San Francisco

John D. Noulton   Public Affairs Director, Eurotunnel

Jeff Simms   journalist with a design, marketing and publishing agency, Picquet Communications

Jonathan Street   Managing Director of Jonathan Street Public Relations

Tim Taylor   solicitor and partner in Hill Taylor Dickinson with experience of several high-profile disaster cases

Francis Thomas   Group Media Relations Manager, The Boots Company plc

Cheryl Travers   lecturer in organisational behaviour and human resource management at The Business School, Loughborough University

Jerry V. Useem   former Research Associate at Harvard and currently on the editorial staff of *Inc.* magazine

1 Introduction

There is nothing new about crisis management. When, in Shakespeare's *Julius Caesar* Mark Antony faced the Roman mob at the Senate House after Caesar's assassination, his handling of the situation was a role model for any modern chief executive facing the glare of adverse publicity.

His technique of (a) coming over as a fellow human being – 'Friends, Romans, countrymen. . .', (b) appealing for a moment of their time – 'lend me your ears. . .', and (c) telling them what they wanted to hear and not what he wanted to say – 'I come to bury Caesar, not to praise him' has only been mastered by a handful of corporate heads when handling crises in recent years.

But crisis handling as a specific management discipline only really emerged in the 1980s, with most observers citing the 1982 Tylenol poisonings in the US as the first and ultimate example of the modern art. Johnson & Johnson, the manufacturers of the painkiller, emerged as heroes because of their immediate and thorough response to the injection of cyanide into some of their pain-relief capsules. They took the product off the shelves nationwide at a huge and visible cost to themselves, pulled all their advertising, set up hotlines and, in short, did all the right things.

It is a sobering reflection on the still-primitive state of crisis management that people get so excited about the Tylenol incident. J & J acted nobly and correctly but they only did the things that any responsible, well-managed company should do in a crisis anyway. What they also demonstrated was that if you do the right things in a crisis you can often benefit from it. Once Tylenol had been reintroduced (in the first tamper-evident packaging) and the furore had abated, both the company's share price and the product's market share recovered to higher levels than before, thus demonstrating that a crisis can become an opportunity.

This contrasted sharply with previous crises where the standard corporate response was to say and do nothing, put up a barricade of lawyers and hope that the problem would go away. In cases like the disintegrating Firestone 500 tyres, the exploding Ford Pinto fuel tanks, and the horrific Thalidomide fertility drug which caused the birth of hundreds of deformed babies, the protection of short-term interests was perceived to take precedence over the much more important considerations of maintaining long-term corporate reputation.

Much of the credit for the shift to sophisticated crisis management techniques has been given to the media because of the increase in sensationalism and investigative journalism. But the role of the media generally has probably been overstated. There has always been sensationalism and investigative reporting, as any student of the eighteenth century British press or reader of the 1930s novel *Scoop*! will know. More, it was the emergence of consumerism, spearheaded by Ralph Nader in the US in the 1970s, and the increasing power through the 1980s of product liability and consumer rights. And underlying these trends was a whole postwar societal shift from an educational and family system in which children were mostly brought up with respect for, and faith in, the authorities and their superiors to one where everyone has a 'right to know' and there is scant respect for those in power.

So Tylenol heralded an era of heavily publicised corporate crises in which the world would watch and take sides. Incidents like Bhophal, Chernobyl, *Exxon Valdez*, *Piper Alpha*, Kings Cross, Lockerbie and a host of other events caught the public imagination and created a discrete art out of 'crisis management'.

One tendency of the art is to adopt the 'King Kong' approach, criticised later in this book, whereby huge manuals are developed to try to cover every possible contingency. Apart from being very expensive to produce, they seldom work in real life. Another common failing is to think that 'crisis management' is just about media training when it is about a great deal more.

Some managements – notably in the oil, food, chemical and airline industries – have superb procedures, and senior managements who are shining examples of how to do it well; they are a joy to work with. Then there are the other 95 per cent. Most companies still do not even *have* a proper crisis procedure. There can be few areas of management where so much time is wasted on so little. It was always said that Colman's made more money from the mustard that people did *not* eat than from the mustard they *did* eat, that is from the mustard taken with the best of intentions but left on the side of the plate.

The same happens with crisis management. Typically, a company has a near miss or sees a rival going through the hoops so the knee-jerk reaction, understandably, is 'we must have a crisis procedure.' So the company goes into a frenzy of crisis planning for a few weeks . . . and then loses interest in the proceedings.

The careful observer can see, spread across the world's corporate map, the rotting hulks of half-written crisis manuals, and the empty shells of crisis communication centres.

The pressures to do something about crisis planning are increasing, and it is a foolish company' that continues to put it on the back burner. Consumerism, single-action pressure groups, legislation, product liability, class actions, investigative media – they are all growing in scale and strength. Even the standards people are in on the act: ISO 14004 requires a company to have an emergency response plan which includes internal and external communication plans.

It is hoped that this book will encourage more companies and organisations to join the centres of excellence and approach their crisis management in a modern, professional and practical manner. It demonstrates that successful crisis management is more of a *psychological* discipline that a *procedural* one – and that it really is very simple. If you can instil the right attitudes into the senior management and take a simplistic, pragmatic approach to your crisis planning then you will be making an immeasurable investment in salvaging and perhaps even enhancing your goodwill *when* – not *if* – you are hit by the real thing.

2 *Definition – 'I Have a Crisis Every Day'*

We have a 'crisis' every day – anything from an angry customer to the factory catching fire. So when does a 'crisis' become a Crisis?

Something as big as a factory fire might be put out quickly and the outside world does not get to know about it. So it is an incident, not a crisis. Yet the minor incident of an angry customer complaining about a single product might turn into a major crisis if that customer goes to the press with 'evidence' that your product can kill.

Most organisations are geared up to handle the physical side of things like accidents and product defects by, for example, knowing which levers to pull, liaising with the emergency services or initiating a product recall. What this book is about is the much bigger task of handling the *threat to reputation* that a crisis can bring. In Figure 2.1 the box represents the volume of resources, people-hours, money, experience and expertise that have to go into the *physical* handling of a crisis (for example putting the flames out, getting the product off the shelves, or having the finance director investigated by the fraud squad).

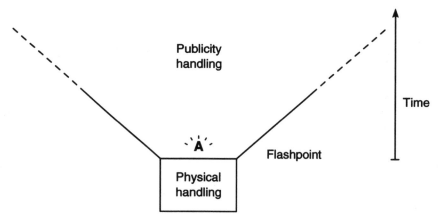

Figure 2.1 Crisis handling

4

The area above the box shows the volume of resources, expertise and so on required to handle the *publicity* element. If we assume that 'A' is the flashpoint – the moment that the crisis enters the public domain – then the demands on those resources grows exponentially with every passing hour. The longer the press and public are left in the dark or not satisfied with a company's version of events, the greater the problem becomes. The area above the box is a sort of 'information vacuum', and the sooner it is filled the quicker the crisis of reputation will be brought under control.

So for the purposes of this book it is the presence or threat of *publicity* that turns a 'crisis' into a Crisis. There are many definitions of a crisis but one of the most useful is:

A serious incident affecting, for example, human safety, the environment, and/or product or corporate reputation – and which has either received or been threatened by adverse publicity.

Perhaps the simplest definition is: '*Unexpected Bad Publicity*'. And it is usually the publicity that can sink a company, not the damage from the crisis itself. But it is wise not to get too bogged down with definitions as there are no clear boundaries with crises. There is seldom a single, definable point at which we can say that a minor problem has become an official crisis. From the earliest stages we have to exercise a balance of judgement – and judgement is essentially what good or bad crisis management is all about.

As a general guide it is best to have a low threshold when defining a crisis. In other words, take even the small episodes as potential big threats and at least be *prepared* for an incident to escalate into a crisis, even if you do not actually press the panic button. While each crisis is different, there are also some common features for it to have occurred and been seen as a crisis:

- Someone is to blame. If lightning strikes your head office and it burns down, it is an accident and people sympathise. But if it burns down because the lightning conductor was not in working order – or if people die because your evacuation procedure is inadequate – you have a crisis. In almost every case human error or malice is in there at the start of it.
- Something is at stake – for example profit, reputation, survival.
- Someone finds out.

And in most cases (except major political and financial scandals) the publicity is much bigger if:

- it concerns the person in the street
- it is geographically close to home

CRISES AND ISSUES

There is also the question of the threat posed by an *issue* as opposed to an incident or crisis. Crises and issues have much in common. Both are developments which threaten you in some way, be it your reputation, your bottom line or your licence to operate. In both cases the greatest danger comes from hostility by one or more groups of people who dislike you and what you do. And almost always the problem is exacerbated by adverse publicity which generates more widespread outrage against you.

Typical **crises** might be:

- product recalls because of defects or extortion
- life-threatening incidents
- health scares
- damage to the environment
- high-profile fraud, or
- computer crash

while typical **issues** are:

- prospective legislation which will damage your ability to operate
- consumer campaigns
- environmental concerns
- health concerns
- negative media campaigns

The bottom line for all of these is the same: the only significant difference is in the time scale. Usually a *crisis* arrives out of the blue and we have to do things in a hurry – and initially with very little knowledge of what is going on, whereas with an *issue* we have more time to analyse the impact, prepare our response and conduct a rescue programme.

Indeed, many of the crises discussed in this book started life as an issue and developed into a crisis because of early neglect by management, or because of an event which triggered it into crisis status. Examples include Opren, BSE and *Brent Spar*. At its simplest:

A crisis is an issue in a hurry!

There are some differences in the way we would prepare for and handle an issue as opposed to a crisis, but they are relatively superficial. The fundamental skills such as identifying and understanding our audiences, communicating effectively, and using 'champions' and credible third parties are exactly the same and it is disturbing to think that there are organisations around who would *not* use broadly the same communications professionals to handle both areas.

This book is therefore deliberately top-heavy in favour of crisis management, with a later section on what the key differences are for issues management – and what to do about them. Because of its immediacy and memorable case studies, crisis is the more interesting and demanding subject to learn – and once we have a grasp of the core principles it is a simple and straightforward process to apply them to issues management.

3   The Nature of Crisis

Crisis is one of the most challenging and fascinating communication disciplines. Information is scarce and there is often insufficient time for proper research and assessment – experience helps but new ground is still being broken. There is usually no black or white, right or wrong choice. One course of action will open one load of problems and another course will open another – and the normally cohesive management team is pulling all over the place as each member tries to protect his/her widely different interests.

Sadly, some crises have tragic consequences and no-one could derive any stimulation or satisfaction from the legal and communicative game of chess that follows. But, happily, the majority of crises do not involve injury or loss of life and the perceived 'villain' does have a case worth representing. In such cases, helping a beleaguered organisation to communicate effectively and restore its reputation, often in the face of increasingly hysterical, hostile and biased groups with a paranoid mission to attack anything big or corporate is immensely demanding, interesting, and ultimately satisfying.

LEARNING THE LESSONS

The best way to understand the nature of crisis – and how best to handle it – is to study other people's crises and see what we can learn from them. Instead of just looking on in sympathy and amazement we should also be asking ourselves:

- What happened?
- Why did that crisis get the amount and type of publicity that it did?
- How did the management handle it? What seemed good and bad about their response?

A useful exercise is to bracket similar types of crises together and see why one turned out differently from another. For example: How did Pan Am come out of Lockerbie compared with British Midland at Kegworth? In what way did the crises differ and how did the two companies respond? How did the different characteristics of the incidents – and the companies' reactions – influence the way the public perceived them?

The same analysis can be conducted with, for example, King's Cross and the *Marchioness*, Tylenol and Opren, *Exxon Valdez* and the *American Trader* – and many others. In the case of the King's Cross fire, for example, the public horror was greater because travelling on the Underground is a daily occurrence and everyone could relate to the awfulness of it. Ironically, 20 more people died just as tragically in the sinking of the *Marchioness* pleasure boat on the River Thames but the public could not relate to that form of death as strongly as they could to a fire on the Underground.

Johnson & Johnson (Tylenol pain killers) and Eli Lilly (Opren arthritis drug) both had pharmaceutical products which were believed to be causing deaths. Because of the obvious and immediate severity of cyanide poisoning, J & J recalled the product immediately and enhanced its corporate reputation in doing so. But because the 'dangers' of Opren were not (and never have been) proven, Eli Lilly kept the product on sale pending further evidence – but public and media pressure forced them into withdrawing the product in a welter of opprobrium.

The damage done to Exxon's reputation with its alleged 'too little, too late' approach to the *Exxon Valdez* pollution is world famous. But the world outside the US hardly heard about the massive 300 000 gallon oil slick served up on the California beaches a few months later when BP's *American Trader* managed to hole itself. This was because BP visibly went into immediate 'apologise and clean up' mode and ended up being praised by the US coastguard and the media for the speed and responsibility of its response.

And do not just examine old crises. Whenever a company or product has a rough time in public, analyse it as it goes along and see what you can learn about good and bad crisis management. Here are some of the key features and lessons of modern crisis management:

IT'S A MOVING PICTURE

Crisis is always a step ahead. There are new challenges all the time, so a flexible approach and frequent reviews of procedures are essential. Some of the developments which have changed the face of crisis management in very recent years are as follows:

Society is Changing

Only a couple of generations ago there was more general respect for authority, and the media seldom attacked icons. A freeing-up of society was long overdue – but now it has gone too far the other way and the media has acquired the power to destroy organisations whether they are guilty or not.

Legal Developments

The law and lawyers are increasingly on the side of the victims in a crisis. This is not in itself a bad thing, but it does mean that big companies and organisations face ever bigger penalties when something goes wrong.

In just a few years we have seen the evolution of the 'class action', whereby groups of victims who could not individually afford to sue can pool their resources and take the 'villain' to court. Hot on the heels of the class action have come groups of lawyers who make a specialisation of representing the groups of plaintiffs. Now we are starting to see some of these lawyers actually creating the 'crisis' by advertising in the press for 'victims' who were previously unaware that they had anything to sue about. And we have seen a bunch of people in the US suing a chemical company for PTSD (post-traumatic stress disorder) simply because it made the fertiliser that a terrorist used in the Oklahoma bomb, which went off near them. In the US, product liability has reached levels of high farce – and other countries are catching the same bug.

Britain is on the verge of corporate manslaughter legislation, and 1995 saw the first case in Britain of a chief executive being jailed because of deaths caused by his company (the Lyme Bay canoe tragedy). It will not stop there.

Heads Must Roll

We live in an age when people no longer believe in accidents – someone must be guilty. Only when some hapless company chief or other perceived villain has been brought before the mob and publicly hanged, drawn and quartered, does the whole thing die down. But until then the press, politicians, pressure groups and the public will be unrelenting in their search for a 'head'.

The 'Enemy' is Getting Smarter

Pressure groups have become more and more streetwise in recent years. They have learned how to create the kind of story that the media will love – and to play on human emotions. Again, this is not necessarily a bad thing. We need extremists to blow the whistle and start doing something about the uncaring, the grasping and the irresponsible, but it is a foolhardy company nowadays that regards a pressure group campaign against it as no more than a thorn in the side.

In his book *Crisis Management in the Food and Drinks Industry* (Chapman & Hall), Colin Doeg describes the resources that Greenpeace laid on for journalists when it took a party of them to the Arctic as part of its campaign against seal culling:

- satellite transmission of video and sound reports back to their own stations
- facilities to process films and wire photographs back to news agencies, newspapers and magazines
- a crew comprising nationals drawn from the countries represented by the media
- shifts planned so that appropriate nationals were on watch when the journalists concerned might want to transmit live interview with them
- a regular flow of news releases to supplement those of journalists on board
- availability of photographs and video footage shot by Greenpeace photographers and cameramen

How many companies have facilities anywhere near as sophisticated as these? Greenpeace has a staff of 1000 and a budget of $150 million; no corporate crisis team in the world comes within a fraction of that resource.

Nor is it just the pressure groups. Politicians, campaigning lawyers and the media, too, are learning new tricks all the time. One recent example in a crisis involving a multinational company was for three journalists from the same news desk in London to call three top executives of the same company in three different countries simultaneously so they could play on any discrepancies in their stories.

(Chapter 8, Dealing with Pressure Groups, gives useful advice on dealing with 'enemy' tactics.)

Disgruntled Employees

In an era of 'business process restructuring', 'downsizing', 'right-sizing', 're-engineering' and other redundancy programmes, many crises involve the disgruntled former employee who comes out of the woodwork after the event and says 'I warned them'.

There is also more danger of a redundant employee with a grudge sabotaging or poisoning your products and/or hitting you with an extortion threat.

Management Awareness

Happily, it is not all bad news. There is increasing awareness of the need for better public relations, and issues and crisis management – and there are many examples in this book of companies who have handled things well. Indeed, almost all the best practice recommended here is culled from observation of companies and organisations handling crises successfully in real life, not from text books.

An investment in sound crisis and issues management will pay for itself hundreds of times over and could even save the organisation from oblivion.

> The asset which we may call 'reputation' accounts for a significant part of the difference between the book value of a business and its market worth. It surfaces as 'brand value' or as 'goodwill' and it can often be the single most valuable asset which a business owns. Very considerable sums of money may be spent in creating reputation and in establishing ownership and benefit from such a reputation. Yet the discipline of formally defending this asset against risk remains in its infancy. (Peter Sheldon Green, *Reputation Risk Management*, Pitman 1992)

Perhaps the biggest single barrier to professional risk, issues and crisis management is the lack of management incentive and reward. If you focus your efforts on selling more widgets you get promoted and the City analysts and stakeholders are happy. But if you invest time and money in preventing something from going wrong there is no visible benefit. Indeed, the *better* you do the job the *less* people will notice you!

This is again a *communications* issue. If companies did more to make their stakeholders aware of the importance of protecting reputation then the investment in time and resources would be accepted. Yet I do not know of a single annual report which describes the company's investments and skills in this area.

WE LIVE IN A GOLDFISH BOWL

Whether we like it or not, we live in a very small global goldfish bowl. Agencies such as CNN, Reuters, WTN and a burgeoning host of smaller local agencies are everywhere. Even small towns increasingly have at least one freelance 'stringer' with a video camera and a satellite transmitter, as the following examples show.

Not long after the Coode Island chemical fire had panicked the whole of Melbourne and sensitised the populace to industrial fires, a paint plant on the outskirts of Melbourne had a fire in the night.

Though impressive (burning paint on a large scale looks rather spectacular in the dark), there was no danger as the factory staff had started to get the fire under control. But a nearby resident called the fire brigade, which arrived accompanied by a video journalist from a local news agency. The duty manager went to tell the fire brigade that everything was alright and when he saw the reporter filming the fire, told him to stop filming immediately.

It was a quiet news night, not just in Melbourne but worldwide. So CNN were delighted to buy some footage of a blazing factory from the local agency. That morning, the chief executive of the paint company, who was on a business trip to the US, was getting dressed in his hotel room in Lousville, Kentucky. Spotting a factory fire on the CNN world news his professional interest was aroused, especially when he realised that it was his factory – and even more so when he saw one of his managers remonstrating with the cameraman!

* * *

And in 1993 SmithKline Beecham had to recall its Lucozade drink in the UK because the bottle necks could shear when undoing the cap. The problem was local to Britain, it was well handled and quickly got under control. But in Singapore shoppers were rushing to the supermarkets to return their (perfectly OK) Lucozade bottles! The story about the British Lucozade bottles had gone out on the Reuter newswire; the *Straits Times* had picked it up and suddenly there was a new panic.

The Internet has added another new dimension. Consumer and pressure groups use it for disseminating information, swapping notes – and even for petitions. With the media there is a degree to which you can get at the source of information about you – in other words you can develop relations with key journalists and brief them with your side of the story – but the Internet is wide open for anyone to say what they like about you.

You will increasingly need to keep up to date with techniques for deploying your own web site and using the Internet to monitor and communicate in a crisis.

Armchairism

Along with the growth in media channels has come a growth in the need for 'expert opinion' to appear in their pages and programmes, as exemplified by Shell's attempted deep-sea disposal of its *Brent Spar* oil rig in 1995. There was a deafening chorus of criticism for Shell's handling of this immensely complex and fast-changing crisis from several 'experts' with minimal knowledge or understanding of what was actually going on.

Country Differences

Be aware, though, that although the world is a global village as far as *information* is concerned, there are still major *cultural* differences between individual countries and the ways that they and their media view a crisis.

The Eurotunnel fire was a good example of this. In France the in-tunnel fire in which a trainload of people had come close to incineration was reported as a minor incident in terms of media exposure whereas in Britain it was covered as a headline crisis.

Watch for the *changes* in cultural differences, too. In Germany, for example, the media have been traditionally very responsible, covering both sides of an issue in depth and allowing the equally responsible German public to make up their own minds. But their coverage of the *Brent Spar* incident certainly did not obey this tradition.

PERCEPTION IS REALITY

The Mecklenburg County Environmental Department in Charlotte, North Carolina used to buy mineral water in the local supermarket to use in their tests. Then in January 1990 they accidentally found minute traces of benzene in a test they were running and realised that it came, not from the item they were testing, but from the mineral water itself. They alerted the water producers, who assumed it was just a local bottling problem, and issued a statement to that effect.

Thus began the Perrier saga. It started in a small way and no-one was in any danger – there was more benzene in a single cup of non-freeze-dried decaffeinated coffee than in a bottle of contaminated Perrier. Yet here was a crisis waiting to pounce. All the lessons were there with hindsight – especially the need to act quickly and be seen to act (which was done well in the United Kingdom) – but the most important lesson was that whether or not the product was actually dangerous was completely irrelevant to the crisis.

For a crisis is not what has *happened*, it is what people *think* has happened. Probably no-one knows the real dangers or otherwise of the redundant *Brent Spar* oil platform, or BSE ('mad cow disease'), or pthalates in baby milk, or the arthritis wonder drug Opren, which was forced from the market by possibly unfounded hysteria. But a potential scare story together with a lack of knowledge of the facts is a potential recipe for crisis.

Of course there is nothing new about this – nor is it unique to crisis. Our own 'reality' as individual human beings is nothing more than a 'meaning structure' created from all the genetic and external influences that make us what we are. Each person's reality is different from that of others; and there is a booming trade in revisionist history as people discover that most of our 'knowledge' of everything from cave painting to World War II consists not of facts but of other people's perceptions put on record.

More than at any time, in a crisis it is vital to recognise that *perception is reality*, and to identify and address people's *concerns*, not the *facts*. It sounds simple, yet the vast majority of victims of crises have addressed the facts and not the perceptions.

Intel, the microchip giant, learned this lesson the hard way when an almost insignificant flaw was discovered in its Pentium microprocessor in November 1994. The person who first discovered it was a mathematics professor who was using his computer for highly advanced calculations – and for the average Pentium user it would take 27 000 years before they were ever likely to encounter the problem. Besides, all new microchips have some sort of flaw.

Intel's response seemed logical enough: they set up a helpline so that worried Pentium users could describe the kind of work they did and Intel would replace their chips if they were likely to be affected by this 'floating point divide' problem.

But that was not enough. By now the media had got hold of the story and, worse, for the first time a crisis was played out on the Internet. Intel's customers felt that they were being cheated and, in the end and after much damage, Intel offered a free replacement for anyone who wanted one, regardless of whether or not they were affected by the flaw. The company had to set aside nearly half a billion dollars to cover the cost of the replacements. (There is a full case study on this crisis in Chapter 9.)

The perception/reality issue was also of paramount significance in the first 'Mad Cow Disease' scare of 1990. In fact, the affected cows do not go mad but the words 'mad' and 'cow' fit into a tabloid newspaper's headline space a lot easier than bovine spongiform encephalopathy (BSE).

It was not until the second, bigger, scare in 1996 that the connection between the bovine form of the disease BSE and the human form CJD (Creutzfeldt-Jakob disease) became so positive. But the story was out. The nation was worried – and was starting to become hysterical – and the assurances of the government were not enough to appease the public's anxiety people are not placated by being told: 'we know best'.

Ironically, when the second BSE scare hit in 1996 the government started to address the 'perception/reality' issue. They called an immediate symposium of the leading experts and announced that, subject to their findings, they would destroy the beef herd if necessary. This was potentially good crisis handling as it was (a) transferring some of the message-making to visibly independent sources (b) being seen to take it seriously (c) acting quickly and (d) being seen to act. But by this time they had lost their credibility because of their mishandling of stage one.

When people think they are in danger – even if you know they are not – platitudes and statistics often do not work, indeed they can make things worse. Instead people need to believe that something is being done, and they will only believe reassurances that come from visibly independent and expert sources.

A leading world expert on this subject is the risk communication specialist Professor Peter Sandman of Rutgers University in the US. He lists a number of 'outrage factors' which convert an acceptable risk into an outrage in the public's mind. According to Sandman (extracted from *EPA Journal*, November 1987), some of these factors are:

- **Voluntariness** – a voluntary risk is much more acceptable to people than a coerced risk because it generates no outrage. Consider the difference between getting pushed down a mountain on slippery sticks and deciding to go skiing.
- **Control** – almost everyone feels safer driving than riding shotgun. When the prevention and mitigation are in the individual's hands, the risk (though not the hazard) is much lower than when they are in the hands of a government agency.
- **Familiarity** – exotic, high-tech facilities provoke more outrage than familiar risks (your home, your car, your jar of peanut butter).
- **Diffusion in time and space** – hazard A kills 50 anonymous people a year across the country, while hazard B has one chance in 10 of wiping out its neighbourhood of 5000 people sometime in the next decade. Risk-assessment tells us the two have the same expected annual mortality: 50. 'Outrage assessment' tells us A is probably acceptable and B is certainly not.

And he lists many others in an invaluable analysis of this important subject. The last point about diffusion can be seen in many walks of life; the death toll on the roads of Britain alone in single week is the equivalent of an airliner crashing and killing all passengers – except that on the roads the deaths are often slower and more agonising, and more children are involved.

Our irrational response to risk is further explained by Sandman:

> In the history of language, 'Watch out!' was almost certainly an early development. 'Stop worrying' came on the scene a little later, as it reflects a less urgent need, but both poles of risk communication – alerting and reassuring – undoubtedly predate language.
>
> So does the discovery of how difficult risk communication is. If there is a central truth of risk communication, this is it: 'Watch out!' and 'Stop worrying' are both messages that fail more often than they succeed. The natural state of humankind *vis-à-vis* risk is apathy; most people are apathetic about most risks, and it is extremely difficult to get them concerned. But when most people are concerned about a risk, it is also extremely difficult to calm them down again. (*The Encyclopaedia of the Environment*, Boston: Houghton Mifflin 1994)

Few organisations recognise this fundamental truth; most make the mistake of (a) leaving communication until it is too late, and (b) believing that communication is just a matter of issuing facts and figures. It is not.

TELLING PEOPLE WHAT THEY WANT TO HEAR

As mentioned in the introduction to this book, Shakespeare highlighted this technique more than 400 years ago when he wrote the speech by Mark Antony on the steps of the Senate after Julius Caesar's assassination. Brutus had just persuaded the Roman mob that Caesar was not the hero they all believed him to be and that he deserved to die.

Now Mark Antony had the unenviable task of convincing them otherwise. The crowd were in a nasty mood and he knew that if he contradicted Brutus directly, they would kill him. So he used a series of devices which even nowadays are only taught on the very best interpersonal skills courses. First he appealed to them in their own idiom – 'Friends, Romans, countrymen. . .' – because we tend to find people who are 'one of us' more credible. Then he used the 'just a second' technique, '. . .lend me your ears. . .', followed by a message they wanted to hear: '. . . I come to bury Caesar, not to praise him'.

At this point in the script, Shakespeare has the crowd calling out to hear what Mark Antony has to say. He is over the first hurdle, and after some more subtle message work he ends up with them baying for Brutus's blood.

> A modern equivalent of Mark Antony was Bob Reid, the Chairman of Shell, at the time that one of their refineries polluted the River Mersey in England in the 1980s.
>
> His immediate response was to hold a press conference and apologise to the nation for what had happened. Having done that he reminded us of how essential oil was, and explained why these sort of accidents sometimes happen. The messages succeeded because the public had been softened by the initial apology.

It sounds simple but have you every tried telling a corporate lawyer that you are going to say 'sorry'?! Yet in almost any crisis you can at least say something which shows that you see it from the other party's point of view. It is not being suggested that you should automatically say 'sorry', as it can be a very expensive word in court. Words like 'regret' and 'concern', however, are not necessarily admissions of culpability but they can go a long way to restoring goodwill.

If you are a waiter and the customer complains that the food is cold, when you know perfectly well that it is piping hot, what do you do? If you argue back you lose the customer. But if you say 'sorry' and go through the motions of taking the food back to the kitchens for 'replacement,' you keep the customer.

We all go through life with our own personal 'attitude barriers' and when someone tries to break down one of those barriers by force (that is facts, figures and counter arguments) it only serves to reinforce it. But if they first say something that we want to hear, then we lower the barrier and they cross over into our space with a better chance of convincing us of their side of things. Figures 3.1–3.3 illustrate this progression.

Figure 3.1   Attitude barriers

Attitude barriers: As we go through life we develop attitudes and beliefs through experience and persuasion – and they are hard to shift. In this example the 'audience' on the left believes, both from painful experience and the media, that big businesses are unethical. You (right) are a big business type and you want to persuade him/her otherwise – but the barrier is well entrenched.

Figure 3.2   Attitude barriers

If you simply say the opposite to the audence's beliefs you will only reinforce the barrier as we feel comfortable surrounded by our beliefs and do not like to change. To do so may change our 'meaning structure'.

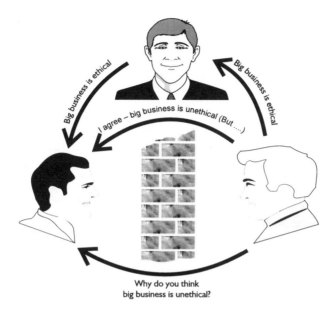

Big business is ethical

Big business is ethical

I agree – big business is unethical (But....)

Why do you think
big business is unethical?

Figure 3.3   Attitude barriers

Ways to break down an attitude barrier (or to get the other person to lower it) include:

Undermining: asking questions that make the audience question his/her own beliefs.

Hopping over the barrier: agreeing with their viewpoint (initially) to soften them up for your own arguments.

Credible third party: getting them to hear it from someone they believe and trust.

CRISIS INTO OPPORTUNITY

The Chinese pictogram for 'crisis' consists of two symbols, one meaning 'danger' and the other 'opportunity'. And in most crises the seemingly unwelcome glare of publicity is also an *opportunity* that you would not otherwise have had. We spend large amounts of money and whole PR departments on constantly trying to attract the gaze of the public – and now suddenly we have millions of pounds worth of free advertising! The content is not what we would have chosen if we had *bought* that advertising space – but the old saying 'There's no such thing as bad publicity' is almost entirely true.

However, to qualify the word 'almost', every now and then a crisis can actually destroy a company (for example Gerald Ratner's injudicious 'crap' remark about the jewellery sold by his company) but these are the exceptions. Indeed, not only do almost all organisations *survive* a crisis, many of them actually *benefit*. This is partly because of the message of care and responsibility that the company is able to put out – Johnson & Johnson's Tylenol recall and Mike Bishop's handling of the Kegworth air crash being two famous examples. But, being cynical about it, just the publicity itself is usually of some benefit as people have minimal recall of what they have seen or read in the news, and after a short while they remember the name of the product but not why they remember it.

It is worth reflecting that:

- Stena Line bookings went *up* after one of its cross-channel ferries was stranded miles off course on a sandbank.
- Hoover did not lose any market share after its massive 'free flights' marketing fiasco. . .
- . . . and when a Soho pub was voted 'Worst Pub in London' by *Time Out* magazine it proudly announced the fact on a huge banner outside the pub – and takings went up by 60 per cent!

As a general rule, it seems that the actual *crisis* seldom does you any harm – but it is your subsequent *handling* of it that can shift your reputation up or down.

THE BIGGER THEY ARE. . .

People respond to big names more than they do to small ones. In good times it is to your advantage (in profiling terms) if you are a Ford or an IBM, but during the bad times it can prove a disadvantage.

In September 1992 a chemical factory owned by the relatively unknown company Hickson & Welch blew up in Castleford, England, and five people were killed. It made relatively minor coverage. In *The Times* it was relegated to the third lead on the front page and a quarter of page four, despite a dramatic picture of a blazing factory and emergency workers running in all directions. More prominence was given to the intensely narcoleptic EC wranglings in Maastricht and a doctor who had attempted a mercy killing on a patient. Most papers did not even cover it.

Part of the reason for the minimalist coverage was the excellent way in which the crisis was handled – a role model for openness. But if the plant had been owned by ICI it would have made much bigger headlines.

LUCK OF THE DRAW

In January 1991 the British nation was in an advanced state of crisis because of three massive food scares: *salmonella* in eggs, *listeria* in paté and cheese, and the first wave of 'Mad Cow Disease'. The press talked of little else, and food neurosis gripped the land.

Then Saddam Hussein invaded Kuwait. At a stroke, the collective national hysteria was redirected at the 'Butcher of Bagdhad' and the Gulf War. Everyone forgot about the food scares and returned to eating beef, eggs and cheese.

How the media will report your crisis will depend to a large extent on what else is going on at the time.

British Midland Airways found this to their cost after one of their planes crashed on the M1 motorway in January 1989. It stayed on the front pages for nine successive days – probably a record for a crisis. Why? It was partly because of continuing and unsolved speculation about the cause of the crash; every day a different bunch of experts attributed the crash to a different cause. The broken plane among the trees by the motorway also made lurid pictures for the front pages. But the main reason it stayed as the lead news item for so long was that nothing else was happening.

Then, on the ninth day, a survivor was found in the rubble of the Armenian earthquake, where he was reported to have been for 40 days. Suddenly the paparazzi who had been climbing the drainpipes of Derbyshire Royal Infirmary to snatch photographs of the aircrash victims disappeared in a puff of smoke, to go and glean some 'miracle' stories, and a respectable peace finally descended on the Midlands. (The Armenian 'survivor' subsequently turned out to be a fraud.)

Some of the media quiet periods can be anticipated, such as holidays and Sundays, though unfortunately we cannot usually time crises for a busy period. But sometimes even that is possible. For example, one of the biggest household product recalls in history did not get mentioned in a single newspaper because the announcement went out on the day of the controversial local elections.

FLAVOUR OF THE MONTH

There is an old journalists' saying: 'Once is an incident; twice is a trend . . . and three times is an epidemic!'

It is worth remembering that during a food scare there are actually no more deaths from food poisoning than at any other time – but you might be excused for perceiving this differently if you read the papers. So if the media flavour of the month is, say, a small spate of environmental contaminations, and your factory has a minor leak of a potential pollutant into the local river, you are potentially headed for a crisis.

4 Preparing for a Crisis

Preparing for a crisis can sometimes be harder than actually handling one. Some of the best handled crises have succeeded because of the relatively simple acts of the top person saying and doing the right things – and doing so quickly – while some other organisations with elaborate crisis plans have suffered public-relations disasters despite their detailed procedures.

For example, it was not the crisis plans that made the Johnson & Johnson Tylenol poisonings and the British Midland Airways Kegworth air crash into show pieces of crisis management. It was the attitude of top management and the speed with which they acted. Conversely, Exxon and Pan Am had highly sophisticated crisis procedures in place at the times of the *Exxon Valdez* and Lockerbie disaster – but the single, simple human factor was missing. It cost their reputations heavily.

CRISIS PLANNING

It is probably impossible to strike a perfect balance between over-preparing and not preparing enough. Some organisations have little or no crisis planning in place, and pay the price for it dearly when something goes wrong. Others are stifled by their cumbersome and unworkable procedures.

King Kong Planning

There is a famous sketch by a US comedian in which a janitor is on duty in the Empire State Building while King Kong is climbing up the outside. A giant gorilla's toe has just come through the window and the janitor is phoning his supervisor for instructions as he has looked in the manual under 'gorillas' and 'toes' and he cannot find any instructions to deal with the situation. This happens in real life. The tendency is for inexperienced crisis planners to try to cover every possible occurrence, in great detail, on paper.

The reasons that elaborate procedures – and particularly huge manuals – do not work for most organisations are:

- **They do not have the resources**   The emergency services and the military spend huge chunks of their lives preparing for just that – emergencies and military engagements. It is what their lives are about. Some oil majors and big airlines devote millions of dollars and scores of people to nothing else – handling a crisis. They have large-scale simulations at vast expense. And even then the military, the emergency services and the big corporations have their share of failures such as the *Exxon Valdez* or Hillsborough.
- **People do not have time**   The management personnel you will use in a crisis are also some of the busiest people in your organisation. They simply do not have time to wade through hundreds of pages of a crisis manual, so the bigger the manual the less likely they are to read it. Even if they *do* make time to read it they will quickly forget what they read – and the more time you devote to simulations and crisis training the more they will resist being involved.
- **'Best before' date**   The more intricate the instructions, the quicker they go out of date. Even with a simple crisis procedure it is a big task to keep up with changes in names, positions, 'phone numbers and so on. One of the biggest complaints from organisations with big crisis manuals when they have just had a real-life crisis is that the manual was out of date.
- **Complacency**   'It's all in the manual so I don't have to bother' is a familiar cry! There is something very comforting about a big red ring-binder marked 'Crisis Management Procedures' on the office shelf – rather like a fire extinguisher that no-one has a clue how to operate, and which has run out of foam by the time it is actually used.

And those large companies which hold elaborate *simulations* find that different things go wrong each time. In other words, one simulation uncovers one set of weaknesses, which are corrected – but the next one uncovers a completely different lot of problems which have developed since the previous one. For example:

One of the oil majors held a simulation in which it was found, among other things, that a number of the mobile communicators supplied for the team had gone missing and they were not able to contact each other. So a system was put in place for the communicators to be locked away in a cupboard in the crisis communications centre, with strict instructions for use and labels on each communicator for each team member.

The next year they held a snap simulation, only to find that the person with the key to the cupboard was on vacation and no-one knew where the keys were, so they had to break into the cupboard to get at the communicators. When they did so they found that the batteries had gone flat in the intervening year as no-one had thought to give instructions about keeping them charged.

So, having added a new procedure and another section to the crisis manual, the company was now even less able to communicate than it had been in the first place!

This is not to say that you should not hold simulations – and Chapter 12 in this book describes how to do it properly – but you should do so with an open and critical mind.

However, if one of the cardinal sins is *over*-preparing for a crisis, an even more common one is *under*-preparing. So, if we are to tread the fine line between over-preparing and under-preparing, what *does* work?

CRISIS PSYCHOLOGY

If there is a single key to successful crisis management it is understanding the *psychology* of the subject rather than getting bogged down with plans and procedures – and you cannot learn psychology from a manual. Every member of the crisis team must instinctively understand what it is like on the other side of the fence – for a frightened consumer or local resident, a distraught relative, a concerned employee, an angry customer, an opportunistic politician, a fanatical pressure group – and when you know how they are feeling you base your communications on *what they need to hear*, not on *what you want to communicate*.

This is why the appearance of the top person in public, showing sympathy, concern, reassurance and competence, is often the single most important contribution to getting the PR aspects of the crisis under control.

In many ways a crisis twists and turns more like a big sporting competition than an organised corporate procedure. If you want a sports team to perform you do not give them a detailed manual, tell them to study it and expect them to know how to respond to every eventuality. By its very nature crisis is chaotic; you cannot cover every contingency. To continue the sports analogy: in a successful modern team each member knows how to play, what his/her colleagues are capable of, and roughly what to expect. But then there has to be a high degree of flexibility, with each team member able to fill in for the others.

So proper crisis preparation is not just about creating lists and procedures; the whole of senior management must be involved from the outset in a continuing process. Crisis should be a regular management agenda item. The worst way to plan is to give the whole thing to outside 'specialist' consultants and let them do it all for you. You are missing out on the vital ingredient of *ownership*.

By all means involve consultants for their expert advice but the best way to prepare is for the senior members of the management team to go on a crisis-awareness course and then hold a series of brainstorming workshops in which they address a set of key questions, out of which a crisis procedure is developed which addresses the real needs of the organisation – and where every team member knows the whole picture and can receive and pass the ball freely. In the following sectors we explore the questions to ask (which are summarised on checklist 1 in the Appendix).

WHAT CRISES COULD HIT US?

Meet every few months for a crisis management session and look at what crises have been in the news and ask: could they have happened here? If so, how would we have coped?

And take a good look at all that is happening in your company that might show up vital 'cracks and warning signs' of a possible crisis. Note how much of the coverage of almost every crisis is devoted to how the warning signs were ignored. The time to spot them is *now*.

Look at your risk exposure. In what ways might you be exposed to the risk of a crisis: chemicals, machinery, health, environment, sabotage and so on? Do you employ a professional risk manager or use a firm of specialist risk consultants? If not, why not?

There are often underlying causes which lead to a crisis happening. Some examples are:

- low morale
- customer complaints
- poor housekeeping
- staff quality
- panic cost-cutting
- rushed output
- rumour and gossip
- management ethos and attitudes
- rapid change
- complex structures

Are there any signs of these since your last meeting?

The graveyards of corporate history are filled with ignored warnings and inadequate checking procedures. For example:

> Barings Bank's ability to catch the early-warning signals – increased trading activity, the extreme use of leverage, escalating trade amounts, and steadily increasing risk – was thwarted by an internal structure that allowed a single employee both to conduct and to oversee his own trades, and the breakdown of management oversight and internal control systems. The ensuing crisis quickly brought about the failure of the entire bank. (*Across the Board* magazine, September 1996)

And a crisis at New York's La Guardia and Kennedy airports:

> AT & T provides critical information to the air traffic controllers who operate the airports. In turn, AT & T obtains the power it needs to run its computers and communications systems from Con Edison. At the peak of the summer heat wave, Con Ed experienced an unusual drop in power because of the added load due to the operation of so many air conditioners. As soon as power dropped, AT & T's backup generators were programmed to begin operating, but the generators failed.

A backup to the backup, in the form of a single 48-volt battery with a 6-hour life, then took over. As soon as the battery was activated, an alarm sounded a warning that the 6-hour 'clock' had begun. But this alarm was not heard until 6.5 hours later. By this time, airplanes were circling 'blindly' above La Guardia and Kennedy because the air traffic controllers could not land them safely.

While this was not a human-caused crisis (not including all those Con Ed customers who turned on their air conditioners), it was exacerbated by a lack of human response – the best alarms in the world are useless unless people can hear them, are motivated to do so, and can take appropriate actions. AT & T found that the alarm was not heard because their system's operators were in classes learning about a new backup system. (*Ibid.*)

Often the very process of analysing the risks and checking for warning signs can prevent the crisis from happening in the first place. For example:

One leading paint manufacturer was preparing a set of scenarios for crisis training and a local manager came up with a hypothetical situation in which a tanker delivering a highly toxic chemical ran out of control down the hill approaching the factory gates and overturned, spilling its load. An over-zealous employee then turned the hoses onto the chemical and flushed it down the drain and straight into a major British river, thus creating a version of the infamous Sandoz pollution of the River Rhine in 1986.

When the plant safety manager saw the theoretical scenario he went white, realising that he was looking at a real accident waiting to happen. The company installed speed restricting humps on the road and safety traps to the drains, thereby averting a potential wildlife catastrophe.

Having assessed the types of crises that could affect you, the next question concerns the 'audience'.

WHO ARE THE AUDIENCES?

Your 'audiences' in a crisis are those people and organisations who:

- are affected by the crisis
- can affect you
- are involved in it, or
- need to know

It is only when we sit down as a group and start to brainstorm the many audiences that fit into these categories that we realise how inadequate is the school of crisis consultancy and training which teaches that crisis management is just about handling the media when things go wrong. Indeed, if you are any good at public relations in the first place then handling the media is one of your easiest tasks! What about the victims and their families? Your employees? Customers? Regulatory authorities? The lawyers and insurers? Pressure groups? One fire chief lists 31 *official bodies* alone with whom he has to communicate in a major incident.

Each of these audiences has its own agenda, its own communication requirements. Each could play a vital role in supporting or scuppering you according to how quickly and effectively you communicate with them. And each has its own attitude barriers and individual psychology to consider. Your communications must address not just the *audience* but also its *concerns*.

Checklist 2 in the Appendix provides a number of suggested audiences for your list. You will need to add your own, and as you develop the list you will understand the crucial importance of establishing who your audiences are *now*. If you leave it until the crisis occurs you will quite certainly forget at least one important audience.

After a chemical spill at a giant British industrial site the management moved quickly to liaise with the emergency services, issue a holding statement, conduct media interviews and communicate with the regulatory authorities and so on. Then, some two hours into the panic it was realised that the company had no system in place for instant communications with the 3000 employees on the site as they answered to a number of different divisions of the same company. While there was a regular site newspaper and team briefing system, there was no procedure for 'flash' communication across the site.

Within the hour, thousands of employees were going off shift with no knowledge of what had happened other than what they heard via the media and the rumour machine.

So as well as listing prospective audiences, we have to address the question of communications.

HOW DO WE COMMUNICATE WITH THEM?

Are channels of communication in place to be able to inform those audiences immediately and effectively? Some examples are:

- names and 24-hour telephone numbers for key press, Members of Parliament, authorities and so on
- office and home addresses
- telephone
- correspondence
- e-mail
- fax
- mobile radio/telephone
- press statements
- press conferences
- briefing meetings
- PR consultants
- telephone helpline
- (pre-booked) advertising space
- VNR (video news release) and syndicated radio broadcast service
- effective Internet communications

Do you know how to set up a telephone hot-line for concerned relatives and others? There are several specialist agencies (mostly tele-marketing firms) and the time to appoint and brief one is *now*, not when the crisis happens.

In particular, identify (and test if possible) your reporting structures and systems with staff, management, authorities, press and so forth. And it is *essential* to start liaising with key audiences and involved parties such as the emergency services, insurers and lawyers as soon as possible to iron out procedures and messages.

For example, one pharmaceutical company with plants around the UK initiated a 'what-if' exercise with the local emergency services and found that the police in different parts of the country had completely different procedures for crisis communications. In England they assumed that the media spokesperson would be provided by the company while the police got on with their own job. But in Scotland the police said that not only was it their responsibility to communicate with the outside world, but they would actually forbid the company to speak!

Remember that organisations like the police and fire service have highly sophisticated PR machines and if things go wrong between you they can often seize the high ground quicker and more effectively than you can. For example, the British Rail officials at the scene of the (1989) Clapham disaster found themselves completely upstaged by the emergency services. The crash had taken place in a cutting and their only source of communication, their mobile phones, didn't work. Meanwhile the London Fire Brigade had arrived at the scene with a mobile TV editing suite!

This can have several negatives for you. For one thing it is *your* reputation that you are looking to salvage, which means that your audiences need to see *you* as a caring and responsible human being. When the handling of the emergency goes wrong you will need to have *your* lines of communication open to put *your* side of the case, and the messages to be put across need to be thought about and planned in advance.

WHAT ARE THE MESSAGES?

Obviously, the information you put out will depend on the nature and stage of the crisis at the time. Nevertheless, having identified in advance the types of crises, audiences and communication methods, it is possible to anticipate a number of 'core' messages, such as:

- **Human face** The best of all is when you can say 'Sorry', but clearly the legal position has to be considered. If it is obvious that your company is at fault you should seriously consider how best to protect the asset of goodwill, which may be worth far more than is at stake in a legal battle over compensation.

In many cases you cannot actually apologise. But can you express 'regret'? As can be seen from a number of cases from Thalidomide to Lockerbie, 'playing it safe' can seriously damage your company's reputation. Would 'regret' really cost you millions? And what will a seriously damaged *reputation* cost? Be prepared to challenge the lawyers' and insurers' advice.

And in all cases you can certainly show sympathy, concern and compassion. One of the most important things that people want to hear from the faceless corporation in a crisis is 'We care'. So show that you care.

- **Reassurance** People out there are worried and frightened. Could it happen again? Will there be long-term damage? Is it under control? Do they know what they are doing? Remember to reassure them. Try to tell them that everything possible will be done to:

  - put it right
  - make amends, and
  - try to ensure that it cannot happen again

  Where possible, it is best for messages of reassurance to come from a credible, authoritative third party, not from your own organisation.

Think, too, of the other types of message that might be needed, such as:

- **What you are doing about it**.
- **Demonstration of the company's excellent track record** (but keep it credible, this is no time for puffery).
- **Convincing reassurance that this is a one-in-a-million occurrence**.
- **Announcement of a thorough investigation** (preferably independent).

It is useful to think of these messages and list them beforehand because:

(a) It will take up valuable time if you start thinking of them when handling an actual crisis, and it is easy to forget some messages in the heat of the moment. It is amazing how often senior management have cared deeply about what has happened but have not said so, not because of legal considerations but because they have been so wrapped up in the crisis that they have simply forgotten to.

(b)   As mentioned, messages such as sympathy and concern will need sorting out with lawyers and insurers beforehand.

This is also the time to prepare:

- **Background briefs** for the media and other audiences (see checklist 5 in the Appendix). When the press descend on you they have to fill their pages with information about what your company does, how many people it employs, what its products are used for, how they are made and so on. If you can provide these off the shelf you will (a) help to fill their pages with your information, not someone else's, (b) ensure that at least they get that part of it right, and (c) make them feel better disposed towards you as you are being helpful.

As well as the written material, facts and figures, remember that about 40 per cent of a newspaper's pages (and almost all of a television news programme) is filled with *pictures* not *words*. If you can quickly issue off-the-shelf, top-quality photos, camera-ready artwork and video footage there is at least some chance that they will use them instead of something less flattering.

Again, *you will not have time* to collate all these details while actually handling the crisis. The time to prepare your background briefs is *now* – especially appointing production companies to shoot your pre-and-post footage for video news releases (VNRs) and audio tapes.

In preparing these briefs you will almost certainly encounter the 'Why should we tell them?' reaction – especially about items such as financial figures, hazardous chemicals and so forth. The answer is simple: the press will fill their pages with these details whether you like it or not; you are simply choosing whether they use *your* version or *someone* else's.

The next consideration is:

WHO WILL FORM THE CRISIS COMMUNICATIONS TEAM?

One of the more difficult tasks is selecting and briefing the team who will handle the crisis communications.

On the one hand you cannot be too rigid and specific in identifying team members and their tasks, as in real life they will not all be there and the demands of the crisis will not conveniently match their pre-ordained lists of duties. But, on the other hand, it is obviously important to have a team of people who can come together at short notice and know what they are supposed to do.

The key components of a crisis team include the following:

Core Team

- team leader
- spokespersons
- 'gatekeeper'
- media minder
- secretary/admin
- as required, executives with skills in personnel, production, security, technical, safety, media and other relevant disciplines
- group/HQ

The *spokespersons* will consist of a senior spokesperson who will be the official face of the company – and other more junior ones as required to handle telephone enquiries, local and trade media interviews and generally soak up the media workload while the senior one deals with the national, international and other major media.

The *'gatekeeper'* is the single, central coordinating source who has tabs on all aspects of the crisis and filters all questions and information coming in – and is responsible for allocating information, briefs, requests for interviews and so on out to the team. The centralising and control of information is vital.

The *media minder* is responsible for the physical aspects of handling the press, for example arranging briefings, providing them with facilities (especially access to telephones), marshalling them for press conferences, keeping them at bay and so forth.

Note the separation of the *team leader* and the *spokespersons*. It may seem logical to have the top person in charge of the team *and* appearing on behalf of the organisation, but in a full-blown crisis the lead spokesperson will have a non-stop round of interviews to give, each one of them potentially crucial to the course of the crisis and the long-term image of the organisation. So he/she will either fall down on managing the crisis communications or miss some vital interviews if both roles are combined. It is therefore best to select the *best* spokesperson for the task – and if that happens to be the team leader then you will need someone else to take charge.

Increasingly the media are prepared to talk to a more junior person – as long as that person can speak with the full authority of top management, clearly knows what he/she is talking about and can do it well. It is sometimes possible to let the legal advisor act as a spokesperson. When an organisation goes through the full crisis preparation described in this book the PR people and the lawyers should get into a dialogue early on in the proceedings to understand each other's requirements. A lawyer who can come across as informative and sympathetic can make an ideal spokesperson as it shortens the communication/approval chain.

However, there are some crises where the strategic approach called for is a 'Mike Bishop', so-called after the way that the then CEO of British Midland Airways salvaged his airline's reputation in minutes by appearing at the scene of the crash on the M1 at Kegworth and demonstrating his human concern and the fact that he was personally taking charge and responsibility. Clearly, in such a case your spokesperson has to be visibly your most senior executive while someone else gets on with the running of the show.

Also, in many crises there is sufficient time for the same person to fulfil both roles – but you just need to be prepared for dual responsibilities in case of a really big one.

Other Team Members

Other full or part-time members would include advisers/experts in:

- legal
- public relations
- security
- other specialist fields
- stress counselling
- families/victims visitor

List and brief reserve team members in case any key people are sick or on holiday.

In a really big crisis, especially an international one, you may need the services of a specialist PR company – and if there are hundreds of calls to answer or set up you will probably need a telephone marketing firm specialising in running helplines (emergency hot-lines for relatives and so on in disasters can be set up by the police).

Regional/Site Teams

The increasing trend is towards devolved local crisis communications teams rather than handling the crisis 'from the centre', for example head office. Local crisis teams can appeal far more effectively to local audiences which are at the site and need immediate communications – and to national media who appear at the scene – and they are usually more than capable of doing so. The make-up of the crisis teams will vary according to your own organisation and the nature and size of the crisis.

Back-up

Crises have a habit of striking at the most inconvenient times and the likelihood of all the crisis team being available is miniscule. So you will need to identify reserve players for the key roles – as well as accepting the 'sports team' principle of a crisis team playing fast and loose rather than sticking rigidly to set duties.

And a big crisis might soak up most of the time and energy of several senior executives so it worth thinking about who will continue to run the normal operations of the company – and how. Take heart, though, from the episode in World War II when the Messerschmidt factory was bombed: the bombs missed the factory and wiped out the administration building – after which aircraft production increased dramatically!

Crisis Team Types

The most important considerations for selecting the crisis team members are:

● *Executive* status with *full power and authority*, and an understanding of the human and media sides of the issue. He or she must be able to:

  – ask for information and get it – in full – at once,
  – issue instructions and get a response, and
  – be powerful enough to take major decisions if necessary – or to have instant access to someone who can.

- It is essential for the *spokespeople* to be *sympathetic, articulate and trained/skilled* in handling tough media interviews.
- *The right temperaments* to handle a crisis which might involve nights of lost sleep and intolerable pressure from outside audiences.

Spokespeople must also be given space and allowed to get it wrong occasionally. If they are worrying about every word and looking over their shoulders the whole time they cannot come across as sympathetic or as speaking with authority. So they must be given the confidence and backing of senior management, who in turn must be educated in the realities of media PR – particularly the fact that however good your media relations and however perfect your press statements, it will still go wrong sometimes.

And always consider how important it is for everyone who deals with the public, relatives, staff and so on to be sympathetic and understanding. In a serious crisis, especially one involving human suffering, all your employees who answer telephones and meet the public are part of the company's PR. They must be well briefed – and trained if possible – in being human, concerned and patient.

Indeed, if you set enough store by having the right types of people on the crisis team then it is not inconceivable to choose the *people* first and then allocate them tasks. If you are sure that someone is going to be calm under fire and is an empathetic type then they may be worth co-opting onto the crisis communications team even if they work in a field unrelated to public relations.

But how do we *know* if people are the right types? In warfare it is often the timid clerk who gets the Victoria Cross while the braggard cowers behind a sandbag. Similarly, the seemingly tough top manager can become an indecisive wreck when a crisis strikes while someone who you thought wouldn't say boo to a goose quietly takes control.

We spend our lives, let alone our careers, living a lie to the outside world. The smooth, distinguished, competent person that the outside world sees in us (we hope!) is not the real us at all, but a sort of psychological hologram of how we want people to see us. Like the legendary policeman's bicycle that becomes part of the policeman through a lifetime of association, the hologram seems very real, not just to the outside world but to ourselves. But when a crisis strikes we revert to type, to the real us. Unfortunately it is a fact that the more senior and seemingly implacable an executive, official or public figure, the greater the psychological can of worms that their exterior is often hiding (see, for example, the chapter 'Politics and Paranoia' in *Families and How to Survive Them* by Robin Skynner and John Cleese for an enlightening description of this phenomenon).

So in a crisis some strange things can happen as certain key individuals on the crisis team start to panic and allow their true characters out for a rare and not very pleasant airing. While there is no way of guaranteeing that you have picked the right types there are some ways to narrow the odds. For example:

- Just being aware of the personal psychological aspects can help you to be more careful in your team selection. It also helps if someone already has a proven track record of being cool under fire and showing strong empathetic qualities.
- There is advice on preparing people for the stress of a crisis in Chapter 13 on crisis psychology in this book.
- A simulation exercise in which executives are put under real pressure and made to make rapid decisions can help to identify warning signs.
- Some organisations put their crisis team through psychometric profiling to test for the right qualities. This can help, but remember that psychometric profiling is only a useful guide, not gospel.

It is very important to have an empathetic character in the role of spokesperson. Empathy is *the* single most important quality to have in a crisis.

Duties

Try not to get too bogged down with listing the specific duties of the crisis team members. By all means sketch out their general duties – but once you start you will quickly find yourself getting sucked into the creation of a 'King Kong' manual, with pages devoted to each individual, who is then not there when the crisis strikes anyway.

How Do We Coordinate Them?

It must be stressed that the 'crisis team' referred to in this book is the crisis *communications* team, that is the management group responsible for communicating with the outside world and internal audiences. This is separate from the crisis *handling* team, that is the people whose job it is to put the flames out, restore production, recall the product or conduct an investigation.

In a small organisation the two functions might have to be handled by the same team – or even the same individual – but in general it is best to try to separate them as it is seldom possible for the same people to do both things at once.

How the crisis handling and communication teams are constituted and interface with each other is the single most difficult area in which to be prescriptive as it will vary enormously with the size and nature of the organisation. And, as with the infamous ever-growing crisis manual, most organisations who set off on the crisis planning route end up with a complex cat's cradle of team structures and organisation charts, teeming with CCTs (crisis communication teams), COPs (crisis operations teams), CMTs (crisis management teams), divisional sub-teams, regional variations and other recipes for a guaranteed total breakdown in communications the moment a crisis actually happens.

Try to keep any structures as simple as possible. The two teams should be geographically close – in the same room if space permits – and liaison between them must be frequent and regular. Some key figures (for example the chief executive officer (CEO), the head of public relations (PR) and the head of human resources (HR) might have a role on both teams to ensure effective coordination of actions and messages.

Where there are divisional and/or regional and site crisis teams the same approach applies. One small group of individuals at, say, factory level will be busy handling the crisis and liaising with the emergency services and regulatory authorities, while another is dealing with the local audiences and media at the site and liaising with head office to coordinate the national effort. Again, the local teams will be geographically close and have some common members.

Co-ordination starts to get really difficult for a multinational organisation with a crisis which affects more than one country. If the structure is too rigid it does not work, especially as nationals working in the different countries have different attitudes to crisis and different ways of doing things. But if it is too loose you can end up with anarchy. The concept of an international coordinated crisis communications structure in which everyone communicates with everyone, and they all know what they are doing and transmit coordinated messages to all audiences, is a myth. Most seemingly well-handled international crises are much more shambolic at the time than outside observers realise. But that must not stop you from setting up as effective an international communication structure as you can manage – and to keep monitoring it for effectiveness.

One of the best ways to achieve effective communications between operations and communications teams, and between head office and the regions and the international network, is through joint training. At least when the different team members undergo the same training – especially the crisis awareness programme – they know each other and have a common understanding of how to approach things. A typical team structure is shown in Figure 4.1.

How Good is Our Internal Reporting?

In the Second World War a Japanese aircraft carrier was holed in the bow and started to take on water. It sank – not because of the hole but because it kept sailing at full speed. There was no chain of communication between the sailors who were frantically trying to plug the gap and the bridge, who were blissfully unaware of the extent of the damage.

Forty years later the cross-channel ferry, *Herald of Free Enterprise* capsized and killed 193 people for similar reasons: warnings about leaving the bow doors open while sailing had been ignored.

*   *   *

At the height of the BSE crisis a London Council suddenly found itself at the centre of the storm because it was handling the first case in which a sufferer from Creutzfeldt-Jakob disease was linked to eating contaminated beef. It had never occurred to the department caring for the victim that they were sitting on a media and political volcano, or that they should alert the senior Council officials of the case and its implications – so the media were carrying the story before the Council's PR team were even aware of it.

The annals of crisis are filled with cases where someone, somewhere in the organisation was already aware of what was going on. Worse, in many cases that 'someone' then emerges after the disaster and says 'I kept warning them'.

43

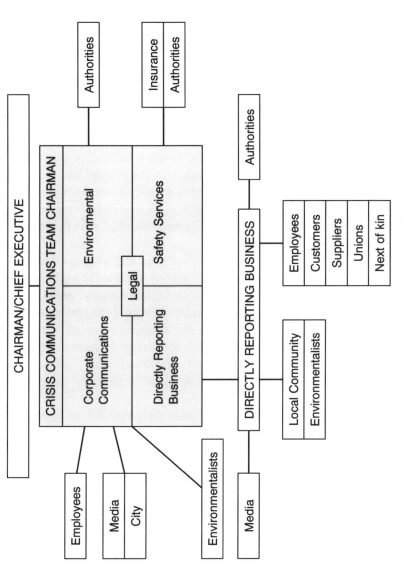

Figure 4.1 A typical crisis management team structure showing lines of communication

Source: Courtesy of Courtaulds plc.

It is not enough simply to issue a one-off written instruction to all staff telling them to alert you if they spot something. Memos are binned and people forget – and are replaced. Your internal reporting mechanism is a major task which will usually include a *regular* item in the team briefing mechanism (if you do not have one you are asking for big trouble come crisis time), *regular* written reminders and *regularly* asking yourselves if the process can be improved.

WHAT RESOURCES AND FACILITIES DO WE NEED?

The smoothness and efficiency of the operation will be strongly affected – for better or worse – by the ready availability of the right facilities. But *what* facilities? Most guides on the subject use the major airlines and oil companies as role models as they have dedicated crisis communication centres with banks of telephones, highly trained staff and every imaginable item of equipment needed for the smooth handling of a crisis.

But how can smaller organisations such as the average industrial company, service supplier, charity or retailer choose the right level of resources that are adequate and useful in a crisis without breaking the bank? The simplest approach, as part of the brainstorming and planning process, is to go through the complete list of what you would have in an ideal world with an unlimited budget – and then choose what your own organisation can realistically afford and operate. Checklist 3 in the Appendix gives a number of possible suggestions.

Out of the huge range of choices some elements are essential:

- You must have somewhere to meet. That 'somewhere' must be big enough – and suitably furnished – to hold the crisis communications team. It should be near to, or shared with, the crisis operations team for more effective coordination. In places like chemical factories there should be an off-site alternative (for example a hotel) in case a fire or explosion prevents access to the crisis room.
- There must be sufficient telephone lines. One of the most frequent public and media complaints in a number of well-known crises has been an inability to get through in the first few hours. If any of your anticipated crises are big enough to need a telephone hot-line facility the time to plan for it is *now*.

- One or two big whiteboards (preferably the ones that produce their own photocopies) can be invaluable, or at the very least have a couple of flip charts.
- You will of course need ready access to all the normal management communication tools: fax, E-mail, mobile telephones and communicators, and mailing facilities. In larger organisations a telephone conferencing – and maybe video conferencing – facility can be useful. And if the crisis strikes in the middle of the night and you do not have a secretary available, do you know how to operate all these tools?
- You will want to monitor TV and radio news broadcasts. This means having a TV, VCR and radio, with spare video and audio tapes, and a list of frequencies for the various stations. Additional information services (for example Reuters) can be useful.
- A simple TV/radio role-play kit can be useful for putting spokespeople through a couple of quick practice interviews before doing the real thing.

Internet Communications

Sophisticated crisis management increasingly includes the Internet as a means of communicating rapidly with audiences. If journalists and consumers know that they can access a web site to get the latest information they will use it. Do you have a web site in place? If not, do you have access to one (for example your PR company)?

As Intel found to their cost (see Chapter 9) negative traffic on the Internet can cause a huge amount of damage to your reputation. While it is much harder to 'control' the Internet than other channels of communication you can do a lot to protect yourself before a crisis strikes. There are four main ways in which Internet users can report your crisis:

- *Newsgroups*: live forums on specialist subjects
- *Web sites*
- *Online publications*: newspapers and magazines with an Internet version
- *E-zines*: magazines only published on the Internet

All of these are interactive so, as well as posting information on your own web site, it is possible to communicate your side of the story back to them. As mentioned in the following chapter, 'What to do When it Happens', your audiences will take this information better from a credible third party than they will from you direct. If you are not set up to monitor all this traffic yourselves there are agencies who will do it for you.

WHAT TRAINING DO WE NEED?

The right training programme can be more valuable than any amount of paper procedures in preparing people to handle a crisis effectively. It can make them more crisis-aware and can play a unique role in team-building. Indeed, for some multinational or widely spread organisations training often provides the only common focus for people from widely differing countries or cultures.

The range of training on offer varies widely in content and quality. The most popular product is media training in which a journalist(s) puts potential spokespeople through a day of being grilled in front of the cameras. Good training is *essential* for anyone who is going to deal with the media. The principles are simple to grasp and will make all the difference between success and failure. People behave completely differently under skillful questioning – especially when they know that a lot is at stake.

Before selecting a media training company for your crisis preparation, check out their credentials as professional trainers and ask to speak to some of the companies they have trained. Look for trainers who understand something about communication psychology and who understand what it is like on your side of the fence. More important still, crisis *media* training is not *crisis* training. Handling the media is only a small part of the picture, albeit a very important one. It is also important to train your people to:

- understand the nature of crisis and the psychologies involved
- know their way round your crisis procedures, and
- practice at simulations or desktop exercises as a team

Here the products on offer are few and far between. There are plenty of conferences and workshops, mostly fronting people who have been involved in well-known crises. Attending one of these will usually be informative but it cannot provide anything by way of the team-building and understanding of the procedures that you ideally need.

Running a full-scale crisis simulation can also be useful, though not as valuable as you might think. Apart from the problems mentioned earlier about different things going wrong each year, remember that a simulation is more of a *testing* day than a *training* one. As with bad media training, if you put a weak link under too much strain in a short time scale, and without any proper development work, it will break. Yet that same weak link could have been one of your strongest if it had had proper training and development in the first place.

One of the simplest and most useful training days is the type of awareness workshop described later in this book. It can impart a great deal of understanding, help with team-building, provide a guide for developing a corporate procedure and introduce delegates to handling the media. There is also an increasing number of computer-based simulation and training products which enable people to hone their skills using an interactive programme which can be tailored to the types of crisis scenarios faced by your company or organisation.

Training is not an easy area. There are few, if any, packaged products that will precisely meet your needs. But one thing is for certain: some training is better than none.

Stress Counselling

Professional stress counselling is an invaluable investment, not just in helping people cope with stress but also identifying in advance how they will behave under fire. The presence of a professional stress counsellor is also valuable *during* the crisis to help both the crisis team and, if appropriate, those affected by the crisis.

THE CRISIS MANUAL

Now for the thorny subject of putting the procedure in writing. In principle there is nothing wrong with putting everything down on paper. It is a sound management discipline and it helps to check that you have thought of everything. But the product you need to pick up and help you in a real crisis must be something much leaner and more practical. It is probably impossible to pitch the manual exactly right. If you try to anticipate every type of crisis and include all the details and instructions that everyone will need, it will be a huge, unworkable document. People do not have time to thumb through hundreds of pages in a panic to find out who does what. But too few instructions and briefing details will leave the crisis team short of vital guidance.

What *is* certain is that the crisis manual should never be produced in isolation as a stand-alone set of instructions. It should simply be a supporting part of a programme of training, meetings, brainstorming and exercises that combine to provide the best and most flexible preparation for a crisis. So the manual is not a prescriptive document but rather a working tool to be used in a crisis by a team of people who already know the principles and what is expected of them. It is best produced as a team effort, with members of the crisis teams having ownership.

The contents of your own crisis manual will vary according to your brainstorming and planning process and the people and resources available, but some typical contents might be:

- *Introduction*: brief description of what is expected of team members in a crisis; corporate philosophy; how to use the manual.
- *Procedures*: brief summary of company's crisis procedures.
- *Crisis team*: names; titles; brief descriptions of their responsibilities; day and 24-hour phone numbers of team and services (legal, PR and so on); details of stand-ins if on holiday or ill.
- *Audiences*: list of audiences and how to contact them; addresses and telephone numbers; emergency numbers for regulatory bodies, employee communications, lawyers, MPs and so on.
- *Messages*: reminder list of the types of messages to communicate in a crisis.
- *Resources*: location of crisis room and so on; what resources there are, where they are kept and how to use them. Instructions in manual or in crisis room on how to operate fax and communicators, how to activate the freephone helpline and so forth.
- *Media*: reminder checklists on handling media and preparing for and succeeding with interviews.
- *Background Briefs*: copies of the briefing notes on company, products, processes and so on. Useful technical data.
- *Useful addresses and numbers.*
- *Other*: any other useful and important information, for example list of frequencies of radio programmes for tuning in and recording in a hurry.

DOES IT WORK?

Now that you have a crisis procedure in place, check its viability and efficiency:

- Check the control and chain of command: who gives instructions to whom? Who must authorise decisions and statements? How does a PRO obtain vital data? How is that data distilled – and distributed? To whom?
- Establish an emergency call-out procedure for assembling the crisis team in a hurry. If possible, test it occasionally.
- Crisis simulation exercises can be useful for spotting weaknesses and honing responses. But, as mentioned earlier, remember that different things tend to go wrong each time, so do not place too much reliance on the results of a single exercise. And successful simulations, like fat manuals, can breed dangerous complacency.
- Desk-top exercises based on realistic crisis scenarios can also be very valuable for testing the system. The value of these is often underestimated; they may not be the real thing, but they play a useful role both in maintaining crisis awareness and keeping crisis front-of-mind and in team building.
- A very simple and useful technique is a 'Crisis Audit', whereby an outside consultant or a senior member of the crisis team drops in unannounced on crisis team members, presents them with a hypothetical crisis and asks what they would do – without checking the manual or written procedures. This keeps crisis front-of-mind and reduces dependence on unworkable and cumbersome written procedures.

BRIDGE BUILDING

We tend to like, believe and trust familiar names and faces. And the better people know and understand you – both personally and as an organisation – the less inclined they are to want to damage you when things go wrong. So an essential part of your crisis preparation is to establish a proactive communication programme with MPs, authorities, key journalists, the local community, support services, PR departments and so on.

The midst of a disaster is the poorest possible time to establish new relationships and to introduce ourselves to new organisations . . . when you have taken the time to build rapport, then you can make a call at 2 a.m. when the river's rising and expect to launch a well-planned, smoothly conducted response. (Elizabeth Dole, President, American Red Cross, quoted by Norman R. Augustine, *Harvard Business Review*, November–December 1995)

And *attitude research* among key audiences now can provide a useful benchmark when you conduct tracking research during and after the crisis (see Figure 4.2).

THE PREPARATION SEQUENCE

Successful and effective crisis preparation is therefore a *process*, not a *dictate*. By working as a team and going through the above questions and guidelines you will develop the procedure most appropriate and useful for your own company or organisation.

An effective flow sequence goes something like the following:

- **Crisis awareness training**: this gets the team thinking about crisis and the psychologies involved. They can agree on a common definition of crisis and be presented with the many questions that will form the skeleton of the crisis plan.
- **Brainstorming**: enables the team to thrash out the many different crises which could hit them – and how they would respond.
- **Planning**: Any written plans are now drawn up – usually in the form of a crisis manual.
- **Media training**: any media spokespeople must be trained in crisis interview techniques.
- **Simulations**: crisis simulations to assess the team's strengths and weaknesses, and to keep them crisis-aware.
- **Audits**: a 'crisis auditor' drops in on individual team members unannounced and checks their top-of-the-head knowledge of crisis procedures. He/she should also check that changeable data in the manual (for example team members, telephone numbers and so on) is kept up to date.

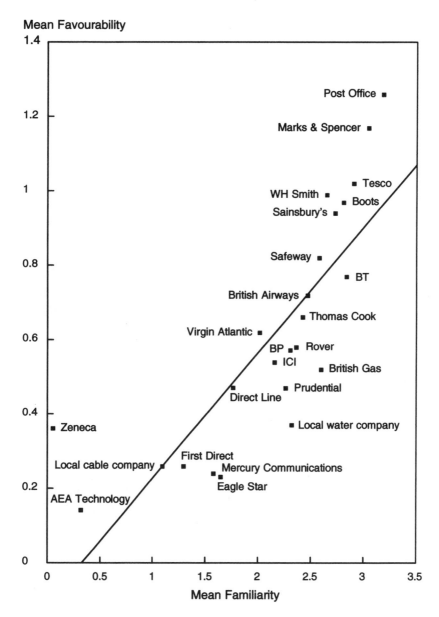

Figure 4.2 A familiarity/favourability chart – the more people feel they know about an organisation the more favourably disposed they are towards it

Source: Courtesy of MORI.

5   What to do When it Happens

No matter how many years of crisis experience you have, when that phone rings and you hear a slightly strained and urgent voice telling you that something big is going down you always feel a knot in the stomach. Unless you are actually at the scene when it happens, at first there is an unreal feeling of calm. It takes a few minutes, sometimes hours, for the affected management to assemble and the real sense of urgency to set in. But, like the period of quiet when the bombardment stops before the enemy attacks in strength, it can be a very false sense of security.

What happens next depends on the crisis itself. With something like a product scare story or a television investigative programme, things usually remain reasonably calm and civilised – even though the outcome could destroy your reputation and the strain and pressure can be just as powerful as in a more spectacular crisis. But in something like a major environmental pollution, an explosion or a fatal transport incident, the crisis room can look and feel like a chicken coop just after the fox has got in the door.

Whether you have a 'false dawn' or a 'big bang' at the start of your crisis . . .

This is your most vulnerable moment.

The reputation – and possibly the very survival – of your organisation or product hangs in the balance. What you say and do in the next few minutes and hours could make the difference between success and failure. *Time is the imperative.* You need time so that you can absorb all the information, make the right strategic decisions, come to terms with the new set of events, and start to do something positive about it.

Most times you will be off to the right start if you (a) do something to buy time, and (b) *think*. The first thing to think about is:

HOLDING ACTION

If there is one simple rule for handling a crisis it is to put yourself in the minds of your audiences – the frightened local resident or consumer, the journalist with a deadline, the opportunist politician, the outraged customer, the mildly unhinged pressure group campaigner – and ask yourself: 'if I were that person, what would I want this company to do and say?' Then do it and say it.

You may not be able to do it and say it in full, but that is the general idea. And when an organisation comes under the spotlight for the wrong reasons what do people expect that organisation to do? They expect them to *do something* about it – and to be *seen to do it*. So when you are faced with a chemical leak, an explosion, an embezzling finance director, ask yourself: is there anything I can do, right now, to show that I'm doing something (and, less cynically, to genuinely make things better). Some examples might be:

- stop production
- close plant
- product recall
- announce immediate, independent investigation
- put someone on suspension pending the outcome of an inquiry

Sometimes you may have to take an action which is operationally unnecessary but which does the vital job of demonstrating to your audiences that you are doing something about it. For example, a leak of toxins into a river might have been fixed and the clean-up underway, so the fact that your factory is still operating does not pose any threat to the community or environment. But think what it looks like from the outside. You have attracted a number of hostile and outraged audiences – and all that they can see and hear is the smoke coming out of the factory chimneys and the hum of the motors. So they assume that: 'You're poisoning our environment. And you're still operating. *You don't care.*'

In fact you might care deeply. It is just that you know that you are no longer poisoning the environment. But *they* do not know that. And you cannot make them believe you just by issuing a statement saying that you *do* care and that there is no danger.

But if you *do* decide to shut down for a short while so as to be seen to be doing something then you may run up against members of your own organisation whose interests run contrary to your own. You will have to fight your corner, and this is the time you will be glad that you involved these parties in the crisis awareness training and the planning process. Often there is no immediate action you can take – but you should at least ask the question and see if there is anything you *can* do from the outset.

The Single Simple Action

In a number of the best-handled crises described in this book and revered in public perception and management teaching, the key to success was the immediate appearance of the chairman or CEO to express concern and demonstrate that something was being done.

As Lockheed Martin boss Norman Augustine puts it in his inimitable style:

> The notion that one person, sitting atop a corporation hierarchy, can regularly and successfully guide the daily action of tens of thousands of individual employees is a pleasant confection created, some would suggest, by academics and certain business leaders. Only the truly brave or the truly foolish would make this claim. However, the one aspect of business in which a chief executive's influence is measurable is crisis management. Indeed, the very future of an enterprise often depends on how expertly he or she handles the challenge. (*Harvard Business Review*, November–December 1995)

And whether or not you can take some sort of holding action. In almost all situations you can issue a statement.

HOLDING STATEMENT

You should at all times be geared up to pen a statement in a few minutes and have it going out via your pre-selected communication channels to the media and other key audiences. Refer to the *Messages* checklist 10 in the Appendix for a reminder of the important core things to say, especially:

- **Details**: as much information about the incident as possible.
- **Human face**: 'We care' – sympathy, concern, understanding; maybe regret; possibly even 'Sorry'.
- **Reassurance**: no further danger; not harmful; what to do if worried; one in a million; and so on.
- **What we are doing about it** – especially a thorough (independent) investigation.
- **Further information**: when and where further information will be available; numbers for information hot-line or helpline.

A holding statement like this puts up a flag saying: 'We're here – and we're talking'. One of the only things going for you in a crisis is that the audiences will come to you first for your side of things. To quote crisis expert Michael Regester, a holding statement establishes you as the 'single authoritative source of information' on the crisis.

The other benefit of taking holding action and/or issuing a holding statement is that it gives you that all-important breathing space while you assemble the crisis team and spend some essential time taking a strategic overview of the situation.

ASSEMBLE THE CRISIS TEAM

This may have already happened in a crisis where you have some breathing space before it gets into the public domain, or the team may still be on their way while just one or two of you have taken the action and issued the statement.

You must be prepared for gaps in the team. Crisis manuals that list every member of the team and an alternate and then assume that all the places on the team will be filled are unrealistic. This is why the flexible planning approach is so important as it means that your crisis managers can act more like a sports team and still play the game and score the goals with substitutions and missing players.

But whatever the constitution of the team and whenever they assemble, it is vital that as soon as enough of you are there to handle the crisis you leave a skeleton staff to handle calls and sit down as a group, away from the action, to take a helicopter view of the situation and develop an agreed strategic approach.

DECIDE ON THE STRATEGY

At this point the temptation to get on with handling the crisis while trying to formulate a strategy as you go along is almost irresistible. Phones ring frantically. People appear from all over the place with urgent messages and requests for information. Key members of the crisis team cannot be found. The media are on the line demanding to speak to someone immediately. And the boss wants to see you right now. But if you cave in to these immediate demands you may make a crucially wrong strategic decision. You may say something you wish you had not. And you will certainly forget things.

So it is absolutely essential for a core group of the crisis team and top management to sit down as quickly as possible, isolated from the crisis and the phones, to take a cool, strategic look at the situation. In an ideal world this would take a good couple of hours. Even if you only take out a few minutes it will be better than nothing. As with the preparation process, if you ask yourselves the right questions the right strategy will evolve. Here are some suggestions:

What is the Crisis and What are the Implications?

This may seem a rather obvious question but it is surprising how often different members of the team have different understandings of what has happened and what it means to their organisation. Even if it only takes a few seconds, make sure that you all have a common understanding of what has happened and what it could mean to you.

Is There a More Fundamental Problem?

Ask yourselves if this new crisis is an indicator of a more fundamental problem. Could it be the tip of an iceberg? Could this incident call into question the reputation of the whole company; the group; the industry? Does it call your safety standards into question? Could this become a broader issue?

For example: when an El Al cargo jet crashed into an apartment block near Schipol airport in 1993 the immediate crisis facing the Amsterdam city government was that of clearing up after the crash. But the accident triggered a storm of anger over the planning policies which allowed the (low income) apartments to be sited in the flight path in the first place. The incident was the beginning of a major political crisis.

Is There More to Come?

Are there likely to be more of these explosions; product tamperings; bent sales executives and so on?

What is the Worst Case?

Look now at the two extremes: the worst that could happen and the 'maybe it's not so bad after all' case. Start by thinking of how bad it could get at worst and think how you would handle it – and keep this possibility in the backs of your minds just in case.

But you should also ask yourselves:

What is Actually at Stake?

One of the worst things that happens in a crisis is the arrival of the first batch of press cuttings. When you see this huge pile of media coverage, all of it saying terrible things about you, it feels as though that is all that people are reading and hearing about. In fact that coverage may only be a small percentage of people's daily reading – and memories are short.

As mentioned in Chapter 3 and the case studies, when Stena Line ran one of its cross channel ferries onto a sandbank, miles off course, it was the lead news item for two days – yet bookings for the company went up because any negative impressions were outweighed by the huge amount of free coverage (helped by the company's positive handling of the situation).

* * *

Or take the case of Manoplax, a heart drug produced by Boots after ten years and £100 million of development. After only a few months on the market serious concerns were expressed in research reports and the company had to recall the product. Yet Boots' share price went *up* on the news because the City's response was to assume that the company would now have to sell its pharmaceutical division, which they had perceived as being a drain on profits.

So ask yourselves: If the worst comes to the worst, what will we actually lose? How loyal are our suppliers, our customers, our shareholders – and will they stay with us in bad times? How long are people's memories? Are we panicking unnecessarily? *But* do not let a positive answer to this question be an excuse for inaction. The natural human reaction in a crisis is to want to get back to normal as quickly as possible, and as unscathed as possible. So while it is an essential part of crisis management to examine the upside as well as the downside, consider this:

> In 1990 a small trade magazine in the US speculated that Reuters had experienced a glitch with a new product and that the launch would have to be delayed. Reuters quite rightly made the point that 'that is what trials are for,' the problem was put right and the launch went ahead. But in the meantime the share price of the company had dropped *20 per cent* on the news – that is four points more than the price of Union Carbide fell after Bhopal.

Do not panic unnecessarily but never be complacent. Most of the potential damage that will happen to you will result from the answer to this question:

What Are the Audiences Likely to Make of It?

This is a vitally important question to ask – perhaps *the* most important one. As has already been stressed, a crisis is not what has happened but what people *think* has happened. Your reputation now hinges, not on what sort of an organisation you are and what you do about the crisis, but on what sort of organisation people already *think* you are and to what extent their opinions change – and in which direction – as a result of your actions.

The simplest way to assess audience reactions is to *ask* them! Where possible, one of my first actions in a crisis is to contact one key journalist in each media sector – tabloid, broadsheet, TV, radio – and tell them what has happened. This has a number of advantages:

- Because he or she is a known and trusted journalist the story will get fairer treatment than it will from several other unknown ones.
- Because they have been given a 'beat' (that is a story ahead of their rivals) it will get more – and fairer – coverage in that publication or programme than it will elsewhere.
- Because someone else has it as an exclusive the other media will be relatively less interested.

The other major advantage is that this gives you an opportunity to ask the selected journalists what they are likely to make of it. Sometimes, happily, you may find that it is not as bad as you thought.

> On one occasion I was advising a manufacturing company who had just had a leak of acetic acid into a major river, killing an estimated 150 000 fish at a time when environmental feelings were running particularly high.
>
> Yet the press hardly seemed interested. Coverage the next day was minimal – and the company's side of things was well-mentioned. Indeed, when I rang a reporter friend on a popular tabloid newspaper the boredom factor was extreme. He did not think they would cover it at all:
>
> 'We're not really interested in fish', he said.
> 'Yes, but I thought maybe 150 000 of them. . .'
> 'No, not really . . . oh, hang on . . . were any children involved?'
> 'No'
> 'You sure? Do children play in the river? Could they be damaged by this acid – could it kill them?'
> 'No. It has steep banks, there are no kids there – and anyway it's only vinegar in incredibly low concentration. It suffocates fish but a child wouldn't even notice it.'
> 'Oh, well we're not interested, then. Thanks for telling me anyway'.

Try to get a feel, both for the positive/negative nature of the reaction and for the level of the response. In other words: 'How well or badly are they likely to take this – and to what degree?'

> On another occasion I was advising a manufacturer of dish-washers who were about to announce a massive recall because of a potentially dangerous defect. My concern – and that of most of the management team – was to communicate the complicated reasons for the recall while protecting the manufacturer's reputation as best we could. But the sales director, while behaving responsibly and professionally in every other way,

seemed remarkably casual about the whole thing. When asked why he was so unconcerned he explained that he had experienced several recalls in his career and that, because of the extra advertising and publicity involved in recalling the product, sales had always gone up afterwards!

* * *

Or take the case of one of Britain's biggest law firms who sacked a tea lady because she had been issuing one biscuit too many to employees in their tea breaks (in fact the reasons for the dismissal were much more complex, but as soon as the press picked up on the 'extra biscuit' angle it became a headline).

This type of 'crisis' was not a problem because their type of client was unlikely to switch their business over one sacked employee, fair or otherwise. So the predictable level of response was zero-to-favourable (as the extra publicity would increase name awareness).

But if they had had to sack a partner for absconding with client funds the response would have been negative and potentially serious because such an event questions the firm's integrity and can affect clients personally.

And if the story – *true or otherwise* – was that a client's affairs had been grossly mishandled, the response would be very negative and very serious. The strategy should be one of major crisis mode.

If you can afford it and have the mechanism in place, *attitude research* among key audiences can be an invaluable tracking tool during a crisis.

What Are the Likely Time Scales?

Try to get a feel for the time scales in which you have to operate. For example, what are the media deadlines? If the crisis has just blown and it is 10.00 a.m., then you have a few hours before the national newspapers will need their final version of your side of things. By all means issue a holding statement and tell them as much as you can, as often as you can, but the first editions of tomorrow's papers will not be available until about 8.00 p.m., so you have a few hours to play with if necessary. But the local evening paper will be going to bed within the next couple of hours – and the lunchtime national TV news will need to have their footage within the same time frame. So sort out your priorities.

Unfortunately this question is becoming less and less relevant, as with the proliferation of world media and communication technology almost *any* newsworthy incident is news *somewhere, now.*

And by when do you need to have established communication with the employees; the regulatory bodies; group headquarters; the insurers? It is also worth giving some thought, now and throughout the crisis, to how long the whole thing is likely to run – the initial burst and then all the follow-up: litigation, clean-up campaign, dealing with pressure groups and so on. Of course, this is hard to estimate accurately and it will change as it goes along, depending on factors such as what else is in the news. But at least if you ask the question – regularly – you can get a feel for what sort of resources you are going to need, and for how long.

Can We Involve Any Allies?

The natural tendency at a time of crisis is to focus entirely on yourselves and your problems. Yet the whole essence of successful, convincing public relations is to get other people to say it for you! That is why the public relations industry devotes itself to getting the media to cover their companies and clients, rather than just saying it in adverts or sending mailshots.

So, would your messages come better and more credibly from, for example, your trade association? An independent research department? If the MP praised you last month for being a good member of the community is he or she prepared to say it again now? The Health and Safety Executive gave you a clean bill of health recently so can you persuade them to put their heads above the parapet on your behalf?

When BP made such a good job of the clean-up after its *American Trader* oil spill, it was the US Coastguard who praised them for their prompt action.

When investment bankers J.P. Morgan offered to buy back their newly issued Turkish government bond on the day the government collapsed, it was their customers, the other banks, who praised them in the financial media for their responsible action.

And the case study in this book on the Odwalla apple juice contamination tells how even the victims' lawyers publicly praised the company for its responsible behaviour.

With friends like these on your side you are well on the way to turning the crisis into a golden opportunity. But it is unlikely to happen naturally – they may need a little gentle persuading!

Often, too, you can involve your enemies in the problem and turn them into allies. For example:

Shortly after the horrific Pan Am crash at Lockerbie in 1988, ITN produced an exposé about how easy it was to plant a bomb on an aircraft. They made an imitation holdall bomb using real Semtex and loads of wires so that even Mr Magoo could spot the thing on the X-ray screen – and they then smuggled it through Heathrow security with a hidden camera in a second holdall filming the whole process. Once the 'bomb' was on a British Airways plane they revealed their hand and invited the authorities to comment.

In earlier days BA would have put up a 'no comment' barrage and fuelled the flames of the ITN report in the process. But after seeing how badly Pan Am had fared after its silence over Lockerbie, contrasted with how well British Midland Airways had come out of Kegworth with its up-front approach, they immediately fielded a spokesman to appear on the ITN News at Ten.

His approach was to congratulate and thank ITN for having discovered this loophole and potentially saved lives. In fact, the security lapse was the fault of airport security and not BA, a point which he mentioned at a suitable moment. He also managed to mention the extreme lengths to which they *did* go to keep passengers safe – but again showed gratitude to ITN for their life-saving actions. The problem went away immediately and the 'bomb' did not get a single mention in any subsequent broadcasts or newspaper reports.

Who Else is (Culpably) Involved?

It is not just your allies who can share the misery. If you stop and think about it there might be other guilty parties such as slack regulatory bodies, suppliers, an extortionist or vandals.

In the case of malicious damage by extortionists and vandals you might be able to transfer public anger on to them rather than yourselves, although if the other 'guilty party' is, say, a supplier or a regulatory body you cannot simply point the finger – you have to be more subtle.

> When the coffee manufacturers had to jack up their prices because of a massive increase in coffee prices in Brazil, most of the companies involved tried to explain about the 'increase in raw materials prices', but this was a pointless exercise as the angry shopper does not give a stuff about your financial problems. But the PR boss of one leading coffee company fed a photograph of a Brazilian coffee baron to Britain's best-selling newspaper. The photo made the front page lead, accompanied by an angry 'shock horror exclusive' proclaiming: 'we name the man who has doubled the price of our coffee'.

Can the Spotlight be Transferred?

If the spotlight of attention cannot be transferred to another guilty party it is often possible to transfer it to a different, more positive, aspect of the crisis story.

Anthony Hilton, City Editor of the *London Evening Standard*, likens a journalist's mentality to that of a two-year-old child heading for the television set.

> If you tell it that it can't play with the knobs it will struggle and scream and stop at nothing to twiddle them. The secret is to find another toy that has tinselly bits on it and makes an interesting noise. If you then shake this new toy just out of reach in the periphery of the child's vision, and pretend that playing with the TV is allowed but this new toy is not, sure enough, the child will toddle over to the tinselly toy and become happily absorbed with it.

Light-hearted and cynical, perhaps. But based on a lifetime of experience from a hardened journalist with a track record of uncovering stories.

A classic case of successful 'spotlight transference' was the near disaster that occurred when a British Airways BAC 111 airliner lost its windshield at 12 000 feet as it took off from Birmingham airport. The rapid decompression sucked the co-pilot out of the window – but miraculously one of the crew managed to hold on to him and they were able to land safely at Southampton Eastleigh airport with the unconscious co-pilot draped over the fuselage. There was pandemonium in the passenger compartment but the cabin crew kept people calm and acted like heroes.

For the next couple of days the media trumpeted the heroism and efficiency of the BA crew and praised their procedures to the skies. There were interviews with crew members, the recovering co-pilot and grateful passengers, while only a much smaller proportion of the coverage dealt with the question of how a BA windscreen blew out at 12 000 feet. If BA had refused to comment the coverage would have been about little else.

*   *   *

Airlines are proving themselves masters of the transferred spotlight British Regional did it when one of their ATP turboprop aircraft had to land on one wheel at Manchester airport in August 1997. It was all there: press conferences, video footage, hectares of media coverage – all devoted to the heroic pilot and crew. It was brilliant PR. The media, sated with human interest material, forgot to ask why the port wheel did not come down as it should have done. And a few months later, Virgin achieved similar results at Heathrow.

*   *   *

Eurotunnel tried something similar after their Channel tunnel fire. They drew as much attention as possible to the way that the staff had calmly and correctly got the passengers to safety at some risk to their own. This did not detract completely from the negative coverage – but it helped.

Again, the Stena Line case study covered in this book is an example of the spotlight of attention being transferred to a different story: how the crew kept the passengers happy. The 'passengers' story far outweighed the crucial question of how a giant ferry landed up on a sandbank miles off its correct course. Nor did we ever find out.

And there have been many others – from the positive coverage after a series of Boeing crashes of how their airliners are kept safe, to a positive in-depth look at chemical plant safety after a major explosion had killed five people.

There may be times when there is not another story to transfer the spotlight to – or when the best way to kill the crisis is to take the blame yourselves and make an issue of your apology and/or the independent investigation to follow.

How Can the Crisis be Contained?

In a broader sense: how can our actions attenuate the speculation and publicity as quickly as possible and stop the crisis running out of control? Remember the earlier Figure 2.1 showing how a crisis expands exponentially from the flashpoint as long as nothing is being said or done. The more you do and say, and the quicker you do it and say it, the faster and better the crisis will be contained.

In a narrower sense, ask yourselves if there is a way that the crisis can be identified with a single plant, a subsidiary or a product. If you only refer to, say, the geographical name of the plant and give all spokespeople a title relating only to the subsidiary, you can sometimes keep the name of the parent company and/or its other products out of the picture – or at least reduce the damage.

Whether it was deliberate or not, the massive chemical plant explosion in 1974 in North Yorkshire which caused a number of horrific deaths has always been associated with the name 'Flixborough' and not the owners. And for months after the *Herald of Free Enterprise* disaster at Zeebrugge, all the blame was directed at Townsend Thorensen and not at their owner, P & O.

Do try, though, to be a little more subtle than the Australian wine merchant whose sales of French wines plummeted as a result of the public protest at French nuclear testing at Mururoa Atoll in the South Pacific. To 'contain' the crisis he removed the labels which said 'French Drinking Red' and re-labelled them 'Bordeaux'!

The strategic overview involved in deciding on strategy might last anything from a few minutes to several hours, depending on how long you have. And it will need regular review as the crisis develops. From it you can now formulate a broad strategic approach, which is then communicated to everyone on your side who is involved in the crisis. Having agreed on a broad strategic approach, the next task is to:

IDENTIFY THE AUDIENCES

Go through your audience checklist and check off which ones you need to communicate with in this crisis. You will in any case have done a quick check when selecting targets for the holding statement – but now you must make a strategic assessment of:

- Who is affected by this crisis?
- Who can affect us?
- Who needs to know?
- Who else should be informed?

DECIDE ON THE MESSAGES

Again, the crisis plan will have a checklist of core messages to communicate. These will be the messages in your holding statement, that is:

- details
- human face
- reassurance
- what we are doing about it
- further information

plus other messages such as:

- track record – and the good your company/product does
- background briefs – details of products, processes, chemicals, company and so on

Select the appropriate messages for this crisis, clear them with other key players such as legal and insurers (you should, of course, have already cleared them in principle as part of your preparation), and start the communication process.

Review both the audiences and the messages regularly as the crisis develops. They might change.

PREPARE AND EFFECT A PLAN

You now have a strategic approach and the crisis team is busy getting things under control. If you have time, try to put some flesh on the bones and draw up instructions detailing what needs to be done, who does it, where and when and so forth. Review and update the plan constantly.

BRIEF RELEVANT PEOPLE

As well as the more formal communications with the selected audiences it is essential to hold regular – preferably personal – briefings with senior management and your front-line staff such as security, switchboard, reception and so on. And try to expose the remote decision-makers to reality. Cold, corporate attitudes and decisions can change dramatically for the better when the decision-makers personally see the victims and grieving relatives, and are subjected to intense grilling by persuasive journalists.

Again, it is a simple matter of psychology. Terms such as 'fire', 'explosion', 'victims' and so on are just words. The words do not convey the full impact of what has happened, so the principle response is still one of 'how can I defend the organisation?' But when the same person actually sees the victims with their injuries, or meets the grieving relatives, or sees and smells the charred remains of the factory, then the response becomes one of 'my God, how can I make amends.' And *that* is the attitude that a responsible organisation should demonstrate in the first place.

CENTRALISE INFORMATION

Try to ensure that all information comes into – and goes out from – a single source throughout. The ideal communication process should resemble an egg timer as shown in Figure 5.1. The central co-ordinating point is often a single person such as the 'gatekeeper' in the crisis team – or at most a small group of people working very closely together and keeping each other informed all the time.

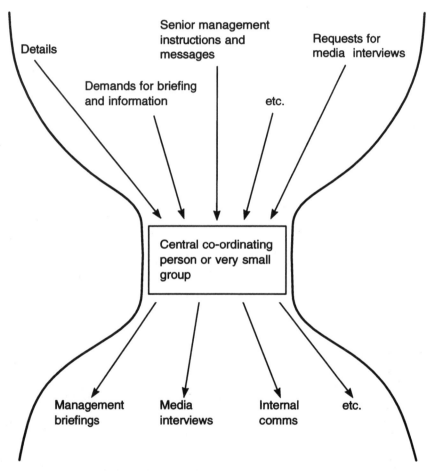

Figure 5.1   The communication flow in a crisis: try to ensure that all information input goes through a single coordination point before it becomes an output – this ensures that everyone knows what is going on and avoids the organisation appearing to 'speak with forked tongue'

Without this discipline things can go wrong very quickly. One of the features of the Perrier crisis was that the company had a devolved management structure and each country was doing its own thing and putting out different messages. As described in Chapter 3, journalists will often contact executives of the same company in different countries simultaneously to see if they can identify any discrepancies for their headlines.

UNDERSTAND YOUR AUDIENCES

Probably the biggest single failing of a company at a time of crisis is a lack of empathy. It is what is *received* that matters, not what is *communicated*.

Describing a chronic cancer cluster controversy, Peter Sandman paints the picture of a hysterical mother holding her leukaemic baby in the face of an engineer who is armed with a sheaf of computer print-outs. It says it all. Both parties are convinced of their case – the mother genuinely believes that the company has in some way caused her child's illness; the engineer's figures tell him that it has not. Worse, his calm *makes* her more hysterical; her emotion *makes* him more impassive. It is perfectly possible that *both* are wrong but they are never going to accept the other's point of view.

It is worth remembering that the antagonistic parties in a crisis usually believe whole-heartedly in their cause. It is only when you understand these people's concerns and get inside their minds that you will start to do and say the things that will help the crisis to subside.

GIVE INFORMATION

There is a very simple and obvious crisis psychology adage:

> *The less you tell people, the more they think you are holding something back. The more you tell people, the sooner they lose interest.*

When a former intelligence officer, Peter Wright, wrote a book in 1987 called *Spycatcher* which allegedly exposed the inner workings of the British intelligence service, the government banned it from sale in the UK. For weeks people all over the country were paying anything up to ten times the cover price to obtain illicit copies smuggled in from Australia, where the book was published.

When the book was allowed on sale, however, it was quietly 'remaindered' three months later by the publishers as no one could be bothered to read it.

* * *

Or take the case of the major chemical company in France which was constantly under attack from the community living near one of its big factories. There were frequent damaging rumours and reports of dangerous leaks, sloppy practices and cover-ups. So the company announced an 'Open House' programme whereby anyone with a legitimate interest or concern – community, pressure groups, media, politicians – could turn up at 15 minutes' notice at any time of day or night and be taken anywhere they wanted in the factory to see for themselves what was going on.

Once the programme was announced the hostility disappeared. And by the time the scheme was quietly dropped a year later not one single person had actually visited the factory!

At a time of *crisis* your audiences have a much bigger demand for information and that demand is going to be satisfied by *someone.* There is nothing you can do to stop it. The pages of the newspapers *will* be filled; employees *will* talk about it to family and friends; concerned relatives and residents *will* talk among themselves; action groups *will* be formed. The vast information vacuum will be filled by your potential enemies unless you provide enough information direct from source.

Remember, too: if they discover something for themselves that you should have told them, then your credibility will be ruined for the rest of the crisis.

Information and openness can be used as a *weapon* as well as a *defence.* Put out as much information as you possibly can, using your prepared channels of communication such as press releases, briefings, mailings, video and audio news releases and the Internet. As well as setting up a crisis information section on your web site you can also monitor any Newsgroups, on-line magazines, 'E-zines' and other web sites that are talking about you (or use an agency to do the monitoring). If you decide to participate in a Newsgroup remember to follow one of the leading principles of good crisis PR and try to get any positive messages conveyed by a credible third party.

Although advertisements are less credible than editorial, do not overlook the possibility of *advertising* to inform the public and get some of your key messages across. Avoid the temptation to justify yourselves because if the copy is too defensive or self-interested it will have the opposite effect to the one intended – it will only incense the public more.

> A good example of using advertising effectively was the Israeli airline, El Al, after the Amsterdam air crash in 1993. Their message was 'Sorry is not enough' – in other words, they told people what they wanted to hear.

If you still feel like clamming up in a crisis, heed the words of C. Northcote Parkinson:

> The vacuum caused by a failure to communicate is soon filled with rumour, misrepresentation, drivel and poison.

If you look at the *Sun*'s coverage of a crisis (a train crash) – see the plate section to the book – you will find that the journalists have filled seven pages in a matter of hours with facts, figures, eye-witness reports, photographs and speculation. A few hours earlier those journalists were faced with a sea of blank space. The point to make to CEOs, lawyers and other 'Don't tell them anything' types is that in a crisis those pages are **going** to be filled whether you like it or not. The only choice you have is whether they fill them with what **you** say or with what **someone else** says. And if they fill them with what someone else says you are not going to like it!

RESIST COMBAT

Easier said than done! It is often hard to be polite to an irate public figure 'demanding to know', or to resist throwing a brick at a press photographer who is climbing a hospital drainpipe to get photographs of the victims. But you must always be polite and dignified.

Again, think of the *psychology*. What *motivates* them? Why do people like politicians and pressure group campaigners spend large portions of their lives putting up with hostile opposition, attending endless meetings and working all their spare time on quixotic causes while sane people are happily playing golf or chatting with friends in the pub? Some politicians and campaigners are driven people who *need* your crisis or they'll have to look for another cause. Remember, too, that we do actually need these extreme types to balance the awfulness that would happen to the world if it was left to the industrialists. *Your* company might care about people and the environment. Many do not.

Reporters and investigative journalists are slightly different. Most do have other motivating forces – namely an editor and a deadline – and if they do not come back with a story for the one, before the other, they will not have a job. Journalists have their senses of responsibility and conscience put to the test at the start of their careers. An early task is to be sent on a 'collect pic' call, where some local kid has been killed in a tragic accident and the paper needs a photograph for tomorrow's front page. This means visiting the grieving relatives and asking for a snapshot from the family collection, which in turn means having to justify this unacceptable behaviour to yourself.

To be fair to the journalists, there is no other way. If *you* do not do it there are plenty who will. And your bosses will not accept a refusal. If you want to stay a journalist you have to do it.

BE FLEXIBLE AND THINK LONG TERM

A crisis can twist and turn. So can the requirements of your audiences – especially the press. You may have to adapt the plan and re-brief people several times.

It can be tempting to try to protect the short-term interest – but it is often best to be prepared to take a short-term loss to protect your long-term reputation. Throughout the crisis, ask yourselves: 'How will people look back on this event a year from now? Five years from now? What will their impression be of our organisation?'

When you step outside the crisis and into the minds of your audiences – *and* look back from a year or so hence – the idea of closing the plant for a day or so, ordering an independent inquiry of recalling the product 'just in case' does not seem so unthinkable. And once you can draw breath from the immediate panic, start thinking as early as possible about the longer-term plan. Good communications and intelligent handling of a re-opening or relaunch can turn crisis into opportunity.

'THEY THINK IT'S ALL OVER. . .'

Once the crisis is over the team should meet to discuss what was learned from it, to prepare a report and to agree on any improvements to the crisis procedure in the light of what has been learned.

A crisis can keep coming back to haunt you long after you think it is over. *You* might want to forget it and get on with normal life again but some of your *audiences* have a vested interest in keeping it boiling. Sometimes the aftershocks come without warning, but most can be anticipated by establishing a forward diary of events such as:

- anniversary
- legal battle (especially if specialist disaster lawyers are involved)
- inquest
- report

6   Handling the Media

While crisis management is about much more than just handling the media, it is also true to say that they can play the single biggest role in a crisis/opportunity. First we need to realise that we are all media 'experts'. We spend a large part of our lives reading, watching and listening to their output. We are immersed in the media – so it only takes a small extra step to be able to understand all we need to know about them. And that step consists of *analysing* the media instead of just using them for information, education and entertainment.

Next time you find yourself half way through a press article or absorbed by a TV interview, pause for a moment and ask yourself why. How did they attract your attention to the piece in the first place? How did they keep you on the hook when your own priority was to get through the paper as quickly as possible? How was the story constructed? What sort of questions was the interviewer asking? And why?

Look at the front page of a broadsheet newspaper and ask yourself: 'If this newspaper were my own commercial business, what would be the most important item on this page?' The headline? The picture? No, if you stop and think about it it is the advertisement in the bottom right-hand corner – for the newspaper would go out of business in a matter of days if it relied solely on the cover price for its income. So the prime purpose of a newspaper business is not to sell newspapers – *it is to sell advertising space*. Which leads to the newspaper proprietor's first big problem: we do not buy newspapers to read the advertisements; we buy them to read the news. So if you look carefully at that front page you will notice that items like the picture and the headline are designed to grab your attention and get you reading more, so that eventually your eye falls on the advertisement.

Notice how the ads are mostly at the bottom of the page and not at the top. This is not coincidence. If the ad was at the top of the page your eye would be more inclined to reject it because you want to read the page for news and features, not the advertisements. But once you are on the hook you are more likely to glance at an ad lower down the page.

The editor comes up against the invisible 'So What?' barrier that every reader has. We are subconsciously asking ourselves: 'What's this got to do with me?' If the story grabs us in some way by appealing to our fear, our greed, our sense of humour, our morbid curiosity or some other human motivator, then we keep reading. But if it does not crash our 'So What?' barrier we turn the page and our eye does not fall on that all-important ad. And if no-one spots the ad and responds to it then the advertisers stop advertising in that publication and it goes out of business. And it is the same for radio and television. Notice, for example, how they will give you a 'teaser' of what is to come just before the commercial break in a TV news broadcast. So there is a 'commercial imperative' running right through the media. Everything is driven by the unseen hand of selling advertising space.

Further down this harsh commercial ladder we come across the journalists. Their role is similar to that of production managers in a factory – they are turning a raw product into one that is ready for the consumer, which is then handed over to the packaging department. Early in their careers journalists are told that the only way to write is with a grabbing first sentence, all the facts condensed into the first two paragraphs, and the whole thing written from an angle which tells only a fraction of the full story, and which meets the editor's definition of 'newsworthy' – that is, written in a way which ultimately helps to sell advertising space.

The 'commercial imperative' varies from country to country. It is strongest in Britain, the US and Australia, where there is intense competition among newspapers and programmes. In some countries, such as France and Germany, the public expect to be given more information and to be allowed to make their own minds up – so the newspapers, for example, can get away with a sea of text which no British reader would tolerate.

It is worth bearing national differences in mind when dealing with the media. But it is also true to say that if you apply the relatively high British or American PR standards to the media in other countries they will use your material more as a result. Indeed, if anything the 'British disease' of sensational journalism is spreading slowly to other countries, especially where a free market pertains and titles and programmes are competing for the same audiences.

So if the media are driven by this commercial imperative what *can* we do to gain some kind of control over what they are reporting? The answer is to be helpful, give them what they want and learn to work together. You will seldom get them to do it all your way but you can vastly improve positive coverage and diminish negative coverage about you by following two very simple rules:

- know the journalists; and
- give them a story.

Know the Journalists

Be aware of the different requirements of the different types of journalist, for example:

- editors
- news editor/news diarist
- page/section editor
- correspondent/specialist
- reporters
- picture editors
- local media
- trade
- broadcast

All have different needs, different deadlines and different places in the pecking order.

Above all, be aware of the vital importance of *human chemistry*. If you want to do business with a major customer do you do it at arm's length? Of course not. We do business with people we know, like and trust so we go to great lengths to get our key audiences to know, like and trust us – everything from the golf course to dinner with respective spouses. Journalists are no different, yet even a high proportion of PR professionals try to do it all by telephone and press release. If you want to win them over you must look for every opportunity to get to know them face to face. Once you do, you will find that they differ from each other as much as people do in any other walk of life, so some you will simply get on with alright, some you will not get on with at all, and some you will click with and cultivate an invaluable mutual relationship.

These principles also apply to journalists who approach you 'cold'. Instead of just responding, ask yourself if this journalist might be useful in future and look for an opportunity to build the bridge with a meeting or a follow-up to the story. Of course, when a crisis actually strikes you cannot expect to develop relationships with every journalist likely to be working on the news desk that day. What you *can* do, though, is to:

- Try to establish *some* sort of relationship via face-to-face meetings and briefings and by coming across to them as a reasonable and helpful human being.
- Feed your regular contacts with exclusives and thorough briefings. Sometimes a specialist journalist who knows your subject or organisation will take over the story.

Creating a Story

Before you can give the journalist a story you must first have a story to tell! Take as much time and trouble as you can to prepare yourself an interview brief consisting of:

- **Message**(s): *you* might have several points to make but your *audience* (reader, viewer, listener) will not remember more than two or three items at the very most. The less you say, the more they will remember. Identify 'hot buttons' – items that will appeal most to the audience. In a crisis, focus on the most important of the core crisis messages which are described in Chapter 4.
- **So what?**: now picture the audience reading or hearing your message for the first time. Will it overcome their subconscious 'So What?' barrier and make them want to know more? If not, why are you saying it? Once you can overcome the *audience*'s 'So What?' barrier you will automatically overcome the *journalist*'s barrier, too.
- **Distil them**: Take time to work out the most clear, succinct and articulate way of expressing the message(s). Pascal wrote at the end of a letter: 'I have made this letter longer than usual, only because I have not had the time to make it shorter'. It takes time, effort and imagination to say it in a few words. This is the famous 'sound bite'.
- **Give examples**: one example really is worth a thousand words. Find a single, detailed, graphic example/anecdote to back up every assertion.

During the furore about long hospital waiting lists, press releases about the percentage decrease in numbers of patients waiting for certain categories of operation, spending increases in real terms and so on fell on deaf ears. But when a single Member of Parliament announced that an old lady in his constituency had had her leg amputated because she had contracted gangrene while waiting too long for an operation, all hell broke loose. It was on the main television news and the front pages of the national newspapers – and it said more about hospital waiting lists than all the statistics in the world. This is because we can relate to a granny losing her leg – but we do not *relate* to statistics.

While the 'sound bite' is useful for conveying a brief, memorable catchphrase, the longer, detailed, interesting and relevant *example* has far more impact.

- **Analogy**: another form of graphic support is to ring a bell in the audience's mind. Relate abstract terms, dimensions and so on to everyday images (for example converting hectares into numbers of football pitches). As you go through life spotting useful examples, anecdotes and analogies store them in a 'treasure' chest to draw on at any time.
- **Advice**: in some interviews, a useful device is to give the audience (and the journalist) a few hot tips on how to get the best out of something or avoid disaster.

An industry spokesman was being given a rough time by a hostile TV interviewer about the sugar content in children's drinks. His company was one of the 'villains' charged with not adequately warning parents about the added sugar content and the potential danger to children's teeth. He briefly explained his side of the labelling issue and quickly moved on to his prepared ground:

We put as much information as we can on the labels – but my advice to any mother watching this problem is: don't leave things to chance. Brush your children's teeth twice a day, check them every week; don't give them dummies with sweeteners on; take them to the dentist every six months. . .

No editor could leave it out.

- **Simplicity**: use simple, spoken language; not jargon, business-speak or techno-babble.
- **Anticipate questions**: interviewees worry too much about being asked a 'surprise' question. Journalists are only human and there is a finite number of questions that can be asked on your subject. But more importantly:
- **It is your show**: every interview is a golden opportunity to get your side of things over to large numbers of people. In thoroughly preparing your brief you are preparing the messages you are *going* to get across to the audience, no matter what the questions are.

Building your 'Islands'

A media interview is like a stretch of dangerous water that you have to cross. Between the safe shores at the beginning and the end are huge waves, fierce currents, whirlpools, sharks – all the dreadful things that could lead to your gruesome, and very public, death during the minutes that you are in the water (Figure 6.1(a)).

The trick is to build 'islands of safety' in advance. These are the pre-scripted and carefully rehearsed sections, following the above guidelines, where you are on home ground. You know what you want to say. You know how to say it. And the material is colourful, anecdotal and – above all – *interesting* both to the audience and to yourself. While you are on an island you will not drown and the sharks cannot get at you (Figure 6.1(b)).

Thus, while you cannot totally pre-script a media interview you *can* prepare large chunks of it – and then use 'bridging' techniques (described later) to spend a minimum amount of time in the water and the maximum amount on your 'islands' (Figure 6.1(c)).

HANDLING BROADCAST INTERVIEWS

Checking the Ground

As described earlier in this book, a crisis is as much an *opportunity* as it is a *threat*. The same applies for media interviews. If your best-selling product has just been hit by a major, unfounded, scare story, for example, and ITN have invited you to be interviewed for a piece that they are broadcasting tonight on 'News at Ten', the item will be

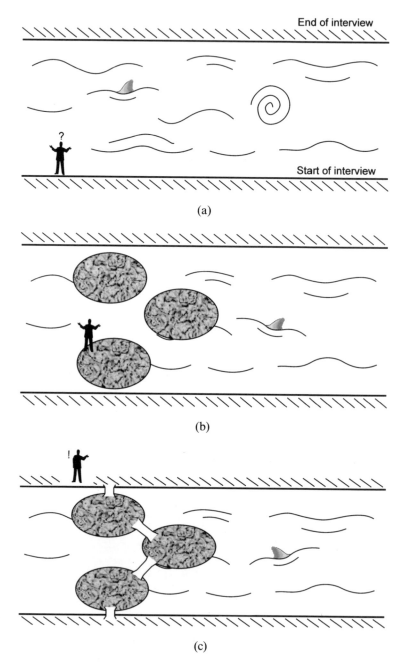

Figure 6.1 Islands of safety

typically one to two minutes long with about 30 seconds devoted to an excerpt from your recorded interview. If you wanted to buy that 30-second slot to put the record straight it would cost you around £250 000 – and here you are getting it for free! Moreover, more people watch the news than the commercials – and editorial coverage is far more credible.

It is staggering that so many organisations turn down opportunities to be interviewed on the usually spurious grounds that they will be 'set up'. It is extremely rare nowadays for recorded interviews to be distorted so that you appear to be saying something different from the original – and it is also prohibited by the producers' own official guidelines.

As you will see from this chapter there is nothing to fear from the questions. As US statesman Dean Rusk said: 'There are no embarrassing questions – only embarrassing answers'. And you can almost eliminate the dangers by preparing your messages and thoroughly checking your ground first. Before accepting an interview, find out all you can by asking:

- What is the programme/item about?
- Who is doing the interview?
- Is it live or recorded?
- When is it being transmitted?
- Who else are they talking to?
- Is there anything you need to know about beforehand that they are going to confront you with? (They are bound by their guidelines not to spring a surprise during the interview.)
- What do they want to ask?

There is nothing wrong with asking them for a general idea of their questions but do not ask for a list. It stifles spontaneity – and the interviewer may spot a more interesting line during the interview, which can dumbfound the interviewee who is slavishly following a 'Q & A' routine.

Just Before the Interview

As well as checking the details and preparing your brief, you can ask the interviewer (and others) questions and get into a dialogue while you are waiting for the interview. Ask them questions like:

- How much do they know about the subject?
- How long will the interview run?
- How much of it are they likely to broadcast?
- What do they want to ask you?

You can ask them about their TV careers, training, interests, where they come from, and so on. The benefits of getting into a conversation based on your questions are:

- It can give some idea of where they are coming from and alert you to likely questions and angles.
- We all need a few minutes' 'warm-up' time in an interview or speech before we start performing at our best. In a TV interview you do not *have* any warm-up time. A discussion with the production team and/or interviewer just beforehand can help you to warm up and prepare for the interview.
- A conversation can also help to relieve nerves. But do not worry if you *are* nervous. You should be. Nerves are valuable adrenalin. *Use* them.
- As with all crisis audiences, human chemistry plays a major part in winning them over.

Appearance and Manner

The way you look on television is *quite* important – but not as much as people make out. Dress smartly, of course, and think of the image that you want the viewer to have of you or your company. Some colours to *avoid* are reds (they 'bleed'), tight stripes (they strobe), black (funereal) and black/dark and white (they throw the colour cameras).

More important than your dress and face, though, is the *personality* you project – and you do this by the way you sit/stand, the way you look at the interviewer and the way you talk with him/her.

Sit up

People look and sound more alert and dynamic when standing – so do the interview standing up if feasible. If seats are essential, then get your back off the back of the chair and sit *upright*, head and shoulders up, maybe slightly forward.

The bar-room interview

Try as hard as you can to pretend that you are not in a TV studio but in your favourite, bar or club – or wherever you most prefer to relax away from work and home. Picture the decor, picture the table or stool you are sitting at – and imagine you have just got chatting with a stranger who starts to ask a few questions about you, your company, your products and so on, and is showing an interest in them.

How would you talk with this stranger in the bar? Would you worry about your 'performance'? Would you worry about whether your legs were crossed or your hands moved and were 'in shot'? Would you pontificate about 'I would like to reassure the viewers. . .'? Of course not. You would come alive naturally because you would want to communicate, to share your belief with your interviewer, and get what is in your brain over into his or hers. You would instinctively lean forward, look him or her in the eye, use simple language, practical examples and anecdotes, modulate your voice and speak with enthusiasm and conviction – or, in the case of a crisis, with genuine concern or sorrow.

If you unknowingly had the cameras on you at this point you would be giving a perfect 'performance' because you would not be *trying* to *perform* – you would be *wanting* to *communicate*! And if you go into that studio wanting to communicate you will do just that. There is nothing they can do to stop you. The only thing that needs 'faking' is your voice in a radio interview. If you slightly exaggerate the highs, the lows and the inflexions you will sound just about right to the listener.

So treat the interviewer as you would that person in the bar:

- Look him/her in the eye (this is very important as wandering eyes look shifty on television).
- Make it a one-to-one conversation with lots of 'you's. By talking personally to the *interviewer* you are talking personally to the *viewer*.
- *Want* to share your knowledge and belief in your subject with him/her.

Handling the Interview

It is much harder to interview than to be interviewed. The interviewer has just as much to lose as you do – often more so. The interviewer knows less about the subject than you do. He/she can only take up a small percentage of the discussion – and any argument has to be turned into questions, not statements. He/she is sitting there with a list of questions to ask, having just been told exactly how long the interview is to run for.

The interviewer is privy to all the background noise and problems of the studio – and if you have ever heard a studio in full cry you will wonder how a programme ever gets out at all. Once the interview starts, the interviewer has to listen to your answers at three different levels:

1. To check that you have dealt with the question.
2. In case you inadvertently answer a subsequent question. For example, if the first question is 'How did the explosion occur?' and you say: 'It was caused by a leak from our solvent tank but happily the fire brigade was on the scene in seconds and got it under control', and the interviewer then asks Question 2: 'How did the emergency services respond?' the producer will not be terribly pleased.
3. To see if you say anything interesting which is worth following up. So if, again, the first question is 'How did the explosion occur?' and you respond with: 'It was caused by a leak from our solvent tank and we're expecting several deaths from inhaling the fumes', the producer will be even less pleased if the next question is: 'How did the emergency services respond?'

This may sound laughable but the poor interviewer has so much to concentrate on that it often happens.

The only real weapon the interviewer has is that he/she is *asking the questions*, which tends to make us defensive. You can overcome this attitude by treating each question not as a *threat* but as an *opportunity* to get on to your own agenda, your prepared messages. Some questions will enable you to get straight on to your own ground, some will require a little more discipline on your part – and some will call for a 'bridge', where you answer the question and move on to a 'bridging theme' before trotting out your prepared message.

Here is how these different approaches work. Say, for example, that you have had a factory explosion and you want to tell your audiences, via the media, that your safety standards are normally second to none and to reassure them that you will try to prevent a recurrence:

Straight answer:

Q. How good are your safety standards?
A. Only last week the Health and Safety inspectors checked our factory from top to bottom and said it was one of the best in the industry. So now we're going to hold a thorough investigation to find out what went wrong and do everything we can to ensure it doesn't happen again.

Although this is a straight answer to the question, you are still seizing the high ground. In particular, note that *you* saying your factory is safe is non-credible – as are BS numbers, ISOs or even the abbreviation 'HSE' (Health and Safety Executive). The above answer carries more credibility.

Bridging

The 'bridging' technique involves moving from a *question* that you do *not* want, to an *answer* that you *do* want. If you are going to bridge you must first be seen to answer the question – and then use the answer as a platform from which to launch your next message via a related theme. For example:

Q. Are you going to compensate the neighbours whose property was damaged by this explosion?
A. We'll certainly look at any claims that come in – but our first priority is to find out how it happened, especially as we normally have such a good safety record. Only last week the Health and Safety inspectors checked our factory from top to bottom and said it was one of the best in the industry.

One message that you can communicate up front in a crisis, without the need for bridging, is the 'human face' one of care and concern. In response to almost any first question it is perfectly in order for you to preface the answer with something like:

May I first say how very concerned we are that this has happened and assure you that we are doing everything we can to find out what happened and prevent it happening again.

Once you have the feel for getting your points across whatever the question, everything else is easy. Most interviewers just want to get the best out of you anyway, but if you do meet a hostile one here are some tricks to watch out for:

- interrupting
- asking multiple questions
- introducing a question with a long, negative statement
- pregnant silence
- wrapping up with a negative

In each case, if you maintain your ground, the interviewer is helpless. If he/she interrupts and you keep talking he has to wait for you to finish. If you are asked two questions at once, you can simply answer the one you want and force the interviewer to have to remember the second one.

But also remember that the 'tricks' might be for your own good. An interruption might be a warning that you are being boring; a multiple question might be an opportunity to wrap up your messages in a single answer. And always remain polite and friendly. Avoid combative language. Take the high ground and do not criticise the competition.

Different Types of Broadcast Interview

There are many different types of television and radio interview:

Live

Relatively few interviews are live – but you should welcome it if you get one. The knowledge that it is for real can enhance your performance. And it also guarantees that nothing can be lost or misinterpreted in subsequent editing; what they broadcast is what you say.

Recorded

Most interviews are recorded – but you should treat them just as though they are live. The experts will tell you that the first take is almost always the best – and you will be less effective if you relax in the knowledge that they might do it again. However, you can ask them to do it again – especially if they do something offside, such as introducing new evidence that you were not advised of.

Panel

This is where there is more than one person being interviewed – sometimes a whole studio audience. Obviously, the more interviewees there are the less of your own messages you will get across. So as you may only get one go at it, have your most important message crystal clear and front of mind. Seize opportunities to jump in – do not wait to be asked.

Down the line

This is where you are in a studio in town A talking with an interviewer in town B. At first this can be very distracting as you no longer have someone to talk with – just a disembodied voice and the self-consciousness of talking into a camera. Sometimes, though, you will see the interviewer on a monitor and be able to talk to the picture, which helps.

The best tip for a down-the-line interview, apart from getting used to it with practice, is to remember that you are simply talking via a microphone and a speaker with someone you cannot see – and that you do just that all day long, on a thing called a telephone! So, just as it helps in the studio to pretend you are in your favourite bar, in a down-the-line interview it helps to pretend you are talking to this person on the telephone.

A down-the-line interview is the only time that you may have no choice but to look into the camera. But because this type of interview is an accepted norm and the viewer subconsciously knows that you have no choice, you do not lose credibility in the way that you would if you looked into the camera during a one-to-one interview.

When they come to you

The advice so far has dealt with studio interviews but they will usually come to you with a camera or tape recorder. The techniques are just the same but it can feel different in some respects. People feel more at ease on their own territory and perform a little better. This is particularly true if you are standing up, especially out of doors.

But watch for the positioning of the cameras as they will try to create a visual confirmation of the nature of the story. In other words, if there is a scare story about toxic leaks from your plant they will try to position you in front of the pile of white drums with nuclear hazard signs and skulls and crossbones all over them.

Doorstep

In exceptional (usually controversial) circumstances they may 'doorstep' you by appearing from nowhere and trying to throw you into an instant interview. Unless you have just been rehearsing your messages you will inevitably be tripped up without the benefit of preparation.

State at once that you *are* prepared to talk – and immediately give a good reason why you cannot do it just now (going to an urgent meeting and so on). Or if it is outside your home or offices you could invite them to come in, so that they have to dismantle the camera and set up again – during which time you can ask them some penetrating questions and prepare some messages.

PRINT INTERVIEWS

Preparing for a print interview is the same as for a broadcast one. And, as with radio and television, you should never go into an interview cold or get engaged in a doorstep interview.

The main differences in handling a print interview are:

- A broadcast interviewer has to both inform and entertain at the same time. But a print interviewer has only to get the information from you – and then he/she goes off to make it entertaining. This makes a print interview potentially much more dangerous than a broadcast one.
- A print interview is usually longer than a broadcast one. This means that you can explain complicated subjects in more depth. But do not get carried away. Like the viewer or listener, the reader will only notice and remember two or three main points. So be sure to get your key points over at least once – backed up by examples, colourful imagery and quotable quotes. It also means, however, that you cannot bridge quickly from the question to what you want to say. You either have to actually answer the question or say why you cannot. And if you do not know, say so; do not speculate or only say 'no comment'.
- There is no audience. This means you can take a little longer to think of your replies if necessary.

Print journalists may use several different tricks of the trade. They can trap you by:

- Being disarmingly nice when you were expecting hostility. Do not let your guard drop.
- Trying to put words into your mouth, such as this famous real-life example in which, after a complicated explanation from a British Rail spokesman about why the snow clearing had failed, the reporter asked:

Q. So, what you're saying is that it was the wrong kind of snow?
A. Well, I suppose so . . .

Headline: 'IT WAS THE WRONG KIND OF SNOW!'
- 'Going fishing' for information:

Q. How much have you personally gained from this windfall profit?
A. Sorry, it's our policy not to disclose that sort of information.
Q. I've heard a figure of half a million being bandied around
A. Oh, it's not as much as that. . .
Q. But over a hundred thousand?
A. Well . . .

Now the journalist has a 'bracket' of between 100,000 and half a million which has virtually been confirmed by you, even though he/she completely made up the bit about having 'heard' a figure of half a million. What if you still refuse to comment?:

Q. I intend to state in my article that you have made around three hundred thousand out of the windfall profit. Would I be seriously wide of the mark?

When the journalist is on a fishing trip don't give an inch.
- Claiming to have already spoken to a colleague or industry source and 'just asking you for confirmation'. This is why it can be important to coordinate media enquiries – usually via a PR department – and to have a company media policy.
- A related trick is 'taking a flier':

Q. How do you feel about your finance director being arrested by the Fraud Squad?
A. How did you know that?

The journalist had simply heard an unconfirmed rumour. Now you have confirmed it.

Some other tips for press interviews:

- Help them by providing plenty of facts and figures. And they will use more of *your* story if you can come up with a good *picture* – a photo or camera-ready artwork.
- Never go 'off the record' – except with a known and trusted journalist, and only then for a very good reason.
- 'Non attributable' (that is, 'you can use this information but do not quote me as the source') can sometimes be used – but again, only with a trusted journalist and for a good reason.

MEDIA HANDLING IN A CRISIS

As far as possible, try to deal with journalists individually as they are much harder to handle in a group.

If a crisis is big enough to attract too many journalists for you to handle individually you must quickly assign someone to look after them full time. This must be a cool-headed person who can remain polite under fire. He/she must make it clear from the start that they are not there to give interviews but to relay as much information as possible, as quickly as possible, to arrange interviews and to look after the journalists' physical needs such as accommodation, a place to meet and work, access to faxes and so on.

This has two advantages:

1. It helps you to know where the media are and what they are looking for and gives you some degree of control.
2. It makes the journalists feel better disposed towards you if they feel they are being well looked after.

An excellent example of such media handling is the Stena Line case study at the end of this book.

Press Conferences

Avoid press conferences if you can as a 'feeding frenzy' develops. If you must hold a press conference ensure that the top person is capable of handling hostile questions and, very importantly, keeping his/her cool. Use a moderator to welcome the media, set the scene, distribute the questions and bring the event to a close. A single roving microphone can help to keep questions to one at a time rather than a barrage.

WHAT TO DO WHEN THEY GET IT WRONG

There are numerous occasions when they get it wrong – usually more from genuine mistakes than out of malice. A journalist might mishear or slip up or, more often, the mistake is made somewhere else along a complex production chain which includes sub-editors and headline writers, all of whom are working at high speed and under pressure.

I work to what I call an 'Eighty Per cent Rule'. That is, if they use what I give them 80 per cent of the time – and if when they use it they get it *right* 80 per cent of the time – that is perfection. For reasons already explained, it is essential to deal with the media – but in the process they *will* get some facts and details wrong and you *will* sometimes be misquoted.

So, whether it is by design or accident, what do you do when they get it wrong?

First, make an unemotional assessment of what actual damage has been done. Remember, there is *almost* no such thing as bad publicity. And also remember that your audience will forget in minutes – can you remember the second lead story in yesterday's newspaper? By and large they remember the name and not the deed – hence the earlier examples of sales going up on the back of a crisis story.

So the best policy is usually to let it go – but at the same time to treat the mistake as an opportunity to build a further bridge with the journalist. So by all means call him/her and point out the wrong-doing, but do so in a constructive manner rather than a vindictive one. Most journalists pride themselves on their professionalism and will respond positively to the idea of meeting up to get to know each other so that further mistakes can be minimised and the way opened up for some future positive stories about you.

However, if the error or mischief is big enough to cause you actual damage, then it is time to apply pressure. A *retraction* is almost pointless as:

- It will appear in an obscure corner of the publication in tiny print.
- It will repeat the incorrect assertion and probably do more harm than good.
- The moment a publication or programme issues a retraction they are liable, so they do not like doing it.
- It will make a lifelong enemy of them for very little reward.

The best option is to pressure them into redressing the balance by publishing a positive story about your company or organisation.

Negative coverage can also be neutralised to some extent by simply asking to meet journalists who criticise you and telling them your side of things and ensuring that they are thoroughly briefed. There is also a half-way house in the form of the Broadcasting Complaints Commission and the Press Complaints Commission.

Dealing with the hard Cases

While the majority of journalists, however bad their behaviour may seem, are only out for a story and will treat you better if you give them one, a small minority can actually inflict lots of damage. The easiest way to spot them is to watch their programmes and read their stories. A high proportion of the sensationalist campaigning and 'consumer' journalists – including their researchers and producers – are more concerned with a good story that suits their preconceptions than they are with minor inconveniences such as the facts. A 'no comment' or a written statement will provide them with a carte blanche to say what they want about you and to use your guarded response as 'proof' of your guilt.

Know your ground

Get hold of copies of the ITC Code of Conduct and the BBC Producers' Guidelines (the latter is on public sale at the BBC Bookshop) so that you know the restrictions under which they are supposed to operate. You will find, for example, that they are not supposed to 'doorstep' you unless they have had a previous request for a formal interview refused; that they may not produce any material during an interview of which they have not given you prior notice; and that an edited programme must reflect the points of substance made by an interviewee in the full recording. These sort of things are useful to know.

Ask them questions

At all stages – before, during and after the interview – check your ground with them. You are fully entitled to know about the nature of a programme, who else is appearing on it, the areas of questioning and so forth. Get this in writing and if they mislead you take them to the relevant complaints commission with the evidence. You do not have to be confrontational, but your thorough and professional approach at this stage will help you to obtain advance warning of their angles so that you can mould your response accordingly.

Use specialists

One malicious programme or article could cost you millions, so it is worth investing a few thousand in PR and legal advice. It is essential that these are specialists with media experience. And call them in from the outset, not when it is too late to change things.

Agree to be Interviewed

Agree to be interviewed and keep tight control of the interview (for example by having your PR advisor and lawyer present to keep an eye on things). Not appearing can be far more damaging than appearing. The public (that is your customers, shareholders and so on) will be left to draw their own conclusions.

By being interviewed you will at least limit some of the damage by showing a human, caring face. And sometimes you can neutralise the impact – or even make it positive.

When Boots ran a playground voucher scheme it made an ideal target for the BBC's campaigning consumer affairs programme, 'Watchdog'. Boots had got their sums wrong and a member of the public spotted that they would have to spend £7000 on Boots' products to pay for a set of Hula Hoops or £35 000 for a tiny kiddies' climbing frame – so they informed 'Watchdog'.

The company accepted an invitation to be interviewed and fielded a spokeswoman who simply agreed that the scheme was fundamentally flawed, admitted that they had got their sums wrong, thanked 'Watchdog' for spotting it and promised to put it right. It took all the sting out of the BBC story and portrayed Boots as caring and human. As you cannot buy advertising space on the BBC that subliminal 'advert' was beyond price.

7 How to Work with Lawyers

Tim Taylor[†]

RECENT TRENDS

Although the conduct and style of legal proceedings in England is different to the United States, there is no doubt that personal injury and other plaintiff lawyers have paid increasing attention to the work of their American cousins over the last 10 years or so. In the United States, the growth of personal injury litigation is largely the result of a contingency fee system, where one successful claim can produce fabulous monetary rewards for the lawyer acting for the claimants, and the willingness of the courts to allow group actions in which the resources of a group of plaintiffs are pooled. The concept of a high-profile plaintiff's lawyer is a comparatively new phenomenon in the UK. It is an increasing trend which is likely to continue.

One of the first cases in England in which the advantages to the claimants of joining forces with other victims became apparent was the Manchester air disaster of 1985 in which 55 people died. Since then, the same handful of specialist firms of solicitors have acted for claimants in most of the recent UK transport disasters including the King's Cross fire, the Clapham railway disaster, the Pan Am crash at Lockerbie, *Piper Alpha*, the *Herald of Free Enterprise* and the *Marchioness* passenger vessel disasters. More recently, they have appeared for victims of the Ramsgate walkway collapse and the grounding of the *Sea Empress* at Milford Haven. In the non-transport area, similar group action has been a feature of other claims such as those against the manufacturers of Opren, Thalidomide and Myodil, and also following the pollution of the River Camel at Camelford.

[†] Tim Taylor is a solicitor and a partner in Hill Taylor Dickinson, with offices in the City of London, Piraeus, Dubai and Hong Kong. He and his colleagues have been involved in several recent high-profile disaster cases, including the *Marchioness*, *Piper Alpha*, *Achille Lauro*, the Ramsgate Walkway Collapse, *Sea Empress* and *Exxon Valdez*.

There are several reasons for this trend:

- The high profile plaintiff's lawyers recognise at a very early stage the power of collective action. Traditionally in England individual claimants, particularly if they are not legally aided, have very slender financial resources and are therefore without access to the best advice and restricted in their choice of experts. Collective action enables those slender resources to be combined and put to best use. It is now possible for conditional success-based fees to be agreed in personal injury cases in England and this is now being done by UK claimants in actions against the tobacco companies.
- The plaintiffs' firms which have come to the fore over recent years are all first-class litigators; they know their way around the legal systems in England and abroad and if they become involved in cases which are beyond the scope of their own expertise they are not embarrassed or unwilling to obtain that specialist expert advice from others.
- The effective plaintiffs' lawyers are also relentless manipulators of the media. There is no doubt that, on some occasions, defendants have been shamed by media pressure into making payments greater than those to which claimants would have been strictly entitled at law.

The pattern of tactics developed by the prominent plaintiffs' lawyers include:

- Making repeated calls for criminal charges to be laid against the company or individuals (or threatening private prosecutions). This happened in the *Herald of Free Enterprise*, the *Marchioness* and *Sea Empress* cases. Indeed it is interesting to reflect that within 24 hours of the loss of the *Estonia*, before there was any informed evidence at all as to the cause of the sinking, there were calls in Estonia and in Sweden for criminal charges to be brought. That now seems to be a standard public reaction, no matter what the evidence may be – or even when no evidence has yet been obtained. Indeed, when there are no charges the public are surprised and do not understand why not. This is all part of a fundamental social change which reflects an increasing willingness to sue when things go wrong.
- Calling for generous flat-rate payments to all victims regardless of the merits of each claim. This is often coupled with a refusal to

identify the claimants represented by the group or to provide any adequate information from which the value of individual claims can be properly assessed.

- Identifying and approaching political figures who may see it as being in their own interests to take up the cause of the victims of the disaster.

- If the defendant is a publicly listed company or part of a public group of companies it is becoming increasingly common for individuals to buy a modest number of shares in the company in order to have the right to attend the company's annual general meeting and put potentially embarrassing questions to the directors.

All these developments from a potential defendant's point of view are going to get worse rather than better.

PROBLEM AREAS

The Facts

There is nothing that can be done to change the facts. All that a defendant can do is to make certain that all helpful evidence is fully deployed. What is important is that before any irrevocable decisions are taken in the immediate aftermath of a crisis, those decisions need to be taken on the very best possible intelligence as to precisely what has happened and where the responsibilities and potential legal liabilities may lie. If lawyers are involved in and control that investigation process, the results of their labours will attract what is known as legal professional privilege and can be protected from becoming public knowledge. That is not always the case where, for example, an 'internal investigation' is carried out.

This is very important and means that the statements that the lawyers obtain and the opinions that they give and the analysis they provide with the assistance of the clients' own staff – and possibly outside technical experts as well – will be confidential and protected from disclosure to third parties, including potential claimants, government inquiries and the police. If lawyers are not involved in that investigation process, there are two risks:

1. that the work of the internal investigation, whether damaging or not, may well become available to the public at large; and
2. those conducting the investigation, while they may be very well qualified in their own particular areas, may have insufficient knowledge of the legal framework within which they are operating and they run the risk of making things worse.

The Police and Criminal Proceedings

In any case involving significant loss of life or personal injury, it is virtually inevitable that there will be some sort of police investigation, even if only for the purposes of a coroner's inquest. There may also be other investigations by official bodies such as the Health and Safety Executive or the Marine Accident Investigation Branch of the Department of Transport. Other countries have very similar investigatory procedures.

In a crisis situation, there now appears to be an immediate media-driven desire to find fault and to pin blame on individuals and urge criminal prosecutions almost indiscriminately. This is far more worrying.

Examples include the prosecution brought against the directors and senior employees of the owners of the *Herald of Free Enterprise*; the prosecutions which failed against the owners of the *Bowbelle* following the *Marchioness* disaster; and the prosecution of the driver of the train which crashed at Purley causing loss of life. He pleaded guilty to manslaughter and was jailed.

There have also been prosecutions of an electrician who wired up a house so that the domestic bath became live and the occupier of the house was killed, and of doctors who have made mistakes treating patients. There have been prosecutions of operators and managers of truck companies operating trucks with allegedly defective brakes. These are not perfunctory summary proceedings where the company, if convicted, might escape with a fine of a few hundred or a few thousand pounds. These are serious prosecutions exposing the directors and managers to unlimited fines and imprisonment. The designers of the Ramsgate walkway which collapsed were fined £750 000. Lloyd's Register, who merely checked the design, were fined £500 000. The prosecution's costs paid by the defendants totalled £723 000. This exposure must be taken extremely seriously.

Very recently, charges have been brought against the Milford Haven Port Authority and the Harbour Masters following the grounding of the *Sea Empress* tanker. The prospect of such prosecutions a few years ago would have been very remote. Now they are very much a reality in the disaster situation.

From my perspective, following a crisis where there have been injuries, I would be less concerned from a legal point about the extent of claims for damages from injured parties, that is civil claims which are probably fully insured, but far more concerned about potential criminal charges and how a criminal investigation should be handled – as well as the potentially adverse impact on the company's business in public relations terms. This has very important consequences from the point of view of contingency planning. In a bad case, there may be a number of different people in the frame. It would not be impossible for charges to be brought against the company, the managing director, the plant manager or technical director or people in that category. Their interests may not coincide exactly.

Someone needs to decide who is going to coordinate the defence, and the person probably best equipped to do this is a lawyer. The last thing that a company in the midst of a crisis wants is their own senior employees running off to their own lawyers in an uncontrolled way.

This raises another question as to who is going to pay for the lawyers. In a simple case, a company might look quite reasonably to its insurers to engage a lawyer to defend the claims but not all insurance provides this sort of cover. In a genuine crisis situation, this is not enough. In such a case there is a risk that the lawyer appointed by the insurers, owing his or her primary obligation to the insurance company, would seek simply to minimise the amount of the civil claims. He or she may care little if anything about restoring the credibility of the brand or seeking to restore confidence in the mind of the fare-paying public. The insurers almost certainly have no interest in those matters at all. It is vital that the company has its own advisors quite separate from those of the insurers so that its own particular interests are protected.

A far better approach is to enter into a dialogue with insurers as part of the contingency planning process so that these problems and the potential areas for conflict are talked through and resolved in advance. There has been an increasing trend for this in the maritime industries but other industries still have some way to go. It is vital for a company involved in a crisis to seize the initiative and to decide for itself on the basis of informed advice where it is going, and not to allow events or third parties to dictate the timetable.

Documentation

I would also like to issue a warning regarding the generation of documentation – not the briefings by PR people to the media or press releases, but internal inquiry documents and control of paperwork generally. There is nothing worse than a 'leak' of a document which is damaging when taken out of context. I am not advocating a cover-up approach – if there is damaging material it will almost certainly come out at some time one way or the other. Far better is to take a more proactive approach, to time the disclosures and to be in a position to emphasise the positive aspects at the same time.

Unrealistic Disaster Plans

What goes into a disaster plan has to be a matter for the company and will vary from industry to industry – but what is important is that you do not create hostages to fortune in your own plans. If the plan is too specific as to what will happen in a given situation, you can be absolutely certain that if there is the slightest departure from that plan some smart lawyer will seek to argue that not only is the company liable for whatever crisis has been brought about, but it has actually made the situation worse by failure to follow its own plan. The key here is flexibility.

Employees/Witnesses

In the aftermath of a disaster there will be huge media pressure for interviews with eye witnesses. This is an area where a lawyer who is closely involved with the company and its business, and who has established the facts, will be able to give some practical advice. In general, I would be very reluctant to allow eye witnesses to be exposed to the media. It is extremely unlikely that they will have had any training in how to deal with media questions or necessarily appreciate the significance of what they are saying. Far better in my view would be again to seize the initiative and for a senior company spokesperson to be put forward to give a detailed (and accurate) briefing on what has happened and what has been done to put matters right.

By the same token very great care needs to be taken with any disciplinary proceedings of one's own staff. This could have serious consequences as far as liability is concerned.

Some years ago, I was involved in a case on behalf of the insurers of a company. We were advancing an argument that the particular accident had been caused without any negligence on anybody's part. A piece of machinery which was brand new, and had been very carefully tested, apparently failed for no good reason in a way that no-one could have predicted.

As the claim progressed, and as the documentation came to light, it turned out that the personnel section of the company had carried out a staff review without consulting the lawyers and had issued a mild reprimand to the individual most closely concerned with the events on the basis that he was guilty of slight negligence. That was, in my view, rather harsh. What was worse was the conclusion, which completely destroyed the defence that was being developed.

The moral here is that you should resist the temptation to start disciplinary proceedings against your own staff without thinking through the consequences. Legal advice is vital.

The Claims

In a crisis situation, the potential for claims is obviously very important – but not as important as some people think. The assessment of claims is usually quite straightforward and there is usually adequate insurance to meet them. Obviously if there is clear liability and no insurance there is always the risk that claims might financially overwhelm the company. Little can be done in the crisis situation to solve that problem.

On the other hand, even if the claims *are* insured, if the other actions necessary to protect the interests of the company – its brands, its reputation and so on – are not taken, there could be equally serious consequences for which no insurance is available. I therefore repeat what I said earlier regarding the importance of establishing a dialogue with your insurers so that if and when a claim arises the insurers will not conduct themselves without regard for the other interests of the company.

HOW ARE LAWYERS BEST INVOLVED IN THE CRISIS PLAN?

For those organisations that have a crisis plan, it is highly desirable for a lawyer or panel of lawyers to be selected in advance. There are some good reasons for this:

- It means that the lawyer is familiar with the client's industry and the culture of the company, and enables the company to select a lawyer who has the experience and skills necessary to deal with the crisis situation. The lawyer who does a great job on your company acquisition work or your conveyancing may not be quite so skilled at dealing with a disaster situation and a criminal investigation. Selection of the lawyer in advance gives both lawyer and client the chance to agree the shape of 'human face' messages which are vital from a PR point of view in any crisis situation.
- In cases where a client does not have a properly trained spokesperson, it is possible for the lawyer to be that spokesperson, subject to having the right training, experience and knowledge of the client.
- Lawyers can be very useful with their contacts in influential areas, such as legal journalists, politicians and captains of industry.

In my experience, even when the PR people and the legal team are working well together and understand each other's priorities, there can be other layers of management in the client organisation who feel that they must interfere because of the importance of the case, because of the seriousness of the crisis and the importance to the company – or simply to save their own skins.

It is absolutely hopeless for the PR people and the lawyers to agree a course of action, perhaps a press statement, and then for that decision to be second-guessed by several layers of senior management. There will inevitably be significant delay and, at the very least, the impact of the message will be lost. A mechanism must exist for decisions to be reached by someone with the necessary authority quickly. If the lawyer and the decision makers have an existing working relationship and they know and trust each other, these problems can be avoided.

HOW CAN THE PR AND LEGAL SIDES WORK TOGETHER?

Why Do Lawyers Think as They Do?

Lawyers are cautious animals. They are trained to think before they act and only to commit to a course of action once they have established all the facts and researched the law. This makes them very awkward customers to deal with in a crisis situation which is developing fast. In such cases, a measured legal response can be worse than no response at all.

So a client selecting a lawyer for the purposes of crisis-response needs somebody who is not only sufficiently confident in his or her knowledge of the law as it affects that particular client's business and is prepared to give speedy advice on the developing situation, but somebody who is also in tune with the public-relations requirements of the client and can assist the PR people in going about their business by not obstructing what they need to do, unless it is absolutely essential. Unfortunately, there are far too many lawyers around who are unwilling to come to terms with these competing pressures.

Key Dates

In a typical disaster situation there will be several events which bring the matter back into the public eye once the immediate crisis has passed. These often have a legal flavour – such as a coroner's inquest, the publication or announcement of a public inquiry, criminal proceedings, the anniversary of the accident and settlement of the main claims. In each case it is vital for the lawyers and PR people to work together so as to anticipate the likely media interest. In some cases it is not difficult to predict what is likely to happen, and it is possible in some cases to pre-empt hostile comment from third parties.

Not Seeking to Defend the Indefensible

Nothing looks worse than an organisation which attempts to defend the indefensible. If it is inevitable that the client will almost certainly be found liable for the particular incident, quite apart from the saving in legal costs, credit can be obtained from a PR point of view in making an appropriate concession. Obviously, one might be cautious about doing so in respect of liability for civil claims for compensation if there was also a pending threat of a criminal prosecution against the company or its staff, but this is where a lawyer in tune with the commercial objectives of the client can suggest appropriate language which achieves the desired result without any downside.

Building Bridges

I believe the lawyer in a crisis situation has a role to play in building bridges between various levels of management in the client organisation. In some ways, ongoing communications within a client company are of more importance than the message to the outside world. Once the immediate crisis has passed, the media will lose interest within a few days. But internally the position may be very different. Employees will be asking themselves whether their jobs are at risk, whether the company is going bust and whether 'Mr X' is going to be charged with a criminal offence.

All of this is hugely distracting for a client company and leads to loss of morale and a general waste of management time. A company would be wise to explain to its own staff what is happening and why and, at this stage, the lawyer should have significant input in what is to be said. It must be assumed that any documents of this sort will 'leak'. That does not mean to say that they should not be issued, only that the contents should be considered very carefully.

Not Making the Situation Worse

I mentioned earlier a situation where an uncontrolled response from the personnel department essentially destroyed a reasonable legal defence. Obviously, the close involvement of a lawyer can avoid that sort of problem. Another example would be attempts by the media to get junior members of staff in a client company to discuss the case in public without the consent of senior management. I have seen examples of this involving 'friendly' journalists attempting to obtain information from telephonists and secretaries. Preventing this sort of thing from happening is all part of the process of establishing clear lines of communication.

One certainty is that, if a company decides to have no dealings with the media at all, it will be assumed that they have something to hide and the media, quite understandably, will adopt any subterfuge in order to get information, no matter how inaccurate or incomplete that may be.

What Can a Lawyer Do?

In a crisis situation, there are basically three types of case:

1. A case which is going to get media attention whether the client likes it or not.
2. A case where the client may gain some benefit (or not as the case may be) if it comes to the attention of the media.
3. A case which is of no interest to the media at all, either because the story is of no interest or because there are other more interesting stories that particular week.

In the first type of case, the client and its advisors will be met by the usual problems of a high-profile media case. There will be a huge amount of misinformation, speculation as to the cause, the desire to pin blame on someone and the general rumour-mill. It is a major advantage to the client if a mechanism can be developed which provides media sources with hard reliable information at a time when hard fact is in very short supply. Lawyers need to recognise that the press have a job to do and a story to tell. If they are provided with reliable information and this helps them meet firm deadlines, they are more likely to print a balanced account.

There may also be the opportunity to challenge inaccuracies at an early stage and this opportunity should be seized. One problem with a typical crisis situation involving lawyers is that once an inaccurate story appears several times, every time it comes up again, perhaps on the anniversary of the accident or another event, the same old rubbish is repeated because the journalist simply goes to the cuttings library and repeats the mistakes made by his or her predecessors.

There are also cases where the media requires a technical legal response. A recent example of this is the solicitor who represented Colin Stagg, the man cleared of the murder of Rachel Nickell on Wimbledon Common, after a judge threw out the case. That was a good result for the client in legal terms, but what was also very important for the client was his solicitor being able to convince the media that it was not a case where his client had got off on some legal technicality because he had a clever lawyer. He was able to get across the message that the prosecution case was flawed from the very beginning in that the only evidence against Colin Stagg was the psychological profiling. The solicitor in that case was wholly successful because the focus of the media attention then shifted directly towards the police and the Crown Prosecution Service. The general point is that, in some cases because of the technicalities involved, a lawyer may be a better spokesperson than someone from the client company.

That example illustrates the importance, when appropriate, of taking a proactive approach. It is perhaps an extreme example but I am doubtful whether anyone without legal training could have explained the important details of the case.

AVOIDING PITFALLS

It is worth mentioning a number of pitfalls which lawyers involved in crisis management should avoid. Lawyers are cautious beasts and like to take their time to consider all the options. In a crisis situation, although time will be very short, I believe it is important in the interests of the client to be seen to be responding positively. Some positive action must be taken, whether this is to launch an inquiry, clean up the mess or whatever. That will enable time to be bought so that the wider implications can be considered at more leisure.

- Resist the temptation to clam up. It is very difficult to do damage to one's case by saying too much – providing the right person is making the statements. Even in the worst case, there are some positive features which can be explained.
- In a compensation-type case, it is often a good idea to make interim payments, even if these are quite modest in money terms. If an admission of liability is going to be made the sooner it is made, the better.
- Choose your lawyers carefully. Find a lawyer who has some experience in crisis situations and someone who enjoys the confidence of your managing director and knows your industry.
- When preparing your crisis plans, talk to your insurers, establish in advance precisely what is covered and what is not, and remember that the financial exposure you may face in effectively dealing with a public inquiry or criminal prosecution is huge and may quite easily exceed the cost of compensation for the underlying claims.

8   Dealing with Pressure Groups

Colin Duncan[†]

Issues monitoring, dialogue (and that means *listening* and acting on *feedback* as well as talking yourself!) coupled with world-class standards are your first line of defence against a crisis – but sometimes you can suddenly find yourself at the centre of a major pressure group campaign. The fact that you have been targeted like this in the first place is probably due to a failure somewhere within your company – but nevertheless you have to manage the situation as best as you can. Here are a few tips on how to avoid such a crisis in the first place and how best to defend yourself if you suddenly find yourself as the centre of attention.

DAVID VERSUS GOLIATH

First of all let me expose the myth that we are talking about 'David and Goliath'. If you do a search on the Internet you will find that there are hundreds of different pressure groups with an interest in environmental issues alone. And that is before you start getting into animal rights, food and all the other issues that are raising their heads.

So it is a very large and very complex movement that we are talking about. And just to illustrate the myth of this sort of David and Goliath that is often presented in the media, Greenpeace alone have over 1000 professional staff on their payroll. It is going down a little because of cuts and they are actually losing revenue in certain countries now, but they still have around 40 offices worldwide –

[†] Colin Duncan is Director, Public Affairs, British Nuclear Fuels plc.

and that's a huge network. They have an annual income of around $150 million dollars. They have a fleet of ships, they have the resources in shock troops. And they have a real-time worldwide communications system with extensive use of the Internet as well as their own internal IT communication systems.

Generally, pressure groups have a sympathetic media and they are outstanding single-issue managers. They are *par excellence* in their particular area – give them a single issue and generally they will not miss an angle on it, I can guarantee it. They are better at it than any PR people I know. They have been doing it for 20 years, they absolutely excel at this skill and they are, by and large, unconstrained by stakeholders, which is a key point when you are communicating in the heat of a pressure group-orchestrated campaign.

Here are the questions to ask yourself to see whether the industry you work for may in future be a target of a pressure group campaign:

1. **Are you a potential target?**   You may be working for an industry that does not know it could be a potential target so it is not just a simple question of 'yes' or 'no'. Some real single-issue management thinking is needed to decide whether your particular business could possibly end up on a hit list. And that takes quite a lot of analysis and some scenario planning in putting yourself in the pressure group's position. If *you* wanted to bring pressure to bear on *your* industry, where would you go for it? You need to step outside your industry to see whether you could be a target.

2. **Do your activities impact on third party countries who have no economic benefit from these activities?**   This is a very important point as far as a pressure group is concerned, because if what you are doing does impact on third parties – it could be individuals, but it tends to be countries or governments – where there is really no economic benefit from what you do, then you have a major weak link, because that is a fruitful way into your issue.

   An example of this is the whaling industry. The whaling ban was achieved through the International Whaling Convention because a number of countries which had no economic interest whatsoever in whaling joined the International Whaling Commission. They voted for a whaling ban because they had nothing to lose. So those countries like Norway, Iceland and Japan, who had quite a lot to lose economically, were outvoted simply by countries with no interest. This is a simple illustration of how a weak link in your industry can be used.

3. **Is there a latent emotional dimension?** Clearly, the more emotional the subject, the more the pressure groups can make of it with the media.

4. **Can a protest be orchestrated which is telegenic?** The television area is very important for most pressure groups because their survival depends on publicity, which keeps the subscriptions from their members rolling in. If they can't get you on TV then you may find that you are left alone.

5. **Have you been keeping your head down?** There is always a tendency if you think you are a target to keep your head down and hope that nobody is going to notice you. In fact this is the worst thing you can do. I am a firm believer that if you are going to have a dispute you should have it on *your* terms when *you* want, not when a pressure group wants it on *their* terms when you tend to be at your weakest point. Moreover, dialogue is more constructive than dispute. Once you are in the middle of crisis, dialogue becomes impossible as positions become entrenched.

6. **Does the weakest link in your production/supply chain have an international dimension?** In the nuclear industry we have to transport nuclear materials around the world. That is our weakest link because, usually, when you have an international dimension that is where your business runs up against third-party countries that have absolutely no economic interest in what you do. So that is the entrée for the pressure group to begin to build up a head of steam against you. Most industries will find that pressure can be easily brought to bear somewhere down their supply chain.

7. **Can competitor pressure be brought to bear?** If you can find a convergence of aims between some of your competitors and a pressure group, some very unhelpful alliances can start to develop. These convergences of interest can come at you from angles that you least expect – so you need to step outside of your industry and try to see where you might be able to identify one or two of your suppliers or one or two of your competitors who, while they may not overtly go out and join forces with a pressure group to put you out of business, will certainly not help you when the going gets tough.

8. **Is there some scientific doubt about the impact of what your industry does?** Every industry that I know of has some scientific doubt associated with what it does, whether you are making Saccharin or cosmetics, whether you are selling food – no matter

what you are doing, there is scientific doubt about the health effect of what you do.

9. **Can one part of your company be played off against another part?** This is a crucial point over which you should have total control within your own industry. The bigger the company, the more varied the agendas. And the more varied the agendas, the more chance there is that you will find people being played off one against the other. Once these cracks start opening up, the single-issue management groups are very good at getting in there and exploiting them. And once your company is divided in terms of what it should do and what the real objective is – coupled with the fact that you may have one or two of your suppliers or your competitors, while not actually throwing petrol on the flames, certainly not helping you to put them out – you suddenly find that a corporate crisis develops.

So those are the nine checkpoints – and if you can put a tick against four or five of those then you might find yourself a pressure group target at some time in the future.

WHAT ARE THEIR TACTICS?

If you *do* find yourself a target, it is worth looking at the kind of tactics that you might find used against you.

It is usually a good sign that someone, somewhere is beginning to target you when you find unexpected studies coming out of universities or think-tanks or from individual academics – and you really don't know why on earth they are looking at this particular issue. This is because one of the first things a pressure group campaigner needs is to start laying a scientific or quasi-scientific foundation upon which to build, because these studies over the fullness of time become 'fact'. First they become media 'fact' and then they become 'accepted fact'. And before you know it you are spending an awful lot of time trying to disprove a study which appeared three years ago because you did nothing about it at the time.

This is the result of keeping your head down. It is very easy to ignore a little study that appears somewhere because it doesn't get any publicity – but it will come back and hit you in the middle of a crisis exactly when you do not want it to.

Another tactic is for pressure groups to seek representation on international fora which could directly or obliquely impact on your reputation. There are so many quangos nowadays involved in all sorts of different aspects of environmental and industrial ethics that it is very easy for pressure groups to get themselves observer status on these bodies. One of these organisations might pass a resolution which, while not actually closing you down or hitting your bottom line in any great way, can, in future, be linked with a couple of studies that have been commissioned in a couple of places around the world. Your opponents are suddenly beginning to build a prima facie case as to why your industry needs changing. The foundations are being laid for a crisis campaign later. These are the sort of things that will be happening over a three/four-year period before you actually enter into a corporate crisis.

If emotional claims are made often enough they become 'accepted facts', such as the ones in the nuclear industry that we 'kill children with leukaemia' and that 'plutonium is the most dangerous substance known to man'. These statements have been said over and over again by anti-nuclear groups for something like 20 years, so that they have become 'fact'. They are not based on any scientific fact. Indeed, the scientific facts completely contradict these two statements, but they have been said over and over again – and if you say something often enough it becomes accepted.

The core of a single-issue campaign is to turn a scientific problem into a political one by communicating on an emotional level rather than rationally. Pressure group communication therefore contains very few facts or science of substance, but is based upon quasi-science and quasi-facts which come from carrying out the kind of research and laying the foundations mentioned earlier. Many pressure group campaigns contain a sliver of fact with a huge amount of emotion on top. To build the foundations takes a long time – it is not an overnight event. It tends to *appear* as an overnight event because the first we get to see about it is at the end of the campaign when, bang, the newspapers have mobilised and the event is happening. Behind that, there is an awful lot of preparation.

Another tactic is what has been called *the salami principle*, which is about taking your industry and cutting it into small slices and deciding on which bits of the supply chain are your weak parts and which bits of your suppliers or your competitors should be targeted. If you are a big industry you are too big to be tackled as a whole, so they will go for the parts that are weak.

Once these foundations have been laid you begin to see the tip of the iceberg poking up into the tabloid newspaper. But it requires a specific event to trigger the crisis. I worked in the oil industry for nine years before joining BNFL, and North Sea decommissioning was an issue for the whole of the nine years I was there – but it never became a public issue until the actual decommissioning of *Brent Spar* provided the newsworthy trigger.

WHAT CAN YOU DO?

So, what can you do? There are 12 actions you could take:

1. **Do not be tempted to keep your head down when you sense rumblings** To do this is to set yourself up at the end of the day for a bigger fall. If you begin to sense 'rumblings' of a possible problem building up for the future, you have to do something about it *now*, because at an early point you have a chance of debate, dialogue and compromise – all those things which effective stakeholder relations is about. If you wait until it becomes a media issue, where positions are totally polarised, all of those luxuries are out of the window and you are into a straightforward propaganda war where they have the emotion on their side and you have very little in your armoury.

2. **Do not wait for the problem to come to you** If somebody is lobbying a government which has absolutely no economic interest in what you are doing, then don't ignore them. Go out there and meet the government, give them the facts, give them the information, put your case.

   This is a problem that we have all the time in the nuclear industry. For example, we transport nuclear cargoes backwards and forwards to Japan. Anti-nuclear groups have spent years winding up the Caribbean and South American nations that these cargoes are floating Chernobyls, just waiting to devastate their land. We go and brief these governments, we brief their advisors, we brief their heads of government on what these cargoes actually are, so that they get the facts.

   When you do this, then what usually happens is that you get a sympathetic ear because you have actually taken the trouble to get on a plane and go out there and do it, and they get pretty angry at the propaganda they have been receiving from pressure groups because they see how much they have been misled with false information. But the option to sit back home because it is not going to hit you means that you are saving these problems up for the future.

3. **Ensure that your science is first class**   And also ensure that you can communicate it in simple terms. Have your 'emotional sound bites' cleared in advance but make sure they are based on sound science.

4. **Know your weak links**   And become involved in the strategic management of these areas at the highest level.

5. **Keep your international networks warm**   If you do not have one, then build one – across time zones if relevant to your business. The time zone issue is fundamental. I have had two international campaigns to manage where pressure groups have been operating while I have been trying to get some sleep – and it is impossible. You really do have to have people based in the right time zones when you are in a crisis position. With the 24-hour media, if you have not got people in the right place, in the right time zone, to give your response, then you have lost it. It is a crucial logistical issue.

6. **Create strategic alliances with your competitors and your suppliers**   Try to get your competitors to understand that 'if we lose this one we all lose'. And it is essential to make sure that your suppliers operate to the same standards worldwide as you do.

7. **Have a plan**   And make someone senior in your company responsible for ensuring that it works and for monitoring potential 'events'.

8. **Try to have the ethical and moral debate on your terms**   Act early and do not wait until you are in the heat of the battle. Dialogue is better than 'position taking'.

9. **Keep customers and other stakeholders informed before a crisis emerges**   Do not duck the difficult issues – communicate proactively, listening and acting on what you hear back.

10. **Be open and honest**   We have about 200 000 public visitors a year to the Visitor Centre at Sellafield – but we also entertain something like 7000 VIP visitors from all over the world. Among these we host visits from anti-nuclear groups, we show them around and sometimes have constructive talks with them. But don't expect them to agree with you and don't get frustrated when they leave the visit and immediately criticise you to the media. Remember, the price of true dialogue is controversy.

11. **Ensure that you are monitoring international fora** And get yourself a place at the table so that you can put your views across as forcefully as your opponents.
12. **Ensure that all parts of your company are united** Expose any divergent agendas prior to crisis. Resolve them at board level by scenario planning. Don't wait for the media to expose them!

So where does all of this leave us? As I said at the beginning of this chapter – monitoring, dialogue and world-class operating standards should be your first line of defence. Dialogue with *all* of your stakeholders is a key ingredient. Perhaps if you listen to that pressure group which has been sniping at you, there might even be an area of common ground where you can begin a dialogue and find a real win/win!

I hope you never have to use the tips set out here. If you think you might have to, then begin that dialogue now – don't wait to be the target!

9   The Role of the Internet[†]

Joseph L. Badaracco Jr and Jerry V. Useem

INTEL VERSUS THE INTERNET

Intel is the world's leading chip maker. Its microprocessors are the brains of roughly 80 percent of the world's 150 million PCs, and the company's 56% gross profit margin topped the industry. The company sells most of its chips to a handful of large computer manufacturers – Compaq, Packard-Bell, Gateway 2000 and IBM – who then sell Intel-based PCs under their own brand names. Intel's new, state-of-the-art Pentium chip was selling briskly during 1994, accounting for nearly a quarter of the company's unit shipments. Positioning the chip as suitable for both home and heavy-duty workstation use, Intel coupled the Pentium's release with its $150-million 'Intel Inside' advertising campaign designed to heighten consumer awareness of the role of its microprocessor.

In June 1994 Intel engineers discovered a subtle flaw in the way the chip performed division. The Pentium, they discovered, returned inaccurate results in division problems involving long numbers, especially with denominators of nine or more digits, and there was no easy way to tell if the chip had made such a mistake. Intel's engineers, however, concluded that such errors would occur extremely rarely: an average of once every nine billion divides, or once every 27 000 years. We couldn't imagine anyone ever running into it', remarked Intel President Andy Grove. The errors were also very small. Most occurred in the ninth significant digit or beyond, an inconsequential magnitude for most computer applications. Hence,

---

[†] The Internet is an increasingly potent force in crises and issues. It cannot be ignored – and the Intel Pentium crisis in 1994 fired a large warning shot across the bows of all companies and organisations.

    This chapter is extracted from a case study that first appeared in *Business Ethics* magazine, published by Blackwell Business, in January 1997. Although primarily about the Pentium crisis it contains a wealth of valuable observations and advice about the role of the Internet in a crisis. The authors are: Joseph L. Badaracco, Jr, who is John Shad Professor of Business Ethics at the Harvard Business School, and Jerry V. Useem, who is a former Research Associate at Harvard and currently on the editorial staff of *Inc.* magazine.

Intel decided not to inform customers of the bug's existence, and planned to continue selling the 'buggy' chips until an updated version could be released in early 1995.

In the spring of 1994, Dr. Thomas Nicely, a mathematics professor at Lynchburg College in Virginia, was using a Pentium-equipped computer as part of a division-intensive research project. On June 13, he noticed that the computer was incorrectly calculating the reciprocals of the numbers 824633702441 and 824633702443. For four months, Nicely scrutinized the operating system and his own programmes for the source of error, all in vain, until finally he came to the startling conclusion that the problem was the Pentium chip itself. Dr Nicely contacted Intel technical support about the problem in late October, but when Intel failed to provide a meaningful answer within a week, he sent electronic mail messages to several acquaintances and asked them to try replicating the error.

One of the recipients was Andrew Shulman, author of several computer books, who promptly forwarded a copy of the message to Richard Smith, president of Phar Lap Software in Cambridge, Mass. Smith in turn posted the message on Compuserve's Canopus forum. Meanwhile, Alexander Wolfe, a managing editor at the trade journal *Electronic Engineering Times*, saw Smith's posting and immediately e-mailed Terje Mathisen, a computer expert in Norway, asking his opinion on the reported bug. Mathisen wrote a programme to test Nicely's findings and, to his surprise, it confirmed the existence of a division bug on the Pentium. He e-mailed the results back to Wolfe, whose November 7 article in the *EE Times*, although it was the first story to mention the bug, received little mainstream attention. Mathisen then posted a message entitled 'Glaring FDIV bug in the Pentium!' to the Internet newsgroup comp.sys.intel.

Newsgroups, one of the most widely used features of the Internet, are forums for information exchange on specialized topics ranging from Barney to bondage to banjo music. Thousands of them exist on the Internet, including company- and product-specific ones devoted to discussing IBM, Chrysler, Denny's, air travel, cellular telephones or sugar cereals. Intel and its products had inevitably become the focus of a newsgroup: prior to November 1994, comp.sys.intel was a languid newsgroup frequented by computer sophisticates interested in discussing the fine points of Intel hardware. In the weeks after Mathisen's first posting, however, it was transformed into the setting of a heated national – in fact, global – debate, collecting more than 6000 Pentium-related messages over a six-week period.

At first the discussion was limited to a small band of technical users who confirmed the error and determined its magnitude and frequency of occurrence. Then a slightly wider audience of Pentium-users chimed in, with incensed PhD students asking 'How can I publish results that were computed on a defective chip?' The flurry of activity on comp.sys.intel had grown large enough by mid-November so that the controversy began to spill into the national press. It started when Steve Young, a technology reporter for CNN, received e-mail alerting him to the Pentium discussion. Internet newsgroups had recently become popular among reporters as a fishing pond for story leads, and Young logged on to comp.sys.intel several times to read the postings there.

Young's CNN report, which appeared on November 22, initiated a buzz of interest in the print media. Reporters at the *San Jose Mercury* and the San Francisco bureaus of the *New York Times* and *Wall Street Journal* simultaneously started preparing stories on the bug. One of the reporters, who spent time scanning comp.sys.intel with colleagues as he prepared his story, remarked: 'Usually when you have a story about consumer beefs, it's hard to track down unhappy customers. But here you had all these inflammatory statements already in text form. You didn't even have to hit the keystrokes – you could just copy the messages onto your computer'. The *New York Times* article, which appeared on Thanksgiving day, reprinted a maths problem gleaned from the Internet so customers could test for the error on their computers.

Press coverage of the controversy mushroomed in the following days, and Internet users, alerted to the comp.sys.intel discussion by the mainstream media, logged onto the newsgroup in ever greater numbers. As many as 250 people posted messages each day, while thousands more read their messages as spectators. In contrast to the well informed technical users who dominated the early discussion, many of these new posters were less concerned with the technical elements of the issue than with posting angry, emotional, and some-times vicious messages attacking Intel for its failure to disclose the bug and its refusal to replace all flawed chips. Since the beginning of the controversy Intel had maintained a policy of granting replace-ment chips only to high-end users who could demonstrate that they needed a very high level of accuracy in division problems, and these users had to answer questions from Intel representatives before getting a new chip. 'I know it's buzzing all over the Net', said Intel spokesman Howard High. 'But there are maybe several dozen people

THE Sun

Saturday, September 20, 1997 **28p**

MANSLAUGHTER QUIZ AFTER SIX DIE ON EXPRESS

COPS ARREST CRASH DRIVER

Train 'went through red light' probe

By MIKE SULLIVAN

THE driver of the express train in the Southall rail disaster was arrested by police last night on suspicion of manslaughter.

The unnamed driver was held 5½ hours after the horrific smash in which six passengers were killed and 163 injured, 13 seriously.

Transport Police inquiries centre on whether he shot through a red light before his inter-city express hurtled at more than 100mph into a freight train crossing his path.

SHOCK

The driver, who amazingly survived the crash with just shock and scratches, was taking the 10.22 Great Western 125 service from Swansea to Paddington.

He was questioned for five hours at a police station near the disaster scene in West London. He was also breath-tested after the tragedy. The result was negative.

The shaken driver of the freight train was also quizzed after human error emerged as the likeliest cause of the crash.

He was released but may be questioned further later.

A spokesman for British Transport Police said: "The driver of the high speed train was arrested on suspicion of manslaughter. He was questioned in connection with

Continued on Page Two

Rescuers lift a survivor from the mangled wreckage of the express train which crashed at 100mph yesterday **Picture: DOUG SEEBURG**

FULL STORY AND DRAMATIC PICTURES: PAGES 2, 3, 4, 5, 6 AND 7

Escape ... express driver's cab

Driver is held

Continued from Page One

allegations he went through a red signal. We are still in the stages of interviewing other witnesses such as signal staff to establish exactly what went wrong.

"But there is no suggestion the driver was under the influence of drink."

Police freed the express driver on bail shortly before midnight, but he was still inside the police station early today.

A spokesman said: "He is due to return here on October 31."

A Health and Safety Executive probe has also been launched. Investigators will try to find out if the crash was caused by human error or signal malfunction.

CROSS

The 20-wagon freight train had been cleared to cross two express lines to reach a goods yard. It was halfway across when it was hit by the 125, which should have been given a red "stop" signal.

Even if the express driver failed to spot the signal, a braking device known as an Automatic Train Protection System should have cut in.

Expert Richard Hope, consultant editor of Railway Gazette, explained: "Beacons on the track transmit signals to the cab. If the driver fails to slow at a danger signal, the train is stopped automatically."

● THE driver of the train which crashed at Watford in August last year faces a manslaughter charge. Peter Afford, 56, was committed for trial in April but his case has yet to be heard. Journalist Ruth Holland died in the smash.

RAIL CHIEFS KEPT COOL

TWO train bosses were on the express when it crashed.

Great Western Trains managing director Richard George and Railtrack commercial director Richard Middleton were shocked but not badly hurt.

Radio 5 Live reporter Jane Garvey was also on board and told how Mr George kept his cool. She said: "He was excellent. He got up and told everyone not to worry."

I SAW THREE BODIES BY THE TRACK

Rescuers' horror as six are killed in trains pile-up

DISASTER AT SOUTHALL

SHOCKED rescuers told of horrific scenes of carnage last night after an express train hurtled into a line of freight wagons at over 100mph.

Six passengers were killed and 163 injured — 13 seriously — in the disaster at Southall station, West London.

It happened when a slow-moving freight train crossed the path of the 10.32 inter-city 125 service from Swansea to Paddington.

The impact was massive. The engine is thought to have hit the rear of one wagon and its coupling, sending the diesel section of the express and the first carriage leapfrogging over at incredible speed.

Following coaches packed with passengers hit the wagons hard and flew in the air before crashing down again.

Twisted wreckage screeched 400 yards down the line.

Overhead power cables were torn down, causing an explosion and flash fires amid the mangled metal.

And helpers who dashed to the aid of screaming survivors were confronted by terrible sights they will never forget.

The impact was massive. The engine is thought to have hit the rear of one wagon and its coupling.

Encased

One victim was lying across a live cable. The three others who died were still encased by wreckage hours after the 1.30pm crash.

Firemen concentrated their efforts on freeing the injured using heavy cutting gear.

Once that was done, they returned to the dead. One body was lifted clear at 8pm and the two others were recovered just after 9pm.

Locals rushed to the rescue seconds after the disaster. Tony, who works for a newspaper, said:

● I was working on my car when I heard a scraping noise followed by the most enormous bang, which sent a huge ball of smoke into the sky above the rail line.

I ran with two friends straight across the track, calling 999 on my way on my mobile phone.

Two policemen joined us and we immediately realised it was very serious.

One of the first sights that confronted me was a virtually decapitated man who had been flung from the second carriage on to the side of the track. Another body was lying across the track but we

By NICK PARKER and MIKE SULLIVAN

couldn't touch it because it was across live electrical cables.

I'll never forget the sounds of people shouting for help. Some were crying, 'Please help us. Is anybody there? Please, please help.'

Others had obviously been injured and were just screaming at the top of their voices.

We ran to a carriage that was lying on its side and started to pull people through an open window.

I got about 15 out and many looked terribly shocked with blood pouring from their faces.

We did all we could but some were trapped and we felt so helpless. Two of the carriages had virtually disintegrated and were scarcely recognisable as part of a train. It's difficult to believe that anyone got out alive.

Tony added: "As we led some of the walking wounded along the track we had to go past two or three badly mangled bodies.

"Some of the survivors just freaked out when they saw them.

"So we ran off and used curtains from the wreckage and whatever else we could find nearby to cover up the bodies."

The crash was the worst on the railways since the Clapham disaster of December 1988, when 35 people were killed.

The night-coach Great Western express was carrying a full payload of 480 passengers into Paddington.

Its driver, who is on bail after being quizzed by police, survived with barely a scratch.

Though shocked, he managed to run along the track with a red flag to stop a THIRD train ploughing into the wreckage. Scaffolder Darren Eagle — one of the first on the scene — said: "I saw him dash into some sort of control box to raise the alarm. Police and waving rescuers

also helped to bring the other train to a halt in time.

Relieved Darren, 25, said: "God only knows what might have happened if it had got involved. We might all have been killed."

The freight train, owned by the EWS company, was pulling 20 empty wagons from Allington, Kent, to a goods yard by Southall station.

It had been heading westbound on a four-track section, on a "slow" line for freight and commuter trains.

It was guided to the opposite side of the tracks ACROSS two "fast" lines used by inter-city 125 expresses.

But it had nowhere near completed the manoeuvre when the Swansea train thundered into view.

Smashed

The diesel-powered express smashed into the eighth wagon, punching it and three others a quarter of a mile down the track.

At first sight, it looked like the express had been ripped in two by the crossing train.

The freight driver escaped unhurt but was said to be "deeply shocked." A massive rescue operation was launched as emergency services put major incident plans into action.

Firemen battled to free 16 trapped passengers as other dazed travellers clambered out of the carriages and walked slowly back down the line to the station.

A fleet of 30 ambulances and buses with medics on board rushed casualties to six hospitals in West and Central London.

Doctors were flown to the scene by helicopter and police cordoned off the area.

All train services from Paddington were suspended. Some people living near the track at first thought a bomb had exploded. But as soon as they realised what had happened,

they rushed out with blankets, chairs and cups of tea for the walking wounded.

Scaffolder Darren was working with pal Peter Ferguson when the trains collided a stone's throw away.

Peter, 30, said: "We heard a colossal crash of metal on metal it was an horrific sound.

"We dropped everything and sprinted across the tracks.

"The first thing we saw was a man lying dead on the ground with blood pouring from his mouth.

"He looked like he'd suffered terrible head injuries - and we knew instantly there was nothing we could do for him.

"So we moved on to try to help the injured who were crying out in the wreckage. We saw a man who we assumed was one of the drivers staggering around looking dazed.

"We did what we could to help but decided to cover up the dead. There were several on the ground outside the train."

Deputy Premier John Prescott ordered an urgent report after touring the crash site. He said: "The scene is horrific.

"The Prime Minister has expressed his concern and I will be reporting back to him." PM Tony Blair and Opposition leader William Hague sent condolences to the families of those killed.

The inquiry into the disaster will be led by Detective Superintendent Graham Satchwell, of the British Transport Police.

Andy Hancock, acting director of Railtrack's Great Western District, said: "This was one of the fastest stretches of track into Paddington with a potential line speed of 125mph.

● RAILTRACK has set up a special emergency hotline for worried relatives. The number is 0171 934 7777. It should NOT be called for travel inquiries.

I SCRAMBLED OUT THROUGH WINDOW: PAGES 4 & 5

Horror on the line ... firemen clamber up ladders to reach survivors trapped in the twisted wreckage of the 125 express yesterday Picture: DOUG SEEBURG

HOW THE TRAINS COLLIDED

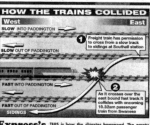

West ← → **East**

SLOW INTO PADDINGTON →

1 Freight train has permission to cross from a slow track to sidings at Southall station

SLOW OUT OF PADDINGTON →

FAST INTO PADDINGTON →

FAST OUT OF PADDINGTON →

SIDINGS

2 As it crosses over the east bound fast track it collides with oncoming 10.32am passenger train from Swansea

Express's fast track to horror

THIS is how the disaster happened. The empty freight train approaches Southall on the west-bound slow line and is signalled to cross over two fast lines into sidings. At the same time the 10.32 inter-city 125 express from Swansea to Paddington hurtles towards it and smashes into the wagons at more than 100mph.

I scrambled half-blinded through 18in window gap

Lucky to be alive . . Dr Hellier with wife Janet

ESCAPE DOC FEARS HE'LL LOSE AN EYE

By TRACEY KANDOHLA

A TOP doctor who suffered serious eye injuries in the train horror told how he escaped by wriggling through an 18in gap in a shattered window.

Consultant physician

Everything was chaos and my only intention was to get out.

"Somehow I managed to wriggle through this tiny 18in gap and then these two very kind gentlemen helped me across to an ambulance which was already

Portsmouth, and Timothy, 25, who is with London's Natural History film company.

Dr Hellier is recovering at West London's Ealing Hospital. He is one of three survivors detained there.

As well as a badly-injured eye, he has numerous face and scalp lacerations, plus broken ribs.

DISASTER AT SOUTHALL

ENGINE IN LEAP-FROG AT 100mph

THE driver of the express escaped serious injury as his engine VAULTED the freight train.

The diesel section is believed to have rammed the rear of one wagon and its coupling. The engine and the first coach then leap-frogged over at incredible speed — leaving first class passengers in the second and third carriages to take the brunt of the impact.

Most of the dead and wounded were pulled from these two coaches, which ended up mangled beyond recognition. A senior officer with the British Transport Police said: "The first class carriages were rammed into the wagons and took most of the impact.

"It appears the passenger train leap-frogged over the freight wagons and came to rest on the other side."

Intact

The third coach — reserved for first class — was also the buffet car. Worst-hit was the second.

But the carriage immediately behind the engine landed on its side almost intact. Like the driver's section its wheels were ripped off.

Some coaches towards the rear of the express even managed to stay on

By THOMAS WHITAKER

the rails. Rescuers were unable to cut the last two bodies free until just after 9pm because of fears firemen could be injured by shifting metal.

Senior divisional fire officer Damian Smith explained: "Until the train was stabilised we could not guarantee the safety of people working there."

Transport Police officially took over once all victims were recovered.

A fire brigade spokesman said: "Investigators will arrive at first light.

"They will have to carry out a search of the site and make it clear for rail journeys."

'Dreadful' says Queen

THE Queen said the crash was "dreadful" and added in a statement: "My family send deepest sympathies to families and friends of those killed or injured, and our thanks to everyone who helped in any way."

GRIM TOLL OF TRAIN DISASTERS

THE crash is the second worst rail disaster in the past decade.

1996: One dead, 69 injured in head-on crash outside Watford Junction, Herts.

1991: One dead, 248 injured when express rammed buffers at Cannon Street, London.

1990: Driver killed, 35 hurt when empty train hit Manchester-Penzance express at Stafford.

1989: Five dead, 94 hurt when two trains collided at Purley.

1989: Two killed, 52 injured as two trains crash in Glasgow.

1988: Thirty-five dead, 113 injured in three-train pile-up outside Clapham Junction.

1987: Four killed when train fell into River Towy in Wales after bridge collapsed.

1986: One dead, 60 hurt when two expresses collided at Colwich, Staffs.

1986: Nine dead, 11 hurt when train hit van on crossing near Lockington, Humberside.

DOOR LOCK TRAPPED US IN CARRIAGE

TWO survivors told last night of their terror at being trapped in a smoke-filled carriage by the "safety" doors.

Businessman Martin Coulson, 49, said black smoke poured in as passengers struggled to open the electric doors for up to 10 MINUTES.

Martin, from Swansea, added: "They wouldn't budge."

Another man said: "We were stuck with smoke rising around us." Police rescued them. The doors lock to stop people falling out of a moving train.

Devastation . . the mangled wreckage of the express and the freight train it hit lies twisted across the tracks after yesterday's high-speed horror crash

Mercy mission . . . ambulance workers tend to seriously injured passengers on stretchers. One paramedic (right) holds aloft a bottle of blood plasma

EVERYONE WAS SCREAMING AS TRAIN FLEW IN THE AIR: PAGES 6&7

How could it happen?

Sell-off brought too many cooks, say ex-BR bosses

INVESTIGATING the cause of the crash will be even harder because of privatisation, claim two ex-British Rail safety bosses.

Last night, as the driver was arrested on suspicion of manslaughter, they claimed there were now too many different outfits involved in running the rail network.

Peter Rayner, who was sacked by BR for warning safety would slip under privatisation, said: "It will be a job sorting out who owns what which will make investigating even harder.

"There is no longer a single line of command. No longer can the Railway Board chairman state the whole matter will be dealt with by the railway.

By JOHN KAY

"Now you have a situation where Railtrack owns the infrastructure, Great Western Trains operate the trains, and the freight train is operated by someone else.

"Great Western doesn't even own the vehicles — they are owned by a company which in turn is owned by Stagecoach.

"Signalling will be maintained by someone else and the track by somebody else on behalf of Railtrack.

Cautious

"The drivers will work for different people.

"Everybody is going to be cautious, everybody will have a lawyer, and everybody will try to protect their own backside.

"It makes the investigation and the management of safety extremely difficult."

Mr Rayner, 62, was chief operating manager of London Midland. He also claimed the privatised rail firms were cutting corners on safety to save money and boost profits.

He said: "This was an accident waiting to happen. Too much money has been spent on the sell-off and not enough on safety. This sort of sprawling privatised railway is virtually impossible to manage.

"There are now too many cooks stirring the broth — and too many concerned about protecting their own positions.

"There are too many vested interests involved. I am a time-serving railwayman and these things hurt me."

Former senior BR safety expert John Child, 62, attacked cost-cutting by the private firms.

He said a friend still in signalling told him this week that many contract jobs were stopped because money ran out.

The estimates were too low. This is happening throughout Southern region and elsewhere.

"Under nationalisation ways were found to provide the money.

"These private railway companies just went to make money.

"Before, it was a public service which was safe and not motivated by profit."

Earlier express had been hit by signal gremlins

THE computerised signal system on the West London line was giving problems yesterday morning — only hours before the death crash.

The 7.54am high speed Didcot to London service was directed into a Paddington platform which was already occupied by an empty train.

A rail supervisor told The Sun the express was held up for almost half an hour, then reversed out and routed to another platform.

He claimed rail chiefs were thinking of switching off the signalling computer and directing trains manually.

By MIKE SULLIVAN

The man said: "There were already gremlins in the integrated electrical control centre.

"A high speed train was routed into platform 12. But the platform is not long enough for an inter-city 125 and there was already another train waiting there."

Railtrack said: "A signalling incident did happen this morning at Paddington.

"The high speed train was travelling slowly and the driver realised the platform was occupied.

"He stopped the train and reversed and moved into a different platform.

"At this stage we don't think there is any connection with the crash because it was a different circuit. But we will leave no stone un-turned and we will establish whether there is any link at all."

Signalling on the track where the train crashed is done by computer from the Integrated Electrical Control Centre at Slough, Berks.

Proved

The rail source said: "A fortune has been spent on the computerised system but it isn't foolproof.

"The incident at Paddington today proved that. They were looking at suspending 50 per cent of the trains from Paddington because of the earlier cock-up.

"Then, all of a sudden, there is a crash. It is too much of a coincidence."

EVERYONE AS TRAIN

Shaken . . . a passenger in a blanket is helped away by police

Stretcher case . . injured traveller is lifted into an ambulance

Cuppa comfort . . . two

Terror for passengers

STUNNED train crash survivors told last night how passengers screamed in terror as carriages were hurled into the air by the massive impact.

Travellers were left shocked and sobbing in the twisted wreckage of the 100mph express.

Television producer **Adam Vandermark**, 35, said: "There was a huge smash and all the luggage flew everywhere. Our carriage careered on for ten or 15 seconds.

"Then there was screaming, with a lot of people shocked and a bit crying. The lights went off and then there was an awful stench of smoke." Mr Vandermark, who works for Channel 4, was among many journalists returning from Wales on the train after covering the devolution vote.

By ANTONELLA LAZZERI and JOHN KAY

He did not realise how bad the accident was until he scrambled from the 10.32 Swansea to Paddington express and saw it had smashed into a freight train.

He said: "Carriages were on their sides and three or four were badly mangled.

The freight train was a mess. It was all over the tracks."

One mother broke down in tears as she told of seeing dead and injured people as she scrambled to safety.

Ann Welfare, 46, travelling home to London with her teenage daughter, said: "There was an almighty bang and we were thrown everywhere. It was complete chaos and confusion.

Smoke

"Everyone was screaming. We clambered out of a door. As we walked along the track I could see people trapped in the wreckage.

"Some were covered in blood and looked dead. Others were injured — it was horrible.

"My daughter has gone into shock and can't speak." Norseman **Mark Cole** told of the moment of terror when his carriage "seemed to fly through the air."

He said: "The windows were smashed and shards of glass flew everywhere.

"I was in the fifth carriage. Those worst injured were in the first-class car-

helt on its side and we climbed to a door and jumped down to the track. There was an almighty mess."

Journalist **Celia Ellecott** told of seeing flames pouring from the express engine as she scrambled to safety.

She said: "We were told to mind the overhead cables. The engine was lying across the track and the first carriage was on its side.

"The next two or three carriages were all tangled up together."

Researcher **Nick Sutton**, 22, said: "As I left the train I saw a man's body lying by the tracks.

"His shirt was ripped and there was blood all over him. There were other people with blood on their faces."

Passenger **Sue Orr** escaped serious injury because she was at the rear of the train in a smokers' carriage.

She said: "There was a massive impact, luggage flew about and we tried to take cover under tables.

"We saw electric cables coming from above and crashing through windows. But we were the lucky ones.

"We were in the last three coaches. Thank God I smoke, that's all I can say."

Builder **Manjeet Singh** was working near the crash scene at Southall, West London, and dashed to help the injured.

Cries

WAS SCREAMING FLEW IN THE AIR

DISASTER AT SOUTHALL

Walking wounded . . . a policeman guides a stunned woman from the scene of yesterday's rail horror   Pictures: DOUG SEEBURG, DAVID BOYLE and JAYNE RU

that this would affect. So far we've only heard from one. It's reasonably rare.' Intel had also initially denied that it was still sending flawed chips to customers, when in fact it was continuing to do so.

On November 27, 1994, faced with a growing chorus of hostility on the Net, Intel's president, Andy Grove, took the unprecedented step of posting his own message on comp.sys.intel. Apologizing for the situation and explaining that 'no microprocessor is ever perfect', Grove pointed out that the bug was far less serious than the flaws that had been discovered in early versions of Intel's 386 and 486 chips. He made several blunders. First, because he did not have direct access to the Internet, he posted his message through a subordinate. Because the message did not bear Grove's address, many Internet users doubted the posting's' authenticity, thereby fanning their distrust and anger. Secondly, he unflinchingly stood behind Intel's original 'one-in-nine-billion' figure – and the idea that the bug was inconsequential for the vast majority of users – when several scientists and mathematicians on comp.sys.intel had posed credible challenges to this assertion. Most importantly, as the technical tone of his message suggests, Grove assumed he was addressing a small colloquium of experienced technical users, when in fact much of his audience was large, growing and diverse, and some of it resembled a lynch mob. Hence, Grove's message added more kindling to the fire.

The final and most celebrated chapter of the affair involved IBM, which was both Intel's largest customer and, as one of the developers of the rival PowerPC chip, Intel's competitor. On December 12, as the storm surrounding the Pentium seemed to be finally abating, IBM made the stunning announcement that it was halting shipment of all Pentium-based PCs, based on the findings of its own in-house study. The study, which IBM posted on-line on its 'home page' on the World Wide Web, claimed that a floating point error would crop up not every 27 000 years, as Intel claimed, but every 24 days. Grove quickly shot back; 'You can always contrive situations that force this error. . . . If you know where a meteor will land, you can go there and get hit'. Many observers agreed that IBM had used unrealistic assumptions for its study, but the shipment halt was nonetheless regarded by many as a strategic masterstroke that would revive the Pentium controversy during the crucial Christmas shopping season.

Indeed, there was a renewed ferocity to the criticism on comp.sys. intel, while IBM won high praise from posters for siding with them and sticking up for the average consumer. Meanwhile, the story refused to die in the press, with the *New York Times* reporting on December 19 that fears about the Pentium were 'growing exponentially'. Thus, the following day, Intel announced that it was reversing its policy and adopting a no-questions-asked return policy. 'What we view as an extremely minor problem has taken on a life of its own,' said Grove. The company ran full-page advertisements in major newspapers apologizing for **its** handling of the situation, and a month later it announced a $475 million write-off to pay for the replacements.

Many viewed this as a victory for the on-line activists 'Internet has spoken', wrote Claire Bernstein in the *Toronto Star* in 1995. 'No one doubts it can spew flames.' Said Alexander Wolfe of the *Electronic Engineering Times*: 'The Internet was the key element in thrusting the story into the public eye. The volume and ferociousness of those communications [on comp.sys.intel] alerted Intel, Intel's competitors (notably, IBM) and the mainstream press that this was an issue with "legs". In summary, without the Internet, the FDIV flaw would have become a quickly forgotten footnote in the history of microprocessor design.' Cleve Moler, one of the mathematicians prominently involved in the Pentium controversy, remarked that 'this whole affair is certainly a creation of the Net'. Intel apparently concurred, for after the controversy was over Grove said that the company planned to strengthen its official presence on the Internet and to monitor Internet discourse on a long-term basis. In January, the company created a new On-Line Affairs Department.

THE EMPOWERED STAKEHOLDER

In Apple Computer's famous, one-time-only advertisement during the 1984 Superbowl, an athlete hurled a javelin at a massive computer screen suggestive of Orwell's 'Big Brother', and shattered it. This was Apple founder Steve Jobs's vision of the PC revolution: small, powerful, independent computers empowering people to free themselves from the yoke of information control, symbolized by IBM and centralized mainframes.

An 'empowerment' scenario provides the optimistic interpretation of the Pentium episode. In essence, the Internet, by breaking down the ordinary pathways of communication and establishing new, more populist ones, will empower customers to hold corporations to higher standards of accountability. Customers, after all, are important stakeholders in companies – especially in firms such as Intel, in whose hardware they have already heavily invested, and on whom they are highly dependent due to the company's dominant market position. In this happy scenario the Internet will allow customers to weigh in on business decisions in instances when their interests might normally have been discounted, all to the benefit of society.

The first way that the Internet can empower stakeholders is to bring together, with astonishing speed, highly talented cadres of experts who can closely scrutinize a company's activities. Especially during the first weeks of the Pentium episode the Internet functioned as a worldwide forum for detailed technical analysis. It allowed experts who didn't know one another to collaborate in instant, special-purpose scientific colloquies, contributing their analytical skills to the problem and trading observations and results. Participants included Vaughan Pratt, a Stanford University mathematician; Cleve Moler, chairman of the Cambridge-based software company The Maffiworks; and Tim Coe, an engineer at Vitesse Semiconductor in Southern California.

Tim Coe's contribution to the analysis was illustrative of how the Net worked as a global technical forum. A week after the bug was first reported on comp.sys.intel, Andreas Kaiser of Germany posted a list of 23 numbers that the Pentium calculated incorrectly. As a chip engineer himself, Coe was able to use Kaiser's numbers to construct a model that he thought would explain the reported division errors. The model, it turned out, implied that the Pentium could produce errors of a much larger magnitude than those reported thus far. Coe therefore created a worst-case mathematical scenario: a pair of seven-digit numbers, which, when divided, would produce a quotient containing an error in the fourth significant digit.

Technical experts, therefore, will lend stakeholders legitimacy and power, for they know what they are talking about and they know they deserve to be listened to.

The second way that the Internet can empower stakeholders is by becoming a source of swift and powerful consumer activism – a vehicle for a new Naderism. That is, not only will high-end technical users gain power, but also average customers – in this case Pentium owners or would-be owners. Consumers can find a louder voice through a form of electronic activism that facilitates contacts among like-minded people and allows them to achieve critical mass rapidly.

The Internet worked as a vehicle for consumer activism in two ways. First of all, it provided a meeting point for people who had a common concern. Without a specialized newsgroup like comp.sys.in-tel, it would otherwise have been quite difficult for dissatisfied Pentium owners to find others like themselves. Secondly, the Internet worked as an amplifier of opinion. That is, once a critical mass of people with a common problem had made contact their efforts to be heard gathered enough momentum that the mainstream press caught wind of the tempest and splashed it across the business pages of the nation's newspapers. The press reports in turn both intensified the Internet storm and afflicted investor confidence enough to move the financial markets; Intel stock weakened as the controversy grew, and the sell-off following IBM's shipment halt was so sharp that the New York Stock Exchange stopped trading in Intel shares for several hours.

The third way that the Internet might encourage positive 'democratic' empowerment is by fostering closer communications links between corporation and customer. In doing so it enables companies to act sooner and respond better. Although Intel was slow to grasp this concept and use it to its advantage, the Pentium episode clearly demonstrated that the Internet can be used very effectively as a focus group, a public relations tool and even a customer hotline. Several months after the affair Grove remarked that on-line services and the Internet 'turn out to be very powerful ways to deliver customer support to a segment of our end customers.

The first, and easiest, way that managers can use the Internet to deal with customer issues is simply to read posting pertaining to their company. Once the story had broken in the popular press Intel began monitoring comp.sys.intel as a way to take the pulse of up-to-the-moment popular sentiment. Far more than telephone calls to a customer service line, which companies usually lump into general categories for their records, Internet messages provide companies with lasting, full-text records of customer feedback that capture customers' attitudes, emotions and technical details. It works something like an instant focus group, allowing companies to form a subtle and complex picture of customer issues.

The Internet also provided an effective means for companies to disseminate helpful information quickly to its customers. Once Intel realized it had a sizable PR crisis on its hands it started posting customer-support information on America Online and comp.sys.in-tel, listing the special telephone and fax numbers which it had set up to handle inquiries about the flaw. The company then shifted its damage-control efforts into high gear, addressing personal e-mails to especially angry comp.sys.intel posters asking to discuss the issue privately by telephone. It was also reported on comp.sys.intel that Intel was quietly shipping debugged Pentiums to especially 'loud' posters – 'Sort of a noisy hinge gets the oil theory', noted one user in Alaska.

Once comp.sys.intel users realized that Intel was responding to some on-line protesters many people started addressing messages to Intel directly, figuring this would elicit a more rapid customer response than a call to the company's free 800 number. Indeed, some people reported that after several days of frustrating telephone discussions with Intel, they posted a message on comp.sys.intel and were quickly furnished with a replacement chip. The newsgroup thus became a conduit for a two-way dialogue between Intel and consumers – an electronic customer hot-line.

The Internet, in effect, peels away many of the layers and filters that normally modulate company-customer discourse: attorneys, public relations staffs, customer service staffs. Intel acknowledged as much when it started staffing its telephone hotline with chip engineers during the crisis – a practice it decided to continue after the affair was over. Comp.sys.intel hosted an unfiltered, first person discussion between customers, scientists, and CEOs, perhaps resembling a direct democracy, where every person, no matter how lowly, has the right to be heard.

With these shifts comes a shift in power. Corporations – this scenario suggests – will get away with less as bottom-up and inside-out information flows replace traditional, top-down control, and as the Internet pokes holes in companies' traditional methods of information control. Increasingly, rather than setting the agenda by holding carefully orchestrated press conferences and issuing meticulously worded press releases, corporations will have the agenda set for them by outsiders who take advantage of the Internet's radical decentralization of power and information. It also does not take too much imagination to conceive of the Internet as a tool for whistle-blowers – the ideal place for employees to post smoking guns and other evidence of corporate misconduct. Companies will find it harder to disappear behind the corporate veil.

In short the optimistic scenario is this: by breaking down the normal channels of communication that companies use to guide and control public understanding of an issue, and by building new ones among customers and experts, the Internet serves as a force for truth and justice, acting as a new source of ethical discipline for companies.

THE VIGILANTE STAKEHOLDER

While the empowerment scenario is quite attractive, there is another, less optimistic view that may capture the essence of the Pentium episode more accurately. On this scenario, the Internet has the tendency of a street mob – to run wild to become electronic barbarians at a cyberspace gate, clamouring to punish competent managers for their supposed misdeeds. As non-issues are fanned into crises by a few on-line firebrands, society as a whole loses. The half-billion dollars that Intel wrote off to pay for the Pentium replacement was an amount that could have built several schools or hospitals, or could have been used to create jobs. Such an enormous loss, more-over, would have destroyed most companies, and would have bank-rupted Intel a few years earlier, thereby depriving the USA of one of its high-technology champions.

The Pentium controversy, at bottom, revolved around a tiny technical flaw of the sort not uncommon to all computer hardware. It is generally accepted that new microprocessors contain a multitude of glitches – most of them minor – that go undetected until after the chips' release. Early versions of Intel's 486 chips, for example, failed to perform trigonometry correctly. In fact, the article in the *Electronic Engineering Times* November 7 about the bug hardly generated a ripple of discussion at Comdex, the computer industry's annual convention that began November 16, indicating that the flaw was simply not that serious. Thus, by holding companies to unrealistic levels of perfection, customers only cheat themselves, paying higher prices for companies to run lengthy tests on all products and waiting longer for new products to appear on the shelves.

This scenario views the Internet as the latest and most extreme evolution of the modern American media. The Net is not, of course, part of the establishment media, the major television networks and big city papers, nor is it part of the so-called 'new media' of radio talk shows, cable television, direct mail, and niche publishing. Rather, the Internet might evolve into another order of media altogether; one that takes the adjectives that describe the 'new media' – diffuse, abundant, populist, unpredictable, rapid and less regulated – to their extreme. It could evolve into a kind of hypermedia, with serious negative consequences.

The Internet, for example, wields its power without any restraints or accountability. Even the most outrageous forms of new media are at some level subordinate to the interests of the organization that produces them: TV ratings, government pressure, shareholder sentiment or public image. Comp.sys.intel, by contrast, was a non-organization with no hierarchy, no permanent staff and a budget of zero. In fact it had no physical location other than its existence in the nebulous information web of cyberspace. It lived a virtual almost metaphysical existence. Thus, while media companies can be irresponsible, the Internet by its very nature is non-responsible; it wields its headless, strategyless, unaccountable power however its users arbitrarily prefer.

Moreover, unlike government agencies and conventional interest groups, companies cannot lobby the Internet, do deals with it, wait for a change in its leadership, make strategic political contributions or try to co-opt it – because there is no 'it'.

The absence of accountability was reflected in the hundreds of angry, unrestrained and often moronic postings that started to overwhelm comp.sys.intel once the Pentium controversy hit the popular press. This was a lynch mob, and the words of one comp.sys.intel user – 'THE HELL WITH INTEL' – summarized the content of most of its flame messages.

Moreover, many comp.sys.intel users were ill-informed about the situation, and a great deal of misinformation spread on the newsgroup and was used against Intel. Once again, a comparison with the main-stream media is illuminating. Media executives, TV producers, newspaper editors work as 'gatekeepers' and have strong incentives to avoid using misinformation to attack another party. And when the press does cross the line and introduce misinformation – for example, when CBS faked the explosions of General Motors trucks for an 'exposé' that accused GM of ignoring life-threatening safety problems – the perpetrator often suffers a severe loss of credibility, and some media executives may have lost their jobs, in part because of this episode. Not so with the Internet: no one guards the gates to cyberspace, and purveyors of misinformation suffer no consequences.

Lawyers are also likely to join in future frays, seeing angry on-line postings as a pool of potential plaintiffs. Ten consumer and shareholder lawsuits were filed against Intel during the affair, accusing the company of a range of offences including false advertising, securities fraud, and violation of certain state consumer protection laws At least one group seeking class action status gathered information for its legal complaint by posting a message on comp.sys.intel.

Finally, Internet 'demonstrations', because they can be seen by everyone, offer stake-holder companies – that is, clients or immediate customers – a powerful platform from which to strike opportunistic blows.

Managers must contemplate and prepare for the day in the not-too-distant future when any disgruntled employee can log on to a bulletin board and complain about their company's labour policies or everyday operations. Information that is not supposed to see the light of day can be paraded before a group of unknown outsiders ranging from nutcases to Nobel laureates, from journalists to members of Congressional staffs. The Internet is a public stage on which just about anything can be posted – a virtual loose cannon on a virtual rolling deck.

IMPLICATIONS FOR MANAGERS

The Pentium case suggests several important lessons:

1. *If companies are not alert to the Internet's multifaceted roles, or attempt to use it clumsily, they can be caught in a meat grinder.*
2. *Histrionic messages may secure disproportionate attention – on the Net and in the media leading managers to dismiss Internet activism in its entirety and thereby overlooking important hazards and disguising genuine opportunities to develop closer, on-line relationships with their customers.*
3. *Although the two are linked, victories and defeats on the Internet should not be confused with victories and defeats in the marketplace.*
4. *The Net's acceleration of information speeds up the decision-making process for companies.*
5. *Companies embroiled in Internet controversies may need to rely heavily on close examination of postings, on managers with some 'feel' for the Net, and on how the establishment media seems to be interpreting the traffic on the Net.*
6. *Posting by companies and executives are fully public; they can and often will be used against their authors.* Because the Internet is a radical new communications technology, both these scenarios are inevitably speculative.

The Net may be to the 21st century what the steam engine was to the 19th century and electricity to the early 20th century. Like all important advances in technology the Internet will bring changes, some marvellous, but some troublesome, some frightening.

10 Preventing the Crisis in the First Place

Christopher Flint[†]

RISK MANAGEMENT

Several factors need to be taken into account if the successful resolution of a crisis is to be achieved. We know from experience how quickly an independent act or series of acts can overcome companies, governments, institutions and multinationals. Unless managed responsibly, effectively, precisely – and with due regard to consumers, shareholders, trustees, the media, environmental and ethnic groups and cultural differences – the negative impact can be devastating.

The Perrier accidental contamination of its water and the malicious contamination of Heinz baby food are but two cases that attracted massive publicity, and both companies, arguably, have had great difficulty in re-securing their market-share. Contrast this to the extraordinarily effective public relations exercise after the alleged contamination with a syringe of a Diet Pepsi can, and the positive impact it had on re-assuring consumers that the production process was secure and any contamination would have occurred post-factory.

The type of threats and risks facing large global companies which manufacture, market and distribute their brands worldwide and employ many thousands of people are no longer limited to extortion, malicious contamination, kidnap and fraud. Increasingly they are the victims of professional diversion teams – especially in emerging markets – commercial espionage, internal fraud, the acts of disgruntled employees and cultural differences. Vulnerability is increased by a failure to implement supplier/distributor accreditation

---

[†] Christopher Flint is Group Security Advisor to Cadbury Schweppes plc. His role there is to contribute to the Group's overall profitability by implementing a strategic direction to security that reduces vulnerability to external threats and risks – and which also enables the Group to respond positively in the event of an incident.

and scrutiny of prospective employees, especially for senior and/or sensitive posts, through a rigorous vetting and pre-employment screening process. The necessity for effective controls to prevent collusion in the award of contracts, the avoidance of excessive debts, and other matters which could reflect adversely on a company or result in litigation, indicates the need for a company policy covering such areas as conflict of interest, fraud, security and related topics.

ANALYSIS OF RISKS WHEN ESTABLISHING AN OPERATION

The company must be aware of the risks involved in investing in commercial operations, especially in developing countries where actual conditions cannot readily be judged, or where the social or political situation is known or believed to be unstable. It is essential that the company takes all reasonable steps to minimise the risks to a substantial investment – and especially to its personnel.

The investing company must address crucial questions about the present and future stability of the country. It must examine any social, cultural, ethnic and religious customs and local attitudes to foreign-owned businesses which may impact on the company's operations. Other considerations should include limitations on foreign ownership, currency restrictions, quotas on foreign nationals, licensing requirements, labour laws and costs, availability of raw materials, available methods of transportation, import and export controls, investment incentives and the potential for product counterfeit or parallel trading in the area.

It is also important that the major commercial and security risks are identified, and the nature and extent of potential, actual or future dangers to the safety of the business and its executives must be evaluated. Research into expatriate accommodation, schools, medical and recreational facilities must also be undertaken.

DUE DILIGENCE

Once a suitable partner has been identified, due diligence is necessary to determine their probity, connections, resources, capabilities, market access and the integrity of the owners and key executors.

Due diligence research should endeavour to establish if the potential partner has been involved in any activity or business practice which could prove embarrassing or a hindrance to your operations at any time in the future. It would also establish if there is any history of bad debt or litigation and if there have been any serious labour disputes or incidents.

GREENFIELD SITES

Project managers must liaise with government departments and local authorities to obtain the required permissions and permits to build. They must prepare specifications and terms and conditions of engagement, evaluate tenders and select and recommend companies to fulfil the contracts. Security must be involved at the architectural planning stage to evaluate and specify security requirements, draw up bid documents, coordinate installation, commissioning and maintenance of the systems. Training must be provided to security personnel who may be required to operate or man the installations.

In particularly unstable or volatile countries the need to identify a reliable local security company is paramount to the successful completion of the project. It is often difficult to do this, and companies should share their experiences and lessons learned. Security managers of companies in such countries, especially Eastern Europe, central and southern America, Africa and so on need to discuss all security issues in a frank and purposeful manner. The sharing of experiences is vital to ensure that the right security company provides a high level of protection, and is accountable.

PHYSICAL SECURITY AUDITS

Security must be regarded as part of the total corporate operation and as a contributor to overall profits. It should be reviewed and evaluated regularly so that outmoded systems can be replaced, procedures streamlined and new risks addressed. If premises are rented or inherited through a joint venture, existing security measures must be reviewed and recommendations made with due regard for the nature of the company operations and appropriate to the local level of threat.

The security survey will consider perimeter and internal site security and include access control, stock control, warehousing and distribution of raw materials and finished product, and will identify critical operations and equipment and assess the impact on production through equipment downtime. There is also a need to assess the availability and efficiency of local security services and their response times, as well as those of the emergency services. The merits of an employed or contract guard force should be evaluated, with guidelines setting out their duties and responsibilities and their management and motivation.

Security at the homes of expatriate personnel must be examined. If necessary, informal instruction should be provided to executives and their families on common-sense routines that will enhance their personal security. Contingency plans must be drawn up for the evacuation of expatriate staff in the event of a total breakdown of law and order.

TYPES OF RISK

Obviously, the types and extent of risks facing companies that operate globally are wide and diverse, but include such things as:

- Product adulteration (malicious contamination);
- Fraud and theft/pilferage (internal and external involving warehouse losses and deliberate spoiling);
- Sabotage by disgruntled employees or for political ends;
- Kidnap and ransom;
- Threats to the operational systems and processes;
- Security of payments and transfers, and security of assets;
- Corruption and patronage, both local and national.

In each of the above, a company can minimise the impact of incidents – or even prevent them – by staying alert to their frequency and growth, the levels to which company executives and assets would be vulnerable, and who are the likely perpetrators. In that way, plans and proposals by which the company can be proactive to each situation can be drawn up and exercised.

It is important to be proactive to prevent loss to the company, whether of assets, personnel, commercial price-sensitive information, IT security, or involving fraud and conflicts of interest. It is far better to prevent an incident from developing into a crisis than to have to recover from the effects of such a crisis.

MANAGEMENT CONTROL

Companies that have dispersed offices and manufacturing plants throughout the world, often in countries that are relatively unstable, obviously require a greater input of management control and supervision than in other more developed areas. It is increasingly apparent that local management may lack the skills and inclination to prevent the occasional and/or systematic diversion of company monies to individuals, whether with or without collusion of external parties. The need for efficient and effective management controls at these smaller – and consequently more vulnerable – work-places is an essential prerequisite of the decision to enter into a particular market.

The importance of systems of management control to prevent and detect fraud cannot be overestimated. If fraud is exposed, it is of the utmost importance that valuable evidence is not destroyed or steps taken which render subsequent investigation and recovery of funds fruitless. Employees suspected of fraud should not be suspended or sacked without a thorough investigation, and it is important to consider whether involving local law enforcement or other resources would improve the chance of recovering funds.

Companies need to be inquisitive about existing conflicts of interest within acquired companies and those who are supplying goods and services to the company. Conflicts of interest which existed when these companies were private or family concerns should no longer be tolerated under new company management, and these must be identified at an early stage.

Security managers should assist in vetting suppliers as well as customers and employees. It is becoming increasingly important to properly vet all entities and people with whom the company does business, especially in those environments where the situation is potentially unstable and the outcomes of business are erratic.

Once an acquisition has been completed, or a joint venture formed, security managers should assist both finance and legal departments during the transition and integration periods. They can arrange for the vetting of senior management of the acquired entity and review local practices to determine whether there are any potentially serious deviations from company ethical standards. Pre-employment screening, for example, can identify unexplained gaps in a personal history as well as other matters. This type of screening is now important. And since Section 8 of the Asylum and Immigration Act 1996 came into effect a new criminal offence can be committed by employers who hire someone not entitled to work in the United Kingdom.

Companies should consider having in place a written global ethics policy which would reinforce its commitment to these matters and an annual certification process, such as is adopted by some companies. This would bring these issues to people's attention on a regular basis and oblige them to disclose any violations or incompatible relationships.

THE NEED TO COORDINATE RESPONSES

There have been too many occasions when companies, usually large and with a significant public profile, have not responded adequately to an incident. It is quite apparent that the coordination of the incident is flawed, revealing to the public a far-from-effective incident management response.

One of the most important aspects of effective incident response is to have clear guidelines in the form of a manual that is clear, concise, and user friendly. There is just no point in having a large, excessively detailed manual that frankly is inappropriate for use during the management of an incident, and is difficult to use as a reference. The manual must contain all contact numbers, and there should be a specific section dealing with product recall. Often this is a delegated responsibility to a sub-group answerable to the main incident management team.

One of the most important persons on the incident team is the public relations manager. The incident coordinator and the PR manager must work in tandem and they must develop a seamless relationship that enables the coordinator to ensure that all members of the team are working both with and for the PR manager to enable the standby and press release statements to be precise and technically accurate. Ideally, the security manager and PR manager should always discuss the possible implications of a potential incident. One way to enable this cooperative link to be established is for the security manager at Group level to be a part of the Group corporate communications.

An effective corporate response, both from the public relations manager and security manager, to ensure that incidents are coordinated effectively is really the most vital element to ensure a successful conclusion to a perceived problem. In my opinion, a failure of both security and corporate lawyers to relate effectively with their public relations department is a sure sign that the outcome is likely to end disastrously.

CONCLUSION

Much can be done prior to the establishment of an investment to evaluate the risks and therefore avoid or prepare for them. In existing operations, issues facing the company should be reviewed regularly by a multi-disciplinary team (security, PR, legal, HR) and contingency plans made.

Incident management manuals should be clear and concise and teams exercised regularly. Crises cannot always be prevented but they can be prepared for and therefore diffused.

11 Organising a Product Recall

Colin Doeg[†]

The unthinkable has happened. The crisis management team is assembling in the board room, which is rapidly being converted into an operations centre. Telephones are being plugged into special sockets. TV sets, video recorders and radios are being wheeled in.

Suddenly the room is empty except for the chairman of the committee and the core members of the team, who represent sales, marketing, purchasing, production, technical services and public relations plus a senior secretary. She opens a new notebook and takes out a pen ready to start a diary of events, recording all the proceedings and decisions, noting the exact times at which they occurred.

The chairman opens the proceedings: 'You all know why we are here. Glass has been found in a small number of jars of instant coffee packed at our plant in the North. What else do we know?'

Production take up the story. 'Five jars out of a batch of nearly 600 000 have been found to be contaminated. They were produced four weeks ago on line-three during the morning shift. There is a record of a breakage at 8.23 a.m. on the day on which they were packed. The line was stopped and all jars in the vicinity of the breakage, both filled and unfilled, were removed and isolated for destruction. The line was cleaned down and production resumed just before 9.00 a.m. It would seem some of the suspect jars found their way into the distribution channel. The factory manager is continuing to investigate.'

Now technical services join in. 'At the beginning of this week we started receiving complaints from consumers about finding glass in their jars of coffee. At first we thought they were isolated incidents

[†] Colin Doeg is a former journalist, a public relations consultant and author of *Crisis Management in the Food and Drinks Industry* (Chapman & Hall, 1995).

because the complaints were from different parts of the country. One came in direct from the consumer, three via the stores from which the jars were purchased, and the other from an environmental health officer who had been contacted by the consumer. We had difficulty obtaining the batch numbers from the stores so we did not get a clear picture and realise the seriousness of the problem until this morning, when we alerted the committee.'

Turning to distribution, the chairman asks: 'How much of this product is still in the distribution chain. Can we get it back and contain the remainder of the situation?'

The head of distribution shakes his head. 'About 80 per cent was delivered to the central warehouses of the multiples and major cash-'n-carries two weeks ago. We must assume most of the jars have been bought and the coffee could well be in use or about to be used.'

Silence grips the room as everyone pictures the consequences of someone drinking a cup of coffee with glass in it.

The chairman is quick. 'Have we any idea how many jars might be out there with glass in them?'

Another pause, then production says slowly: 'Unfortunately, we have no idea. The jars which were put aside have been destroyed. We have no way of knowing how many were put aside. But, usually, when there is a breakage, anything from 200 to 300 jars are isolated and destroyed. In this instance it is unlikely that we are talking about more than a small number of jars that went astray. Indeed, the five complaints we have received might be the only jars that were not destroyed.'

'But we cannot be sure, can we?' the chairman asks pointedly, and everyone is silent again. He breaks the silence by asking: 'What do we do now?' and goes round everyone in turn.

The responses are all much the same: 'We cannot afford to take any chances. Even now someone could be drinking a cup of coffee with pieces of glass in it. We must not delay.'

All eyes turn to the sales director. Confidently, she says that all the major accounts could be contacted within an hour and that all jars of that particular coffee would be off the shelves of all major super-markets within an hour of those calls. Cash-'n-carries would do the same thing but it would be difficult to reach all their customers because they are so scattered and varied. So publicity will be necessary to warn consumers and stockists who cannot be reached directly.

No-one voices the fact that adequate publicity is essential anyway to satisfy the government's department of health (DoH) and its environmental health officers that the company is doing sufficient to forewarn people of the potential danger from the contaminated product. Otherwise, in the public interest, the DoH would take over and issue a product recall notice.

The marketing director interrupts everyone's thoughts by reporting that the advertising agency handling the coffee account is standing by to prepare and place a recall advertisement. A schedule has been drawn up – all major national newspapers and the trade press covering cash-'n-carries and grocers.

As a precaution arrangements have already been made to replace coffee commercials due to run on TV and radio during the day with advertisements for other products. As, presumably, there is to be a national recall, advertisements for other brands will continue to be substituted for the next few days. Arrangements are also in hand to commission market research to determine the climate of consumer opinion should the problem become more serious than it appears to be at the moment.

Public relations begin sliding sheets of paper round the table. 'Here is a rough draft of a recall announcement and also a list of answers to possible follow-up questions – we had a brief warning this might be the situation. We just need to insert a few figures and some other details then we will circulate the draft for approval. Once it is agreed we can cascade the release out to the media very quickly. We'll do television and radio first. We want to get the release out by mid-day. Then we'll follow up with the print media.'

'We will be in a position to respond to media enquiries as soon as we begin to send out the release. However, I would like about another half hour before I am prepared to give any live interviews on television. At the same time, we will rehearse our usual marketing spokesperson' – the marketing director and head of PR exchange grimaces – 'to be ready to do the same thing. That will take less than an hour.'

'We can set up a telephone hot-line to deal with consumer phone calls in a matter of minutes. We have a special number that feeds into the consumer relations department. Our consumer relations people only have to clear their desks and have a few moments to study the press release and list of likely questions and answers. It is unlikely that, on this occasion, we will need to involve the outside organisation

we have in tow which specialises in these facilities. We can cope with
the calls ourselves at this stage.'

*   *   *

That crisp and cool meeting might seem to be a highly idealised
scenario of a crisis hitting a company, but it need not be far from
reality in any business, whether large or small, if it is properly
prepared for such an eventuality.

Recalls of a wide range of products are commonplace today, but a
food company has been taken as an example because food is an
emotive subject – we cannot live without it – and because that
industry has become highly sophisticated in the way it deals with
such problems. Many years ago, its trade association, the Food and
Drink Federation, set up a special committee to help advise member
companies on the latest techniques in crisis management and also to
forewarn them of contentious issues and trends. The Institute of
Grocery Distribution also acted some considerable time ago by
compiling a directory of emergency contact numbers for the grocery
trade, which is regularly updated.

The Department of Health, in conjunction with the Ministry of
Agriculture, Fisheries and Food, the Scottish Office, the Welsh Office
and the Health and Agriculture Departments of Northern Ireland,
has produced Statutory Code of Practice No. 16: Enforcement of the
Food Safety Act 1990 in Relation to the Food Hazard Warning
System. It provides essential advice and guidance to enforcement
authorities and is worthwhile reading for anyone likely to be involved
in crisis management because it reflects the lessons which have been
learned over the years.

The Code describes the system operated by government departments to alert the public and food authorities to potential problems,
both national and regional, concerning food which does not meet
safety requirements. It also advises food authorities of the action they
should take if a potential national or regional problem comes to light
in their areas.

The scenario at the beginning of this chapter highlights the need for
a number of things if a product recall is to run smoothly:

- Firstly, it is essential that a system is in place to monitor consumer
  complaints and warn of any undesirable trends.

- Secondly, it is vital that all possible hazards in production are identified and procedures laid down concerning the actions to be taken if they occur. The opening scenario also underlines the need for every item to carry a clear production code which enables it to be identified quickly and accurately and also tracked through all stages of production and distribution.

  If standard practices require the product to be destroyed at any stage during manufacture or distribution it is essential for an accurate record to be kept of the number of items involved – a shortcoming in the arrangements of our mythical food company which, hopefully, would be swiftly rectified because there is always a lesson to be learned from every product recall and crisis.

- Thirdly, those in the crisis team are obviously well-rehearsed. They are all professionals in their jobs. But regular rehearsals of crisis arrangements are even more important these days, especially in large organisations when many executives are moved comparatively quickly from one role or responsibility to another as part of overall training and development schemes. If these rehearsals do not take place regularly there is a real danger that a group of virtual strangers could be gathering to try to cope with a situation so alarming it could threaten not only their own career prospects but the fortunes of the entire business.

- Fourthly, if the necessary skills are not available within the company it is important that, at the least, contact has already been made with outside consultants who can offer the necessary expertise.

In any product recall, the guiding principle must always be the well-being and safety of the consumer. That should rule all decisions. It is also important that accurate information is available about the problem – that, in itself, can be reassuring because it implies that the company knows what it is doing. The terms in which any product announcement is couched are also important. The announcement should:

- describe the problem
- tell consumers how to identify the product affected
- explain how the situation arose
- accept responsibility
- set out the action the company is taking to rectify the matter
- tell consumers how they will be reimbursed, and

- provide a source for further information if they require more details or reassurance

In the midst of any product recall, whether it involves an electrical appliance, a motor vehicle, a child's toy or a food product, *time* is of the essence. A well-prepared company will rise to the occasion and deal with the problem while continuing to run its business. A complacent company will crumble under the spotlight of media and consumer attention and be in danger of going out of business.

12   Organising a Crisis Simulation

Kate Graham[†]

Regular exercise is good for you! This is true whether you are simply working out in the gym or organising regular crisis management exercises which will enhance your company's ability to cope with crises.

IS PRACTICE REALLY NECESSARY?

In the aftermath of the *Piper Alpha* disaster, the oil industry embarked on some extremely elaborate and expensive emergency exercises. I can recall an occasion when I hired the services of almost 60 'relative response' role-players (that is people posing as relatives) and journalists to participate in one exercise.

Everyone was trying to improve their procedures so that they would be able to cope 'perfectly' with a disaster. My advice to you is DON'T TRY. The fact is that if you and your staff can cope well with what might be termed a more normal emergency, then you will also cope with a more serious situation. Your response teams will be stretched to the limit and beyond. It will be extremely difficult and you will make mistakes but you will cope. I do not believe that any organisation can truthfully say that it has the ability to cope comfortably with any imaginable situation.

You do the best you can and at the end of the day you should review the subsequent media comment and public reaction to your response and vow to do better if it should happen again. Failure to learn from your experiences is foolhardy and can be very costly indeed.

[†] Kate Graham was formerly responsible for Occidental's press and public relations response to the *Piper Alpha* disaster in 1988. She provides consultancy, management and staff training in both relative and media response, and lectures widely in crisis management.

Do not wait for the real thing to happen. There is an ongoing need to test your company crisis management procedures and your staff's ability to carry out their duties. But do be realistic!

CRISIS SIMULATIONS

The crisis management business has grown immeasurably over the past ten years. When I embarked on this subject, 'emergency response' was the term used to cover all aspects of this work. Nowadays there is 'crisis management', 'issues management' and numerous other headings which can be placed under the same banner. However, regardless of the nature of your crisis there are some guidelines which should be followed.

Above all, do not be complacent – test your procedures and your ability to respond and do not lose sight of what it is you are trying to accomplish. Organising an emergency simulation should not be merely an opportunity for a consultant to give vent to an overblown imagination and create a sequence of horrific events which will reduce a client's personnel to quivering, demoralised creatures at its conclusion. The purpose of the exercise should be to test procedures and train response personnel.

There is little point in proceeding with a simulation unless you intend 'playing for real'. It is advisable to use the services of external personnel for role play, simply because your own staff may find it difficult to be completely serious if they recognise the voices of colleagues role-playing as anxious relatives, police, government ministers and so on.

THE SCENARIO

I mentioned earlier that the writing of a scenario should not be left entirely to someone who is intent on writing a script which might have the potential of becoming a successful Hollywood disaster movie! Realism is essential and the purpose of the simulation should be made very clear from the outset. You know your business and you should ensure that external consultants are adequately briefed.

I recently observed an exercise during which a sequence of events occurred which made an effective and efficient response by the company impossible. Every event on its own would have been a very serious incident. The running together of about five such incidents made the situation somewhat farcical, and the response teams resented being placed in an impossible situation. As a result, the debrief discussion was very heated and revealed that little had been learnt, simply because no-one had had the opportunity to satisfactorily complete any aspect of emergency response.

So what was achieved? Nothing positive. The participants were angry and demoralised and believed that their time and efforts had been wasted.

The following suggestions should enable you to create a situation which will at least enable you to produce an exercise with some useful purpose:

- Decide what you want to achieve from the exercise and write a scenario which is realistic and demanding.
- Get your facts right – one technical error in the scenario and those being tested will tell you in no uncertain terms that they should not be expected to cope with situations which could not actually occur.
- Use real journalists. They know how they would pursue a story in real life, so let them do the same during your simulation.
- Choose role-playing personnel who will behave in a realistic manner. Take 'relative response', for example: Most callers do not start off by screaming hysterically at company personnel who are trying to help them. But if a company does not divulge enough accurate information for several hours, then the families and friends of those involved in the incident will become irate and they will voice their criticisms to the media, MPs, police and anyone else whom they believe will help them.

In reality, every call will have to be handled in a sympathetic and understanding manner. However, for every angry and abusive call there will be dozens of others which will be easier to handle. Again – remember that you are training your staff and trying to build up their confidence while they undertake a very difficult role.

DIRECTING STAFF

The police, Coastguard, local authorities and several government departments usually welcome the opportunity to participate in simulations. Such occasions enable them to test their own procedures.

Do give them ample warning, however, and recognise that even if they agree to participate, real events may cause last minute changes to your plans. Also remember that the simulation has been created primarily to test *your* staff and procedures. Do not permit external authorities to override your own personnel and change the entire focus of the exercise.

If the authorities cannot participate, ensure that you use experienced consultants who can provide realistic, worthwhile input. There are those who have retired from your industry, as well as retired police officers, government officials and so on. who can provide excellent role play. The consultant employed to lead the exercise should be able to provide such personnel at a reasonable cost.

Compile exercise instructions and issue these to the major role-players. If participants are not adequately briefed regarding their roles and the purpose of the exercise, then they can hardly be expected to achieve the required goals. Incident status sheets will also form part of the scenario and the progress of the simulation should be closely monitored by the exercise leader to ensure that all objectives are met.

When I leave instructions for role-players, I type in large bold capital letters at the bottom of the page, REMEMBER THIS IS MEANT TO BE TRAINING NOT TORTURE! I would recommend that the organisers of simulations bear this in mind.

THE AFTERMATH

Always conduct a 'hot wash up'. At the conclusion of the exercise, give everyone about an hour to gather their thoughts and note their observations. Then conduct a short debrief during which the exercise leader can note the main points for inclusion in the final report.

This session should be brief – an hour at the maximum. Feelings can run high in the immediate aftermath of an exercise and potential conflict and the apportioning of blame for errors should be avoided at all costs.

FINAL REPORT

A final report – including the valid comments and constructive criticisms of the main participants as well as media stories – should be compiled and submitted to the company within approximately five working days. The stories will reflect media reaction to your handling of the incident and their importance should not be overlooked. If you do not like all that has been written – and even if there are inaccuracies in the reporting – remember that this is exactly what could happen in a real situation.

Occasionally, the exercise leader who will compile the final report may misinterpret a situation which arose during the simulation. Therefore do ensure that a final draft is reviewed by the appropriate person within your organisation. Any contentious issues should be fully discussed and amendments to text made as necessary, prior to the final report distribution.

ACTION

Act on the report recommendations and handle any sensitive issues (for example the behaviour of a responder) in a confidential manner. People make mistakes and can say the wrong things when under pressure and it does not follow that they should always be heavily criticised for their mistakes. Perhaps they need more training, or did not receive sufficient support and guidance during the exercise. Consult your own personnel and discuss the correct course of action.

Occasionally, however, you may identify someone who is just not suitable for an emergency role. While it is never pleasant to have to inform an individual of this, do not forget that leaving him/her in that role may create serious problems in the future.

Finally, do not place the report on the shelf along with the procedures and forget about it! Incorporate the recommendations into the procedures and ensure that those involved are kept appraised of any changes.

13   Handling the Stress

Cheryl Travers[†]

'A real measure of a man is not where he stands at moments of comfort and convenience but where he stands at moments of challenge and controversy.'

Martin Luther King

INTRODUCTION

Just as a corporate crisis is about people's perceptions rather than reality, so the individual stress resulting from a situation very much depends on how an individual perceives it. 'One man's meat is another man's poison.' When attempting to prepare companies for a crisis we need to ensure that the managers involved see the crisis as 'meat', turning it into an opportunity.

There is very little research and literature available on assessing the individual and psychological aspects of a crisis, and this is mainly because crises have tended to be treated in a *passive-reactive* way, that is we only do something about them when they actually happen. Both as individuals and as organisations we need to address a more *proactive* stance whereby we do not wait for the problem to come to us but instead we go to the problem by preparing for it. Prevention is better than cure!

A key question to emerge when examining crises and their effects is, why are some people either paralysed or destroyed by them while others seem to grow from them? Much of the stress we experience is a result of the pressure to perform and always to cope rather than show

---

[†] Dr Cheryl J. Travers is a leading expert and author on stress psychology. She lectures in Organisational Behaviour and Human Resource Management at The Business School, Loughborough University.

weakness. But although a crisis is, by its very nature, an extremely threatening pressure situation, there is no reason why it cannot also be a source of great stimulation and challenge, and one in which individuals can come through triumphant, both individually and organisationally. Many of us would claim to experience a crisis every day of our lives. In order to help a crisis management team to prepare and effectively cope with crisis we need to emphasise that, although a crisis happens from *outside*, the way we react and manage it is largely *under our own control* if we learn how to deal with it and our own reactions to it.

WHAT IS A CRISIS IN PSYCHOLOGICAL TERMS?

'It is in [the] whole process of meeting and solving problems that life has its meaning. . . Wise people learn not to dread but actually to welcome problems.'

M. Scott Peck, *The Road Less Traveled*

The word crisis originates from the Greek *krinein,* 'to decide'. A crisis is therefore a decisive moment, a time of great difficulty or danger in a company's or individual's history. A crisis may have the following features:

- it is an event that is against the usual scheme of things
- it poses a challenges to resources
- it demands attention/immediate action
- it is potentially damaging
- management will have limited control
- individuals will need to act largely on their own judgement rather than follow instructions
- it has a local/international impact
- unpredictable progress may be made
- it is liable to arouse press/public interest
- there is something at stake (for example profit, integrity) which is inversely proportionate to the success with which the crisis is managed

Due to these factors a crisis requires certain key skills, attitudes and behaviours from individuals. In a crisis the key features of threat, urgency and uncertainty are present and these threaten all involved. They provide challenges to effective decision-making in that the crisis team find themselves making decisions which they have not anticipated, and many of the responses that are taken irrevocably shape the pattern of responses for good or ill. Organisations are forced to take crucial decisions in areas where they have little knowledge, and in the heat of crisis, when they themselves are undergoing extremely rapid organisational change.

Depending on the individuals and company involved, the handling of the crisis and its outcomes, there are also *benefits* to be had from its successful management, such as:

- personal growth and development
- a sense of achievement
- stimulation
- prevention of stagnation
- personal opportunity for improvement, and
- organisational growth and success

If the crisis is handled well both companies and individuals may have reasons to be proud and actually benefit from the experience in some way.

THE EXISTENTIAL COMPONENT OF CRISIS

As outlined above, crises affect individuals in terms of what is expected of them and also the way they make them feel. One of the least acknowledged aspects of crisis management is what Thierry Pauchant and Ian Mitroff (*Transforming the Crisis Prone Company – Preventing Individual, Organizational and Environmental Tragedy*, Jossey-Bass 1992) call the *existential* component – talking in detail about the difference between physical and psychological death.

Many writers in the field of psychology emphasise that, for humans in the western world, the most fundamental motivation is to preserve at all costs their:

- sense of personal feelings
- inner view of themselves and of the world
- self-concept
- affirmation of self
- ability to do

- ability to create
- ability to be self-actualised, and
- ability to feel alive

Scholars distinguish between physical death when the body biologically dies, and psychological death when the inner structure of an individual's experience is shattered, destroyed or challenged in a traumatic way. Both types of death are so terrifying that individuals will resist them with all their strength.

Industrial crises can trigger both types of death – though the latter is the kind we are most concerned with in this chapter. Not all company crises result in psychological *trauma* but the threat to psychological *well-being* can be very great. Individual responses to the challenges presented by crises are very personal and it is therefore difficult to predict precisely which of these feelings and symptoms a crisis will trigger. It does seem however, that crisis situations affect the following basic assumptions an individual may hold:

- a sense of certainty about particular issues and the future
- a sense of perfection – and therefore invulnerability
- a sense of connection with others, that one has a 'place in the world'
- a sense of 'righthood', that one is involved in a worthwhile cause, and
- in western companies at times of crisis this may be a challenge to our feelings of competence and effectiveness

WHAT KEY SKILLS AND ATTRIBUTES ARE REQUIRED TO MANAGE A CRISIS?

It would seem, then, that effective crisis management is not primarily a set of tools and mechanisms to be implemented in organisations, but rather a general mood and a set of actions by managers who are not too 'emotionally bounded'. To develop an effective crisis management effort requires much more than the search for self-interest. Crisis managers need to be able to put themselves in the position of all stakeholders and be able to see what impact the crisis may have on their feelings and needs. The most successful crisis managers are those who, when experiencing a crisis, are able to fundamentally question their organisational culture and structure and look for areas where they may be in part responsible. They are able to put themselves in the shoes of the victims, and they can fully realise the impact of actions on all employees.

Therefore, a major skill when dealing with crisis is the ability to anticipate and deal with the stress experienced by *others* – and also to deal with the stress that you are under yourself at the same time. Stress needs to be managed as the crisis war is fought on two fronts: all eyes are on the event itself, and also on how the company and individuals handle the event. Dealing with your own stress is even more important when we consider some of the other key skills which a crisis calls for, such as:

• clear-headed and rational managerial decision-making
• consideration of stakeholder interests in the long term, not just the short term
• involving others in the decision-making process
• communicating clearly
• not being defensive
• being honest but unruffled – being able to admit you do not know all of the answers
• keeping on top of the news
• reacting in a speedy fashion – but not as a panic reaction
• making best use of available resources
• the ability to work under extreme time pressure
• the need to be able to liaise with others and work as part of a team
• the need for flexible and creative thinking, and
• managing stress both in oneself and in others (this is important in order to be able to display all of the skills outlined above

A key point here, then, is that when selecting a crisis management team we may want to look for evidence of these particular skills and attitudes. However, it may also be beneficial to *train* people in crisis management skills in a proactive way, and make them aware of the skills that are needed and the importance of developing these in a training environment.

HOW SIMILAR IS A CRISIS TO OTHER TYPES OF ORGANISATIONAL CHANGE?

When we examine what a crisis actually is we can see that it is in fact a major change that takes place in the life of a company and the many individuals that are involved. It is unlike many other changes that are *evolutionary* in their nature in that it is not deliberate, no one has planned it and it takes people by surprise. One of the major mistakes companies make when managing any kind of change is to assume that individuals are 'over it' and coping effectively when in fact they are still in a resistance phase.

One of the major problems with crisis from a change management perspective is that it is not a *transitional* one which has a clear future state and is implemented within a desired time frame (for example the implementation of new technologies). The point about transitional models of change is that there are a several predictable issues that occur when change occurs. Smooth transitions take place when managers of change take into account these predictable factors (for example peoples' psychological reactions to change). So in order to prepare well for a *crisis* we can draw up a list of the *predictable* responses that will occur, and be able to anticipate how to deal with them as many of these will still be evident in a crisis situation, as with any change:

- **Personal Impact**   When a crisis first occurs, each individual in the organisation who is in any way affected will have a personal reaction. They will wonder 'What does this mean for me? Will I still have a job? Do I like this? Am I in any way to blame? Can I still get ahead as planned? When people are having these reactions, they tend to go inside, withdraw from their situation and stop listening. Important information may be offered, and yet they are so intensely into their reactions that they cannot hear or understand very well. Their feelings will need to be aired, as these reactions directly influence how they will deal with the crisis. Therefore it will be the role of those managing the crisis to ensure that all parties involved get the opportunity to air their views.
- **Resistance**   Depending on people's reactions, they will decide to support or resist the changes imposed by the crisis. Resistance may show up in individuals or groups and it can take active or passive forms. Resistance is always based on perceived threat or fear. To reduce it, find out what underlies it. There is always a vein of truth in resistance which may provide you with some valuable insight into people's needs during the management of the crisis process.
- **Readiness**   When people accept how things need to be done in the crisis situation, they will 'ready' themselves for it. Some will likely be enthusiastic in their support. Sometimes, however, peo-

ple's enthusiasm is extreme and may need to be tempered as uncontrolled enthusiasm can be as difficult to manage as resistance. For the crisis management team a goal is to encourage greater readiness and acceptance throughout the organisation, before a timetable forces people to adapt too soon.

- **Power/political** Because it is natural to want to influence a crisis situation to one's advantage, political dynamics can escalate. People will want to side with the 'winners' and have a say in any possible outcomes. Although it is often difficult to discuss openly, knowing who the political players are is essential. Doing an initial political scan is valuable preparation, as is knowing the key stakeholders and how to manage their reactions.
- **Need for control** Because times of crisis are so uncertain, an individual's need for control emerges. This usually takes two forms: to stay in control of the ongoing business so that things do not fall through the cracks, and to control how the crisis is managed to minimise disruption. Each form requires strategy, planning and support to reduce the feeling of chaos. What makes it difficult is that individuals are not usually in control of the way they feel and act at times of crisis.
- **Cultural impact** Crises can have both obvious and subtle impacts on the organisation. Among the subtle effects is the impact on the culture: people's feelings, values, beliefs, norms and rituals. A cultural impact assessment is a useful step towards understanding what effect the crisis will have on these underlying elements. It will also indicate how committed people are to the organisation.

INDIVIDUAL REACTIONS TO CHANGE

If we examine the most common ways that people attempt to handle dramatic and negative changes – such as bereavement, divorce, major illness, job loss and so on – we can put their reactions in a 'Reactive Response to Crisis Curve' as shown in Figure 13.1. What this emphasises is that a crisis need not necessarily be a negative thing. It may be possible for us to turn a crisis situation into a challenging opportunity in which a company, the crisis team involved, and relevant individuals can step out of the firing line and into a heroic light just by handling the crisis effectively.

What the curve of Figure 13.1 shows is that when a crisis occurs the initial response is generally one of *shock and anger* – 'How could they

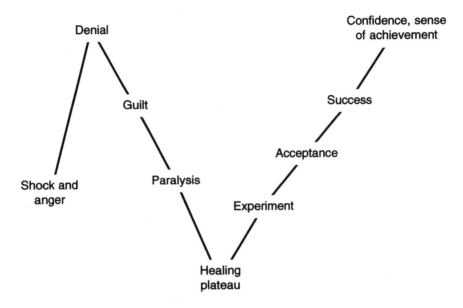

Figure 13.1   Reactive response to a crisis

do this to me?' 'Why is this happening to me?' 'Is this real?' This may then be followed by *denial* – 'This isn't really happening is it?' and then subsequently by *guilt* – 'What did I do to make this happen?' 'If only I hadn't. . .' 'It's all my fault.'

As guilt is largely debilitating, a period of *Paralysis* – 'I can't handle this.' 'I'm going to shut my eyes and wait for it to go away.' may follow which, once acceptance of the crisis has occurred, should be followed by a *healing plateau* – 'Well maybe it'll be OK.' 'We can only go up from here.' 'I'll need some time to think about this.' 'I have every right to feel bad.' This is a very important stage and one which is often denied individuals. They are expected to accept and move on immediately, when psychologically it is healthier to be allowed a period of 'self-indulgence' where the past is hankered after and some wallowing in the horror of it all is permitted. If this is denied these feelings may well surface at a later, more damaging stage.

If the crisis and the individual's feelings are managed effectively then they will move out of this plateau by *experimenting* with the new – 'I suppose we could try it this way, or do that.' This may be followed by an *acceptance* of the need for change – 'I think we can make it.' 'I can cope – this isn't so bad, actually things may be better because of this.' And depending on the *success* of this – 'I managed that really well, people still trust me to do a good job', then a sense of *confidence and sense of achievement* should result – 'I am much better equipped to deal with difficult situations in future', 'I'm really proud of myself for getting through that one'.

Key points to note here are that when dealing with crises we need to be aware of this curve and plan for the fact that:

- individuals will go through these stages and that these are natural responses
- in order to move through these stages successfully and come out the other side people need to be allowed to move through each stage – and that this needs careful management
- people should not be allowed to stay in each stage for too long but attempts must be made to help them move on to the next stage: reassurance and the use of appropriate questions and answers will be needed

FIGHT-OR-FLIGHT RESPONSE

Responses to stress can often have a highly adaptive, valuable effect. What occurs is the famous 'fight-or-flight' response, in which the brain makes its perception of the threat in the immediate environment and then signals to the rest of the body to produce an energy surge to allow the person to flee from the situation of fight the aggressor. With this triggered response, there is a consequent release of hormones (for example adrenalin) into the bloodstream which prepares the body for action by slowing down non-essential functions, such as digestion (hence dry mouth, butterflies in the stomach), and gearing up the heart, lungs and muscles with extra power. Thus the heart beats faster to pump more blood to the lungs for oxygenation, the breathing rate quickens to increase oxygen intake and there is enhanced blood flow to the muscles. Sweating occurs to provide the necessary cooling during this process. We may also think of *freeze* as an alternative to either fight or flight, where an individual may do nothing but stay fixed to the spot, both physically and psychologically.

Although the fight, flight or freeze response is more easily seen in situations where there is real danger (such as an emergency, an accident and so on), it is particularly helpful when trying to understand a range of stress reactions. In most industrial and company-based crises it is a lot harder to physically fight or flee – so where does the extra energy go? The result is often excessive anxiety as the body is prepared to deal with the threat but action not taken. If there is no release then individuals may find themselves in the stress response without a real outlet. Suggestions on how to deal with this will be outlined later on in the chapter.

PREPARING FOR THE STRESS REACTIONS TO A CRISIS

It is normal to experience intense emotional reactions to a crisis: these are understandable reactions to abnormal events. Even if the threat is psychological and not physical the reactions can be just as strong. Many varying crises may occur but the responses to these will be very similar and we are half-way to coping with them if we are aware of them, prepare for them and do not spend most of our recovery and decision-making time worrying that these responses may be in some way abnormal. It is easier to understand and deal with these reactions if they are seen to fit into certain categories:

Physiological Effects

Physiological responses to stressors are related to the fight-or-flight syndrome and include increased heart rate, rapid breathing (hyperventilation), trembling, muscle tension, sweating, faintness and irritation of the digestive system ('butterflies', diarrhoea, nausea), psychosomatic disorders such as eczema, sexual problems, headaches and so on. These effects are mainly part of a normal reaction, and are less likely to have a detrimental impact if the individual is aware of them and sees them as natural reactions rather than illness. They can be controlled to a certain extent by specific stress reduction techniques, based on breathing exercise and muscle relaxation.

Psychological and Emotional Effects

A wide range of emotional and psychological responses can occur as part of the stress response. These range from positive feelings of excitement or alertness, through apprehension and anxiety, to a loss of emotional control. Here an individual can become aggressive, or visibly distressed (for example breaking down crying). A range of possible reactions include surprise, euphoria, anger, sadness, fear, horror, hopelessness, helplessness and depression.

Reactions in emergency situations include such things as non-comprehension of the situation, guilt, a sense of chaos, helplessness and a loss of emotional control. The key thing to recognise in a company crisis is that often, unlike in emergency situations where there is something more tangible to deal with, it may be that these emotions get swept under the carpet in an attempt to appear in control and not to lose face. It is important, however, that these responses are recognised and discussed as far as possible so that they can be dealt with rather than suppressed to do damage later.

Behavioural Effects

'Behavioural effects' are the changes in an individual's normal pattern of behaviour brought on by the stress. Therefore, a level of activity that is normal for one person may be unusually high or low for someone else and may be a symptom of stress. But there are some behaviours that are typically associated with stress that we may expect to see in a crisis situation, for example avoidance, over-zealousness or rigidity (fight, flight or freeze). What is certain is that the type and intensity of behaviours are likely to be rather consistent and somewhat predictable for a given individual, hence the value of exploring typical stress reactions in advance of a crisis in a workshop format so that more effective ways of dealing with the stress can be considered if needed. So the better the crisis team leader's and members' awareness of each others 'stress barometers', the easier it will be to spot and deal with them if a crisis occurs.

Relationship Effects

When a crisis occurs, new friendships and group bonds may come into being. On the other hand strain in existing relationships may appear. It is probably more often that the strain will form in the home relationships as we often tend to want to be with the people with whom we have something in common. This may mean that we have a tendency to exclude family and so we need to be aware of this if we are to manage stress effectively.

Defence Mechanisms

When individuals attempt to protect themselves from painful feelings and thwarted motivations they tend to employ various defence mechanisms to avoid having to deal with complex, potentially threatening situations which, if acknowledged, would overwhelm their ability to cope. Freud and other pioneers of psychoanalysis identified the mechanisms by which the human mind distorts external reality as a way of coping with trauma. There are eight major devices which may be employed:

1. **Denial** – the expressed refusal to acknowledge a threatening reality or realities.
2. **Disavowal** – acknowledging a threatening reality but downplaying its importance.
3. **Fixation** – the rigid commitment to a particular course of action or attitude in dealing with a threatening situation.
4. **Grandiosity** – the feeling of omnipotence.
5. **Idealisation** – ascribing omnipotence to another person, object or organisation
6. **Intellectualisation** – the elaborate rationalisation of an action or thought.
7. **Projection** – attributing unacceptable actions or thoughts to others.
8. **Splitting** – the extreme isolation of different elements, extreme dichotomization or fragmentation – that is, not looking at the crisis overall but trying to focus on certain aspects in order to make it seem more manageable but not being particularly helpful.

RECOGNISING WHEN REACTIONS BECOME ABNORMAL

All of the above responses are *normal* reactions to stress – but we need to be able to recognise when they get out of hand. A typical checklist to help yourself and others to determine whether responses are getting out of hand is as follows:

1. If you cannot handle intense feelings or body sensations and/or continue to have them. If you feel that your emotions are not falling into place over a period of time, or feel chronic tension, confusion, emptiness or exhaustion.

2. If after a month you continue to feel numb and empty. If you have to keep active in order not to face up to your feelings.
3. If you continue to have nightmares and poor sleep.
4. If you have no person or group with whom to share your emotions and you feel the need to do so.
5. If your relationships seem to be suffering badly, or sexual problems develop.
6. If you have accidents.
7. If you continue to smoke, drink or take drugs to excess since the crisis.
8. If your work performance suffers.
9. If you note that those around you are particularly vulnerable or are not healing satisfactorily.
10. If as a helper you are suffering exhaustion.

(Peter Hodgkinson and Michael Stewart, *Coping with Catastrophe*, Routledge, 1991)

THINGS THE COMPANY CAN DO

The following are some of the things a company or organisation can do to select and prepare the right types of individual.

Selection of Crisis Team

In selecting or helping individuals to function effectively in the crisis team we need to examine aspects of their personalities. Where possible you should be looking for those individuals who:

- have a 'locus of control' balance – this is the extent to which an individual perceives that he/she has control over a given situation
- are not emotionally bounded and can discuss and question aspects of crisis openly and without defensiveness
- have positive self-regard
- are hardy – that is committed, in control and confident
- are not neurotic, and
- are good team workers

You can assess some of these via self-assessment and observation of teams working in training sessions.

Psychosocial Care

One way in which the crisis team can be prepared for the psychological aspects of the crisis is to consider the implications for psychological care, who needs it, why, and who can provide it? So part of your crisis preparation is to be aware of, and have contact names for, those in the caring and support organisations. Try to assess the available external and internal support systems, for example counselling services, information packs and so forth.

Training, Experience and Practice

Individuals who feel that they have some grasp of what might happen in a crisis and have already considered the most appropriate reactions are more likely to deal more effectively with the situation when it occurs – hence an argument for crisis management training. It is important to note, however, that previous experience is only really likely to have a positive effect on the confidence and future performance if the previous experience was successful. A badly handled incident or unpleasant experience may well have a detrimental effect on someone's perception of their future ability to deal with stress – so this would have to be explored in training sessions.

Standard Crisis Management Procedures

One important facet of many stress management systems is the need to have some sense of control over events. In the emergency services the use of standard response procedures has been found to assist in providing a feeling of control in an ambiguous and demanding environment. This should also apply with regard to organisations. If the organisation has in place a (workable) crisis manual and a crisis team and has considered the best way to deal with a variety of crises, then individuals involved should have an enhanced feeling of being able to cope, of being able to implement some initial actions, which will reduce stress and also reduce the need for creative problem solving. So, as well as assisting in decision-making and team co-ordination, a crisis manual complemented by training will also help mitigate the effects of stress for those in crisis management positions. Individuals can also have in place ideas and strategies for dealing with their own stress.

THINGS THE INDIVIDUAL CAN DO

Some of the main things that the individual can do to be able to handle a crisis successfully are the following.

Enhanced Awareness

As outlined above, an individual is best prepared to deal with a major stressful event if he/she is more aware of the way they typically react and has already considered ways in which they would deal with both the situation and their own and others' reactions.

Self-Preservation

In the stress field the 'Yerkes Dodson Law' states that stress can result both from *too much* pressure and also from *too little* pressure – which is why people who have too few demands at work may suffer stress as much as those who have too many. It suggests that for the majority of people there is what is called an 'optimum level'- a zone within which demands made can be tolerated – even thrived on – and satisfactory performance achieved.

In times of extreme stress, however, the upper limit of this zone is pushed out and the individual is expected to 'stretch' their optimum level zone beyond what is normally tolerated. This is not so dangerous if it does not happen for prolonged periods of time and as long as the individual is prepared for it by not being vulnerable to its effects. Vulnerability may be enhanced for someone who has an already vulnerable lifestyle – for example a poor diet, no exercise, poor self-esteem, no social support, or an inability to relax. It is important that we have a lifestyle which makes us robust to stress all of the time, but this is especially important at a time of crisis.

Physical Activity

Individuals should be encouraged throughout stressful times to pay particular attention to physical activity – though this should also be part of our lifestyles. Exercise, though a stressor to the body, is a relaxant to the mind, and there is some evidence to suggest that certain chemicals are released in the brain which cause this response. In periods of stress it can utilise the excess energy that may have been built up during the fight/flight response. It can dissipate anger, restore balance but also give individuals some time alone to focus and concentrate – a great asset during a period of crisis. At these times, fatigue will set in and exercise may seem completely the opposite to what is required, but it can be very rewarding and will help keep the individual alert and also make a good night's sleep a lot easier to achieve when the mind may be over-active.

Relaxation

In periods of prolonged stress such as crisis, the sympathetic nervous system may become over-active to the point where individuals are not relaxing naturally (that feeling of anxiety and constant butterflies!) These feelings make people exhausted – but they also make them feel out of control. It is important, therefore, that individuals have a technique which they can use to help restore their balance when needed, that is to override the sympathetic nervous system. This may be in the form of yoga, exercise, meditation, massage, mental relaxation, walking the dog and so on. Companies should make this part of crisis training so that these are available if a crisis occurs.

Seek Social Support from Colleagues, Friends and Family

Social support is crucial when we are trying to manage stress – but often in a crisis individuals withdraw. Individuals need to be able to identify who they can turn to both in and outside of work. Especially during a crisis, it is easy to neglect those who are at home – yet it is crucial to involve these people, partly so that they do not feel left out but also so that they will be there to offer support once the crisis is over.

In summary, the key issues to consider are:

- be aware of individual differences and select those who can thrive on crisis
- be aware of how we react to crisis and recognise the stress signals in ourselves and in others
- encourage positive coping – for example sport versus alcohol
- prepare for extended pressure/stress periods
- keep communication clear, frequent and unambiguous to provide control and involvement
- consult and involve others as much as possible
- prepare to grieve and allow others the same luxury

- use relaxation and social support to counteract anxiety and panic
- aim to be flexible. Expect the unexpected – and never under-estimate the seriousness of the situation
- plan for crisis – be proactive not reactive
- review and learn from the process

CONCLUSIONS

This chapter has discussed the psychological aspects of crisis management. It has suggested that as well as putting together crisis manuals and crisis teams it is essential to consider these aspects so that a crisis will be managed more effectively. If individuals are prepared to deal with their own and others' reactions to stress, then they should experience less negative outcomes. It may be that a company invests in training individuals to manage a crisis and the crisis never happens, but the reality is that these kinds of skills will always come in handy. The key point is that individual members of the crisis team should have a balance of mental, physical and spiritual health in order to cope with any stress that comes their way.

14 Group Behaviour in a Crisis: Symptoms and Cures

In the previous chapter, stress psychologist Cheryl Travers described the effects on the *individual* and how to cope with them. This chapter focuses on how *people and organisations* tend to behave under crisis situations. Once you know to expect this behaviour you can do something about it.

'MUSTARD ON THE PLATE'

Symptom: Just as the mustard that is left on the plate allegedly accounts for more sales than the mustard that is actually eaten, most crisis preparation is a waste of time and money. Companies spend more time talking about it than doing it. They snap into 'We must do something about crisis' mode after they have had a near miss or seen another company suffering from a crisis and, like a driver who has just had or witnessed a road accident, they resolve to sharpen up their act.

For a short time people scurry in all directions, contacting training companies, delegating crisis team members and starting on a crisis manual – usually in the wrong sequence. But after a couple of weeks these good intentions tend to fade. Just as we return to our bad driving habits when the accident is forgotten, crisis planning is moved further and further down the priority list and nothing happens, until the next scare.

Cure: Before embarking on a crisis preparation programme, recognise that it will take up a huge amount of time, resources and commitment. Set aside a realistic budget, make time – and persevere. It will be worth it in the end.

'CHILD'S TOY'

Symptom: The mustard-on-the-plate psychology is a sub-set of the broader child's-toy psychology which affects most businesses when

160

they enthusiastically throw themselves into a new project – only to drop it when they get bored with it. The waste is incredible. Over the years I have seen a plethora of highly expensive programmes – from briefing groups to corporate image campaigns – left abandoned. One company spent several hundred thousands of dollars on a 'corporate image programme'. Six months later the programme was abandoned because sales had not risen. This sort of ineptitude impacts on your crisis management because sound corporate communications are a vital asset when the chips are down.

Cure: Communication initiatives only work if they are *sustained*. Often the results are not measurable, but they are still there – as you will find to your benefit or your cost when a crisis strikes.

'STRANGER IN THE NIGHT'

Symptom: It is human nature to trust someone we know, and to distrust – and even dislike – someone we do not know. If a crisis strikes and your audiences do not know anything about you, you are starting from behind.

Cure: A pre-emptive, proactive corporate public relations programme is an essential part of crisis preparation.

'KING KONG'

Symptom: So named after the comedy sketch in which King Kong is climbing up the outside of the Empire State Building and nowhere in the janitor's manual does it give instructions on what to do about a 40-foot gorilla sticking its toe through a 12th floor window.

This is exactly how most organisations prepare for crisis – trying to cover every possible contingency and ending up with a vast crisis manual which is completely impractical and which, in any case, does not contain the instruction on gorillas' toes – which is the one unthought-of crisis that actually strikes.

Cure: Keep your procedures lean and simple. Teach individual team members to understand crisis psychology, to think on their feet and work as a team. Restrict the manual to a useful working tool to be used in a crisis by people who already know what they are meant to do.

'GOLDFISH BOWL'

Symptom: Nowadays, when a crisis hits an organisation it is everyone's business – both because of increasing public accountability and the proliferation of world media. On a quiet news day your seemingly minor incident can be world news in moments.

Cure: It is essential to have a communication machine capable of reacting quickly and able to contact all the key media and other audiences. Remember the saying: 'A lie can be half-way round the world before the truth has got its boots on'.

'FAMILY HOLIDAY'

Symptom: The natural state of a crisis management team at the height of a crisis is that of a family on the last day of the holiday from hell. They are stranded at some ghastly airport in 90 degrees of heat. The airline is on strike and the money has run out – at which point this normally cohesive group breaks down, with each family member pursuing his/her own agenda.

Cure: It is vital for all senior management likely to be involved in a crisis to learn about each other's agendas, to have respect for them, and to thrash out any areas of potential conflict beforehand. Crisis-awareness training, desktop exercises and crisis simulations can help.

'WHAT YOU SEE IS WHAT YOU GET'

Symptom: The conversion of thought into physical matter has long been the province of psychics and mystics – but it happens every time in a crisis. One of the biggest causes of communication failure is that the organisation behind the crisis is busily pouring out messages based on the *facts*, while the audiences are getting steamed up about what they *think* has happened.

Cure: From the outset, try to assess what people think the problem is and treat that as your crisis, not what has actually happened.

'STAMPEDE!'

Symptom: When it comes to risk and crisis, a 'herd' instinct often does take over.

Cure: Understand something about group behaviour and apply it to your crisis-handling. Watch for the signs of a stampede building up and maximise your efforts to prevent it, for once it has started you are in big trouble.

'DAVID AND GOLIATH'

Symptom: People instinctively tend to support the perceived 'little guy' in a fight. Greenpeace, for example, has a bigger PR resource than any corporation in the world but there is almost automatic public hatred for its targets, not just because they are charged with violating the environment but also because they are perceived as being the big bully taken on by the courageous 'little guy'.

The 'Goliath' psychology influences how people will react towards you in a crisis even if there is no 'David'. If you are a small company or organisation there is a general lack of interest unless you have done something unspeakably dreadful – and even then the media coverage will often talk of 'a local chemical company' without naming you. But the bigger you are, the more people want to see you take a fall.

Cure: Whatever size you are it is essential to develop good communications with your crisis 'audiences' over a period of time before a crisis ever happens. But the bigger you are, the more you must invest in developing a positive corporate image which will be your 'credit in the bank' at a time of crisis.

'FRIENDS, ROMANS, COUNTRYMEN'

Symptom: The first rule of getting an audience to believe you is to tell them what they want to hear. When Shakespeare's Mark Antony told the mob that he had come to bury Caesar and not to praise him, he personally felt the opposite. But it got them listening, from which platform he was able to plant the seeds of hatred for Brutus.

Cure: Next time you have to get important messages across to crisis audiences, start by assessing what it is they most want to hear from you and make that your going-in position.

'WHO BROKE THE WINDOW?'

Symptom: A crisis is like the school playground when a window gets broken and the teacher comes out to find the culprit. If you were the one who threw the brick your punishment will be lessened if you own up immediately – and the other kids will respect you. If it was someone else, you want to make sure that teacher's attention is transferred to the real culprit – but if you are the one who points the finger you will be picked on by the others.

Cure: A public admission gets it over quicker and impresses others with your honesty. But if you can transfer all or some of the spotlight to someone else, look for a subtle way of doing so – such as a confidential leak to a trusted journalist.

'SALOME'

Symptom: It is worth remembering that when a crisis occurs, there is an increasing public need for a head to be served up on a plate.

Cure: As with the playground window, if someone actually *is* guilty it is best to get it out in the public arena as quickly as possible. Even if there is no guilty party, or you cannot find one, the 'constructive *mea culpa*' – at least some sort of apology, for example – can help, as can the various techniques for transferring the spotlight described in Chapter 5.

'SPYCATCHER'

Symptom: *Spycatcher* was the book that the government banned – so everyone wanted to read it, and people paid several times the cover price to obtain illicit copies smuggled in from Australia. Then, when the ban was lifted and the book went on public sale, nobody wanted to read it. This is one of the simplest, most obvious, and yet least appreciated psychologies: *the less you tell people the more they want to know; the more you tell them the sooner they lose interest.*

Cure: Give as much information as you can; as honestly as you can; as quickly as you can. You will seldom do yourself any harm by over-informing but you will almost always make a crisis worse for yourself if you under-inform.

'BUSY BEAVER'

Symptom: If you work like a beaver behind the scenes and do not tell people about it they think that you are doing nothing – which in a crisis will work against you.

Cure: In a crisis you need to *do* something about it – and to be *seen* to be doing it.

'FRIEND IN NEED'

Symptom: One of the symptoms of stress and crisis is to try to do things on your own, even though there are friends and allies all around.

Cure: In preparing for a crisis look for possible allies who can take some of the load and perhaps communicate your messages more credibly than you can. Examples include trade associations, friendly politicians, academics, journalists, regulatory authorities.

'CLEMENT FREUD'

Symptom: Sometimes even your enemies can be turned into allies if you use your brains. This psychology is named after the politician and gourmet Clement Freud whose public attacks on British Rail catering ceased after he was invited to create his own BR sandwich recipes and allowed his signature to appear on the pack.

Cure: As part of your strategic overview, see if it is possible to work with any of your enemies. It may not be as unthinkable as you fear.

'BAAAAAAAAAAAAAAA'

Symptom: Remember that if chemical spills or cancer scares are the media vogue themes of the moment, and you have a chemical spill or your product starts a cancer scare, then the scale of your crisis is doubled before you start.

Cure: None. But take it into account in your strategic planning.

'EMPEROR'S NEW CLOTHES'

Symptom: 'Asking the people who were responsible for preventing a problem whether or not there is a problem is like delivering lettuce by rabbit' (Norman R. Augustine, President of Lockheed Martin Corporation, *Harvard Business Review*, November–December 1995). Like the naked emperor who was conned into thinking he was wearing an exquisite invisible cloak, companies may often not be totally aware of what is actually going on in a crisis. Information is withheld or watered down.

Cure: If you haven't created a management atmosphere in which people are allowed to make mistakes and honesty is rewarded, you will get your just desserts come crisis time.

'HEADLESS CHICKENS'

Symptom: When a crisis strikes it is tempting to rush in and deal with all the questions and commands as they arise. This is a recipe for everyone rushing round in a blind panic and never achieving a strategic approach or a common sense of purpose.

Cure: It is essential for the key players to buy time at the start and to meet to agree on a common understanding of the crisis, its implications and the appropriate strategy for handling it.

15 Training the Team

Training is an essential part of good crisis management for two reasons:

1. **Crisis awareness** training is usually the best way to kick off the whole planning process; and
2. Anyone who will act as a spokesperson **must** be media trained.

There are scores of *media-training* courses – but do vet the trainers first. In particular check out what they offer by way of *print* interviews. Most training courses are run by ex-*broadcast* journalists and it is essential to receive some tuition in the subtle difference of the print interview.

Crisis *awareness* training is much harder to come by, which is surprising as it is so important for everyone on the crisis team and their advisors to understand the nature and psychology of crisis before embarking on a plan. You may have to develop a course of your own with help from outside experts. To help with this process, there follows a description of a typical crisis awareness training day as run by the author's company and published in *Industrial and Commercial Training* magazine (vol. 27, no. 2, 1995).

SELLING THE TRAINING

The first challenge is how to persuade a management to start with a training course when they have usually already committed to preparing a plan first? Indeed, many already have a plan in place, in the form of a huge manual, and the brief is to help them train around it and make sure it works.

Fortunately some organisations quickly grasp the concept of the new approach and are prepared to try it. Other have to be lured into the training in the belief that it fits in with their preconceived requirement. So the 'training' is offered as, for example, media training to help them face the cameras, or a course in how to implement the manual.

THE AWARENESS COURSE

Much hinges on this introductory day. So it has to be good. The ingredients of a successful course are involvement, self-learning, anecdotal material, practical work, team competition, structure . . . and enjoyment.

The best approach is to start with a general analysis – called 'Anatomy of Crisis' and work towards a crescendo of tough television interviews at the end. So in the first session delegates are invited to call out the names of well-known crises and I write them on a board.

I put the names of the crises into similar groups. For example, someone may call out 'The M1 air crash', which I then bracket with 'Lockerbie'. 'Tylenol' is paired or grouped with 'Perrier', and so on, so that in the next stage delegates are asked to analyse why the outcomes of similar crises were so different.

Thus the delegates are having to do a maximum of thinking from the outset. They are also starting to gel as a group and, most importantly, they are discovering for themselves the lessons to be learnt from other peoples' crises.

After the initial 'Anatomy' session the delegates are provided with the bare-bones guidelines for preparing for and handling a crisis – and are then broken into groups before lunch, with each group receiving a different scenario to work on over an extended lunch period. It is important to provide each delegate with clear written instructions on: what their group is expected to achieve, the need to appoint a team leader from the outset, selecting spokespeople and their roles, and so on.

'Seeding' the members of groups is a popular preoccupation in many organisations – but my own experience has been that it does not make much difference. Random grouping (for example as they sit) seems to produce just as good a result as trying to pick the teams in advance.

After lunch the team leaders or spokespeople report back after reading out their scenarios. These scenarios are carefully devised to throw in plenty of the dilemmas that face a crisis team in real life. And they are 'unsolvable' in that there is no obviously single right approach. This ensures that by mid-afternoon every delegate not only understands the general principles but he or she also realises that there are no simple answers. The idea of coming in tomorrow morning and binning the official crisis manual is taking root . . .

Once the groups have selected a winner it is time to move on to guidelines for handling the media, followed by a spokesperson from each group giving a demonstration no-holds-barred TV interview on the subject of the group's scenario in front of the other delegates.

It is important for this exercise to be conducted in the spirit of enjoyment and good humoured badinage which should by now be pervading the delegates so that the interviews can be realistically hard-hitting without the spokespeople feeling intimidated.

I have run many scores of these courses and the feedback has been most encouraging. As well as teaching the subject they encourage the relevant managers to re-think their crisis programme in line with a new approach which, before the course, was completely alien to their way of doing things.

LENGTH OF TRAINING

In companies who take crisis seriously it is even more effective to extend the training over two days and include unfolding scenarios and more specific and intensive media training. It should be stressed that the one day course makes delegates aware of how to handle media interviews but it is not as effective as dedicated media training in which each person has a number of different practice interviews.

INTERNATIONAL TRAINING

Requests often come in for crisis and/or media training in different countries, with the teaching to be conducted by nationals from the country in which the training is being held.

It cannot be done. The standards of media and crisis training – and PR training generally – are vastly higher in Britain, the US and Australia (partly because of the nature of the media in those countries) – but few British, Americans or Australians speak other languages well enough to teach in them. So a compromise has to be found, either by using professional trainers and conducting most of the teaching in English, or employing a mix of professionals and locals.

Crisis *simulations* are also a very useful form of crisis training – though it should be borne in mind that they are expensive to do properly and that the findings must not be taken as definitive. Those organisations who conduct regular simulations find that what went wrong one year goes right the next, and vice versa – so you are still chasing a moving target. But they help to keep people crisis-aware and on their toes. Simulations are dealt with in a separate chapter.

16 Managing Issues

In Molière's *Le Bourgeois Gentilhomme*, the nouveau-riche Monsieur Jourdain hires a professor of language to teach him to speak like an aristocrat. The first lesson is 'Prose' at the end of which the delighted Jourdain proudly tells his family that, thanks to his professor, he can now speak prose. Similarly, issues management is something that many companies and organisations have been doing all their lives but no-one had defined it.

When I worked for Ford in the 1970s and early 1980s we had an 'issues management' programme of which any modern specialist would be proud. There was an informal intelligence network of different departmental managers, politicians and civil servants with motor industry interests, friendly journalists, academics, trade associations and others – so that there was almost always early warning of potential threats. These were discussed regularly by top management, involving the PR and government relations teams, and programmes were then conducted to steer the company through the issue.

For example, when the British Government decided to opt for inward investment, starting by incentivising Nissan to build a huge greenfield site in the North of England, we were facing a massive issue. Taken to the extreme, it could have spelt the end of the indigenous motor industry.

There was no way that inward investment could – or indeed should – be stopped, so an intensive, targeted and highly professional lobbying and communications programme was launched, very quickly and very extensively, to bring a few constraints into the equation. The key feature of the subsequent government policy was a condition that any foreign company manufacturing in Britain must do so with 80 per cent local content.

This local content policy was not only proposed by us, a high proportion of it was actually *drafted* by us and discussed with civil servants prior to being presented to the government in a workable and acceptable form. It was drafted in the early 1980s and still applies to this date.

Nowadays there are numerous textbooks and consultancies specialising in issues management. Public relations practitioner, W. Howard Chase, who is credited with conceiving the term 'issues management' in 1977, gave us a taste of the management-speak that was to come when he defined issues management as: 'the systems process that maximises self-expression and action programming for most effective participation in public policy formation' (F. Seitel, *The Practice of Public Relations*, Merrill, 1989).

Most texts in the area preach the vital requirement of having an efficient monitoring system, but hardly anywhere is there any sound practical advice on *how* to monitor for potential issues, which is extremely difficult to do well and impossible to do perfectly.

THE DIFFERENCES

The great majority of the principles and disciplines of crisis management work equally well for issues because the two are so closely related. Indeed, the two sometimes *are* one and the same thing. For example, a major health or environmental concern whipped up by a pressure group and/or the media, which is in essence an issue, can threaten a whole company's or industry's viability to the extent that it is a crisis. So, to a high degree, they should both be handled in a similar way by the same sort of people.

However, there are several differences between crisis and issues which are worth considering in your planning and handling, which will now be described.

Time Scale

As quoted earlier in this book, a *crisis* is *an issue in a hurry*. You could also say that an *issue* is an *infant crisis*. Both present some kind of threat – to your reputation, your bottom line, your licence to operate and so on – but usually over a different period of time. Crisis management therefore requires more in terms of advance planning, team building, training, simulations and prepared plans. You have to be able to press a button and go.

By contrast, hurriedly pressing a button and going may be the last thing you should do when handling an *issue*. So long as your early-warning system is working and you have spotted the issue developing, it is usually best to *evolve* a response, starting with simple working and brainstorming groups and building up to a specifically targeted programme of the right intensity for that particular issue, and involving the right people. The appropriate team, training and planning will present themselves as the issue is addressed.

Of course, if your early warning system is *not* working and you have not spotted the issue developing, you probably have a crisis anyway! And just to confuse things further, in many 'crises' there is also a reasonable amount of early warning and time in which to prepare your response.

Monitoring

Monitoring is one of those areas that is simple in theory but extremely difficult in practice. There is no single agency, and no internal department, large enough and equipped enough to be able to identify every evolving issue and analyse its implications. So you should not castigate yourself if the odd one slips through the net. However, it is certainly possible to improve your identification of – and response to – issues by establishing some kind of monitoring system. The best approach – in addition to the obvious techniques such as employing a media monitoring agency – is an informal network of people and organisations with some kind of involvement in your field, and who are in a position to pick up the early signals.

This is because issues do not just happen. Someone, somewhere brings them to the attention of the public. That *someone* might be a pressure group, an aggrieved individual, a research body or various other persons or bodies. But it is like the conundrum of the tree falling in the forest not making a noise if there is no-one there to hear it: the someone or someones at the source of your issue have to involve *someone else* for the issue to make waves. And those 'some-one elses' are the sort of opinion formers that you should in any case be involving as a normal part of your ongoing public relations.

So, if you are doing your job properly in the first place, you have already identified your many champions – such as Members of Parliament with a trade or constituency interest, specialist and local journalists, academics with an involvement in your field, and so on – and developed a dialogue with them. They may not be the same opinion formers that the pressure groups and others target, but they work in the same field and mingle with them. And – again if you are doing your job properly – you do not just meet these people for lunch occasionally and send them Christmas cards, you feed each other useful information about what is going on.

Indeed, you can often have a dialogue with your 'enemies'. Many environmental pressure groups, for example, prefer to negotiate with the alleged polluters, giving them a chance to put their house in order before the issue ever reaches the battleground. This also gives you a chance to put your side of things. In the end you might both agree to differ and have a public punch-up – but at least you have an early warning of what is to come.

So the most effective type of monitoring is for the organisation to be fully in touch with the world around them – and to be in touch with each other. If the various internal constituencies (for example general management, public affairs, sales, government relations, R & D and so on) do not already meet and communicate regularly to consider potential issues (and crises), it may be an indication that the organisation needs to look at the root of the cause as a general management issue.

Trade associations should also monitor issues as part of their service to you. And there are increasingly sophisticated ways of monitoring developments electronically. Here Jonathan Church, a specialist in issues forecasting and monitoring, gives his advice:

Issues rarely grow rapidly into threats without a helping hand from an interested party. More often than not, that party is a pressure group, NGO or government department. Through keeping in touch with a wide range of interested parties, it is possible to spot new campaigns before they impact upon an organisation. Once we are able to foresee the efforts being made to move forward an issue, we must look to see where the issue is being taken seriously by those feeding the media.

Good electronic newswire monitoring allows us to see where an issue is emerging into the public domain – usually before it does so (only around one in twenty newswire stories actually makes it into print or onto our screens). The push and pull together provides a rounded picture of emergent issues in a company's current and intended business sectors. The first steps to issues forecasting are:

- List all possibly interested pressure groups/NGOs and regularly update.
- Map their key characteristics and players.

- Regularly check usenet newsgroups which cover networks of pressure groups, such as ECONET. Scour their issue alerts and news reports.
- Physically join the groups who are most active, most influential (or get an anonymous third party to do so for you). Regularly check distributed material.
- Programme search engines to monitor key topics on newswires, in addition to 'issue words' (problem, issue, alert, etc.).
- Bookmark and regularly check all government Internet sites – the UK and EC governments have sites which show the daily output of news releases.
- Check the output, both electronic and printed, of trade bodies and competitors (particularly at times of corporate results).

Chapter 8 Dealing with Pressure Groups, gives further advice on issues monitoring.

Government Relations

Most issues come before the government at some stage as the people behind the issue want to see something enforced by law or government policy. At least here is a (relatively) single focal point for identifying a potential issue and doing something about it. It is also one of the few areas where it actually is worth hiring a specialist consultancy to help with the monitoring and lobbying process. Choose your government relations consultants wisely. Look more for their contacts and influence in the *civil service* rather than among politicians. The real skill lies in spotting a piece of potential legislation before it gets to the Green Paper stage, which is usually the first time that most people realise it is happening and by which time the government has already made up its mind. Many a damaging new law or policy has had a few crucial words tweaked and saved a company or industry from heavy and unnecessary damage. You should still take much of the responsibility for your own relations with relevant politicians and civil servants.

Industry Implications

Most crises only affect one company or organisation while an issue is usually industry-wide. With issues management there is therefore more scope for galvanising an industry-wide response and involving the relevant trade associations.

THE SIMILARITIES

The differences are minor. The common ground is considerable. Both crisis and issues management involve public-relations-led techniques to protect your reputation and/or licence to operate when under threat from negative outside influences.

So if we take the *crisis* preparation and handling checklists and apply them to *issues* management, we end up with very similar lists. The common ground is:

Preparation

- **What** issues could hit us?
- Who are the **audiences**?
- How do we **communicate** with them?
- What are the **messages**?
- What are the **resources** and **facilities**?
- Are spokespeople **trained**?
- Have we built **bridges** with our audiences?

Handling

- **Assess** the situation.
- Select and assemble the **communications team**.
- Decide on the **strategy** and **plan**.
- Identify the **audiences**.
- Decide on the **messages**.
- **Brief** relevant people.
- **Centralise** information.
- **Understand** your audiences.
- Give **information**.
- Give **reassurance**.
- **Resist combat**.
- Be **flexible**.
- Think **long-term**.

The issues communications team will be less structured and more flexible and changeable than for a crisis but it will still involve a number of the same people.

As with successful crisis management, it is not just about *communicating* – it is more about *how you communicate*. As ever, success comes from understanding your audiences, being seen to give some ground, and demonstrating that you see things from their point of view before getting on to your own agenda.

And finally, issues, like crises, can also be *opportunities* as well as threats. Now that you are in the public spotlight you can demonstrate how caring and responsible you are. Normally when you do that it falls on deaf ears.

CASE STUDIES

The following case studies have been selected for the many lessons and examples of real-life crisis management that they contain, providing a rare insight into what the crisis was like for the people actually handling it.

The Stena Challenger Grounding

Jeff Simms[†]

The way that cross channel ferry operators Stena Line handled the grounding of one of their ferries in 1995 is text book stuff. This case study demonstrates a number of the features of a well-handled crisis:

- *The extra volume of media attention when there is not much else in the news.*
- *The importance of responding quickly – Stena estimate that as little as a quarter of an hour could have made a significant difference.*
- *Passenger safety was put before financial considerations.*
- *The importance of being where the media are and not trying to handle them from head office.*
- *Good media control – including regular press conferences and being helpful to them.*
- *Being honest about the negatives.*
- *Every crew member becoming a PR person for the company.*
- *Third-party endorsement – vox pops from happy passengers.*
- *Competitors not putting the boot in.*
- *Crisis into opportunity – a unique chance to demonstrate customer care in the public spotlight.*
- *The prompt, high profile, presence of the managing director.*

* * *

INTRODUCTION

At 10.35 p.m. on Tuesday 19 September 1995, *Stena Challenger*, a 18 523 tonne multi-purpose ro-ro ferry of the Stena Line fleet (then

[†] Jeff Simms is a journalist with the Kent-based design, marketing and publishing agency, Picquet Communications.

Stena Sealink Line), went aground on Calais beach while approaching the harbour. She was carrying 172 passengers, 73 crew, 30 cars and 73 freight vehicles.

None of the passengers or crew was injured but, because of recent ferry catastrophes, international media attention was acute. While the company's operational staff on board and ashore acted swiftly to refloat the vessel and ensure passenger safety, Stena Line's communications team also went in action to minimise negative media coverage and maximise any positive coverage.

This report outlines the media management activity in what has been described by independent PR observers as a copybook PR campaign.

Since the incident it should be noted that Stena Line passenger figures have increased on the Dover–Calais route, with *Stena Challenger* carryings at normal levels.

THE INCIDENT

The beaching of *Stena Challenger outside* Calais port on 19/20 September led to Stena Line – then Stena Sealink Line – putting into action its well-practised crisis management plan.

A copy of this plan – with practical information such as telephone numbers, contact points and clear procedures – is to be found in the briefcase of every member of the firm's senior management in readiness for such an event. The plan is activated by the master of any Stena Line ferry in distress: it is the master who puts into action an appeal for help.

This produces a 'domino effect' at Charter House, the company's headquarters in Ashford Kent, with the ship and port management department, led by Maurice Storey, offering the technical support and assistance necessary to handle the incident and the four-strong PR team, led by director of communications Chris Laming embarking on a media management plan.

The PR operation ensures that the ship management and technical teams are protected from any media interference. These skilled Stena Line staff are, as a result, allowed to get on with their vital work, rectifying the situation and ensuring passenger safety, rather than directing their time towards answering outside questions.

MEDIA ATTENTION

In any such incident, where passenger safety is involved, there is a huge amount of media attention early on. PR executives have to use their experience to assess and direct the media interest but it must also be remembered that the level of interest is governed by outside factors, such as the amount of 'competitive' news vying for front page coverage at the time.

The *Stena Challenger* incident coincided with a quiet news period that lasted over 24 hours. Consequently, the eyes of the UK and Europe were focused on Calais and the plight of the ship. Every major UK national radio and television station carried the story as their lead item for 24 hours, and every major UK newspaper – as well as newspapers in France, Holland and Belgium – attended the scene in Calais.

QUICK REACTION

In this age of satellite TV, digital photography and modem links, the race is on to get TV crews and press to an incident. From the scene, they can transmit by one method or another the news as it happens. TV news coverage is instant reporting.

Satellite teams can be up and running in minutes, broadcasting live to everybody who wants to take it – and seen by everyone watching.

NO DANGER, NO NEWS?

It became obvious very early on in the *Stena Challenger* incident that despite the ship being on the beach, the danger to passengers was not that acute. The obvious first question was how stable was the ship? Fortunately it had a flat bottom and had come to rest on a flat beach so it sat upright and virtually motionless.

There was a force 8 gale blowing from the north east which meant that the *Challenger* was stuck fast on a lee shore and was receiving the full force of wind and wave. As a result, the wind helped push her more firmly onto the beach, adding to her stability, not reducing it. Stena Line operational staff concluded that the ship would not list or topple over.

Having established this, Stena's team then asked themselves how long passengers and crew could be kept on board in satisfactory conditions. The ship is licensed to carry up to 500 passengers but there were only 172 on board and there was plenty of food and drink, so conditions were quite good.

On the evening it happened – 19 September – Chris Laming was attending the travel industry's principal awards dinner – the *Travel Trade Gazette* annual awards – at the Grosvenor House Hotel in London. His public relations manager, Sue Kirk, was at home on call (the company operates a 24-hour on-call system via Vodapagers issued to each member of the PR team) and media-relations manager Brian Rees was on holiday in Spain.

The communications department secretary Mary Lilliott and former communications director Jim Hannah were both, by happy coincidence in Ashford on the night of 19 September and were able to come into the office at short notice. The alarm having been raised by the master, the marine department alerted the duty PR officer – Sue Kirk.

Sue realised immediately that this was a major incident, and decided, without delay, to 'bring in reinforcements'. This critical decision allowed her colleagues and senior Stena Line staff to lose no time in beating the media to the scene. Even a quarter or half an hour's delay at this stage could have altered the course of the media management outcome.

Before midnight, she had called Chris Laming who returned from the London event to head office in Ashford by car at 1.00 a.m. Chris was still dressed in his dinner jacket when he entered Charter House, the company's head office, to find Sue Kirk battling with media phone enquiries, assisted by ship management staff who were able to offer technical advice and support.

Because modern ferries have mobile phones and faxes – as well as ship-to-shore radios – the marine department could remain in constant contact with the ship to monitor the situation as it developed and pass this information quickly to the communications team. At the same time, operational staff had returned to the office around midnight to handle the technical side of the incident.

Company managing director Gareth Cooper was alerted at home and by 2.00 a.m. he arrived, as did customer relations manager Irene Hayward. For half an hour Gareth Cooper listened to Chris Laming and Sue Kirk dealing with phone calls from the media. While he was gathering his notes, Sue and Chris were giving live interviews by phone to national radio and Sky TV.

In under two hours from the moment *Stena Challenger* had hit the sand bank, press and TV crews were broadcasting.

'Doing live TV interviews at 2am are relatively easy', said Chris Laming. 'Few people are actually listening at that time of the morning. Your response to questions may be a little unprepared at first but the more interviews you do, the better and smoother you become – you get your story straight.

Gareth Cooper stayed at head office until 4.30 a.m., by which time it was clear what operational and media management action was needed. Operationally, it was decided that tug assistance was required and the firm agreed Lloyd's 'open salvage' to speed up the release. 'Open salvage' encourages operators with the necessary tug capacity to attend the scene as the successful salvage team reaps a lucrative insurance purse.

This decision could cost Stena Line a great deal of money once settlement by tribunal is finalised but it helped but it helped underline the company's firm stance that passenger safety comes before any financial consideration. Stena Line planned to refloat *Stena Challenger* at 9.30 a.m. on the morning of 20 September, at high tide. But rough seas – a force 8 was gusting – and poor light made it too dangerous to evacuate the ship before or during the attempt. Stena's operational staff have built up an enviable reputation for their dedication to safety and passenger safety was always the guiding criterion here.

GOOD MORNING TV

Media interest was very high and the Stena communications team knew from experience that the media would already be on its way to Calais.

A stranded ferry with inconvenienced passengers and freight hauliers would make the perfect story for breakfast television programmes and it was ideal for Radio 4's Today programme too. Radio 4 had already requested a live interview at 7.00 a.m. when the programme went on air. Radio 5 Live and the independent TV stations all had live breakfast interviews pencilled in.

Taking the adage 'Go where the news is' as his guiding brief, Chris Laming advised MD Gareth Cooper and ship and port management director Maurice Storey to set up a media base in Calais. After all, the cameras would head for Calais whether they were there or not. The ship was there, the passengers were there – so the cameras would be there and any thought of remaining a safe distance from the action was dismissed.

Stena considered the various methods of getting there: chartering a helicopter would be difficult because even though Stena Line has lists of charter helicopter operators in its emergency plan, the same companies invariably get swamped by the media first. What better way to cross than by Stena Line ferry? This would underline confidence in the product and allow on board time to be deployed planning their action on arrival.

The Stena team crossed on the 5.30 a.m. sailing, on board *Stena Fantasia*, arriving Calais at 8.00 a.m. local time. The ship passed close to *Stena Challenger*, giving ship and port management director Maurice Storey the opportunity to assess the situation from close quarters.

ON THE BEACH

During the crossing Gareth Cooper and Chris Laming were able to conduct live interviews via mobile phones. And what better PR could there be for the ferry firm's managing director to talk to the media while travelling by ship himself? By their time of arrival in Calais, many media were on the beach close to the grounded vessel at Bleriot Plage, about five or six miles from the Calais passenger terminal.

Chris Laming warned Gareth Cooper that a media 'reception committee' would be waiting for them in the terminal – all seeking one-to-one interviews This was a critical hour for the PR operation. 'If the press get the feeling you are weak, inexperienced, ill-informed or unhelpful they will make your life very difficult', Chris Laming said later. His initial aim was twofold: to get the press on his side by ensuring they had good facilities in which to work; and to confidently provide them with enough information to satisfy their needs.

By doing these two things he would be able to direct their reporting and prevent them seeking information from other sources. A 'headquarters room' was quickly set up in the Calais terminal so the Stena team could confer in private, plus a conference room for press briefings, away from the public areas of the terminal building.

To ensure the press knew where they could hear reliable information, Chris Laming told them that he would hold regular press conferences, with the first starting in 30 minutes (giving HIM time to gather information, and preventing THEM from leaving the terminal to gather their own information). The promise of a press conference was enough to bring reporters and TV crews from 25 media to the briefing room.

Stena's approach to the media was open and honest but not naive. Laming decided to give them as much information as possible and during the conference he made a point of asking journalists what they wanted. This was a key move: the media hounds were pleasantly surprised to find a helpful response and they warmed to the invitation, requesting a press conference every two hours on the hour.

The press made another request: could managing director Gareth Cooper give a live interview from the beach during the refloating attempt?

Such an interview would make great news if successful: proud MD, happy waving passengers, *Stena Challenger* afloat. But if the attempt failed, Stena's MD would have been caught on camera commentating on a failure. This request was rejected and a second press conference arranged at 10.00 a.m., after the refloating attempt. Forty-five media attended.

REFLOATING ATTEMPT

At the beach, the ship had become the focus of attention for locals and it made a great newspaper picture. Until a ferry is out of the water, it is difficult to appreciate just how big it really is. The sight of such a beached 'whale' gave press photographers a field day and the following day's dailies virtually all carried *Stena Challenger* on their front pages.

The first refloating attempt at 9.30 a.m. was made by small harbour tugs, but only two had managed to get a line on board with the aid of a helicopter. The attempt failed. The weather was still bad and Stena dismissed suggestions of evacuation as too dangerous Passengers would stay on board until the next attempt to refloat at 10.00 p.m.

VITAL CREW ACTION

Passengers were provided with free food and drink and mobile phones were issued so they could make free calls to their families.

Many crew gave up their cabins to allow passengers to sleep in their beds.

Every crew member on that ship that night was a PR man for the company. They were the heroes and their actions prevented what could easily have turned into a customer relations disaster. Well-trained and well-managed, the Stena staff were very caring, very patient and very professional – they did all the right things.

After the first failed attempt to refloat, the media were keen to talk to passengers by phone, so at the third press conference held at 12 noon, the focus switched to what the conditions were like on board ship. The media wanted to talk to passengers and asked for the phone numbers of the mobile phones. Stena refused, saying it needed to keep those phone lines open for passengers to contact relatives and for technical experts to stay in touch with the vessel. Most of the press appreciated why the firm refused this request and perceived Stena's response as that of a caring company action rather than an unwillingness to provide information.

But what worried Stena most was how the press would interrogate passengers once they met them after disembarkation. It was decided that a ground support crew member would meet each passenger before they came into contact with the media. Ground crew would speak to each passenger, offer them free hotel accommodation in Calais and listen to any complaints. They would collect the customer care forms that had been distributed to passengers with details about any inconvenience, and any compensation to which people felt they were entitled.

Some were on a beer dash, some were day trippers, others were travelling on business while others were returning home from holiday in Britain. By asking individual passengers to define their own needs, the passengers on board felt reassured that they were being well-treated. As a result, when they disembarked, the vast majority did not have a bad word to say against the firm – in fact most people said Stena had taken good care of them.

HONEST, UP FRONT

Stena did not however, attempt to tell the press that everything was rosy. At the fourth press conference during the afternoon (some five hours after the first failed refloating attempt and six hours before the next) Stena managing director Gareth Cooper freely admitted that some passengers were becoming frustrated at the long wait and disgruntled at the position they found themselves in.

What the press and public at large did not know was that Stena's directors were meeting French maritime authorities, the military and coastguards behind the scenes to plan an evacuation of the ship if the second refloat attempt did not succeed. Clearly, Stena was ensuring a contingency was in place should the second refloat attempt fail. But with the help of a bigger tug, *Stena Challenger* was refloated at 9.00 p.m., the night of the 20 September – with a further two ocean-going tugs from Le Havre and Cherbourg also on hand in case of need.

As soon as the ship started moving off the beach, the media went back to the terminal and were taken to the quayside in buses laid on by the Calais Chamber of Commerce. When the vessel entered port about 10.00 p.m., Gareth Cooper, Maurice Storey, Chris Laming and other senior Stena managers went on board to meet the passengers.

The most hostile passenger demanded to meet Gareth Cooper and, while everybody else disembarked, he remained behind on the car deck talking to the Stena Line MD. In consequence, this passenger did not come into contact with the media and did not supply them with his negative story.

Before the marine authorities boarded the ship to begin their investigations, Gareth Cooper called the crew together and thanked them for their efforts praising them for the excellent work they had done taking care of passengers. The directors then went to the terminal for a final press conference.

IDENTITY SAFEGUARDED

After a relax in the bar and a good night's sleep, the Stena team dealt with late media enquiries and by midday the following day press interest had waned, signing off with Gareth Cooper live into ITN's lunchtime bulletin as the *Challenger* left Calais en route for a Dunkirk ship repair yard.

Throughout the incident, the identity of the ship's master was protected by Stena: they were not prepared to put him under the media spotlight so he was secreted away from the ship, out of France and taken to a secret location in England where he stayed with his family. To this day the captain's identity has not been revealed by Stena.

Follow-up media interest focused on the damage to the ship. An inspection by divers in Calais suggested no major damage but when *Challenger* was checked in dry dock in Dunkirk it was found that some plates were buckled. The ship was taken out of service and this was covered by the media, with full support from the Stena Line communications team.

GOOD TEAMWORK

The Stena Line communications team had done a tremendous job during the whole operation. The two press centres – one in Calais, the other at the HQ in Ashford – worked very well together. Communications between two press offices in separate locations is difficult but the Ashford team was able to monitor developments by following live TV and radio coverage of interviews being given by Stena staff at Calais.

This is a point for other PR practitioners to note, says Chris Laming: 'It is a valuable tip for others in similar circumstances. Press officers in different locations should use live media coverage to keep in touch with what's going on, and ensure a consistent approach is taken to answering media enquiries.'

INDUSTRY IMPLICATIONS

The ferry industry has been in the spotlight for a long time: the competition with Eurotunnel and the tussle for market share; safety at sea – especially in the light of the *Herald of Free Enterprise* sinking at Zeebrugge in 1987 – and the Estonia disaster in the Baltic; and duty free. They all make front page headlines.

But in any incident, the media will either seek out a story or seek to 'create' one. Take, for example the attempt by the *London Evening Standard* to link the routine replacement of the *Challenger's* bow door hydraulic locking pins earlier in the day on the 19 September with the beaching. Stena had to threaten the newspaper with an injunction before it toned the story down for later editions.

Knowing the press will explore every angle, justifiable or not, has led companies like Stena to develop detailed PR crisis management plans. In Stena's case, this extended to the way customer services also operates in such circumstances.

At Stena, on the morning of 20 September – at about 2.00 a.m. customer services manager Irene Hayward set up a 14-strong telephone response team at head office to answer all non-press calls from relatives, pressure groups and so on. They provided an invaluable service and followed up all compensation claims from *Challenger* passengers. As well as being a genuine service for passengers and their families this ensured that fewer disgruntled passengers approached the media to give damaging interviews.

DAMAGE LIMITED

But there's no doubt that Stena's reputation was damaged. Chris Laming admitted: 'There was no way you can disagree with that when you have your ship aground on a beach. You have to be open and honest and admit it was damaging but I think we came out of it proving that we are a caring company.'

'During the incident we were helped by our competititors, who resisted "putting the boot in". Eurotunnel and the other ferry operators stayed silent and the chairman of a rival company congratulated us on the way the incident was handled. As a damage limitation exercise it was successful and we have had favourable reviews in the *Independent* and the *London Evening Standard* about our efficient handling of the crisis, plus positive appraisals in magazines like *PR Week*.'

A MANAGEABLE 'DISASTER'

Compared to a tragedy like the sinking of the *Herald of Free Enterprise*, the beaching of *Stena Challenger* was a straightforward communications task. But it remains a fact that Stena's PR team did the right things at the right times. As a key point of strategy, they resolved to get the MD in the spotlight very quickly.

In this respect, Stena followed the example provided by Sir Michael Bishop, who took a lead role after the British Midland Kegworth air disaster and won many plaudits for his handling of the incident.

'We regard a high profile for the MD as a vital part of crisis PR strategy', said Chris Laming. I believe the senior management who shirk the glare of the press during a time of crisis are asking for trouble. You have got to be able to stand up and be counted and you must be prepared to shoulder responsibility.'

How quickly does a firm recover after an incident like the *Challenger* grounding? This is difficult to quantify but Stena's passenger carryings show that the incident had little effect on business. And the positive media coverage the firm received about its caring on-board staff has helped the ferry operator limit any damage. In some ways Stena succeeded in turning the incident into a good news story. After all, no passengers were injured, no crew were at risk, everyone on board who felt they merited compensation has been compensated . . . and most important from the press point of view, *Stena Challenger* helped sell more newspapers when news was hard to come by.

Odwalla Apple Juice

Matthew J. Harrington[†]

The handling of a massive and fatal product contamination in the US won the top industry award for the **PR** firm who managed it. The key features included:

- the size and scale of the task
- immediate establishment of objectives
- the role of on-going audience research
- the importance of understanding the company culture
- ensuring that 'communication remains true to the company's core values'
- effective use of the Internet
- the human touch – chairman visiting victims
- third party endorsement – praised by the victims' lawyers!

*   *   *

STATEMENT OF PROBLEM

Late in the evening on 30 October 1996, health officials in the State of Washington alerted the management of fresh-juice-maker Odwalla Inc., of Half Moon Bay, California, that there was an epidemiological link between a number of cases of *E. coli* 0157:H7 and Odwalla fresh apple juice. Within a matter of hours, Odwalla management voluntarily recalled its apple juice and all juice blends containing apple juice – approximately 70 per cent of their product line. The company also recalled carrot juice and vegetable cocktail because they are made on the same press as apple juice. In the early morning

---

[†] Matthew J. Harrington is Executive Vice President/General Manager, Edelman Worldwide/ San Francisco.

hours of 31 October, Odwalla delivery trucks in seven states and British Columbia began collecting juices from more than 4600 retail accounts.

Late in the day on 31 October, Odwalla hired Edelman Public Relations' San Francisco office to handle all aspects of the company's crisis communications. Public relations activities were conducted throughout Odwalla's entire distribution area but were concentrated in the Seattle area, Northern California and Denver because as many as 60 cases of *E. coli* bacteria were ultimately identified and linked to the juice maker in these Odwalla stronghold markets.

We worked continuously on the project from 1 November to 17 December, when Odwalla made a presentation at an FDA meeting on the necessity of mandatory pasteurisation.

RESEARCH

The nature of a crisis obviously requires immediate action, but we simultaneously undertook research on multiple levels to assure that we fully understood the issue, the tone and content of media coverage to date, the potential impact on the company and the best ways to move forward. Further, Odwalla has a very strong culture and company vision that had to be fully understood by the agency and media to help explain the devastating effects a crisis of this nature had on a company founded on the principle of 'nourishing the body whole'.

Research conducted by Edelman included: a full *debriefing on event and company culture* by Odwalla management, an immediate *audit of all media coverage* for tone and content, *review of media coverage* of *E. coli* outbreak in apple cider in New England three weeks prior, *review of all materials* provided by the Seattle Department of Health, *review of background information* on *E. coli*, *review of previous Edelman crisis work* including work done in the San Francisco office on an *E. coli* contamination in dry salami, annual reports and articles on both the Tylenol and Jack in The Box crises, Internet research, a debriefing by Edelman/DC on past Food and Drug Administration actions regarding product recalls, *review of analyst comments* on the crisis to date, *review of consumer calls* to the Odwalla 800#, and *debriefing* with Edelman Denver affiliate agency Johnston Wells and independent Seattle public relations agency Elgin Syferd for perspective on and assistance with local markets.

Over the course of the crisis, we identified acceptance of messages by conducting a *daily media analysis* from sources including an express clipping service, video monitoring service recap reports, an on-site media centre and Internet monitoring of media coverage.

Quantitative research was conducted two weeks into the crisis and also in January 1997 to understand consumer response to company actions. *Qualitative research* was undertaken in December 1996 to probe consumer response and awareness of the crisis and company actions.

PLANNING

Given the breadth of response and action needed in a short time frame, planning was essential. Two Edelman teams were immediately established – a Half Moon Bay (HMB) team in charge of overall crisis response that worked in constant contact with the Odwalla Director of Public Relations and Director of Marketing, as well as agencies Johnston Wells/Denver and Elgin Syferd/Seattle and a San Francisco (SF) team responsible for handling media response.

Objectives were outlined immediately and included:

- establishing dialogue with consumers about the incident
- communicating the recall
- neutralising potential press criticism
- responding to all media inquiries within deadline, with information and/or an interview
- advising retail trade partners of Odwalla's actions and remaining available products, and assuring them of the company's long-term viability
- communicating the company's dedication to nourishment
- communicating company sorrow at the outbreak of illness
- establishing Odwalla as the pre-eminent authority on fresh juice
- ensuring that all communication remains true to the company's core values
- protecting Odwalla's position in financial markets

We identified the following target audiences:

- media
- Odwalla consumers
- retail trade partners

- employees
- families of afflicted persons (nearly all children)
- health departments (national and state)
- investment community

Key messages were developed about:

- the investigation into the source of the contamination
- concern for families affected
- changes made to assure safe juice in the future
- adoption of a previously avoided process – pasteurisation
- product re-introductions
- long-term company viability

The following communications channels/vehicles were tapped for disseminating information:

- newswires/press releases
- fax lists of interested reporters
- internet/website (newly created and updated daily by Edelman)
- expanded customer response 800#
- in-store communications/Odwalla cooler advisories, retail trade partner information packets
- conference calls (employees, investment community)

Other planning activities vital to the smooth implementation of the crisis management plan included: *establishment of a media centre* at Odwalla to monitor local and national television and radio coverage; *development of a media tracking, response and interview/information request relay system; daily team meetings* to discuss strategy and assignments; *scenario planning* to anticipate developments and prepare; daily *executive summary packets* for Odwalla senior management, including media analysis, representative media clips, strategic message points and daily news releases; and *regular updates from Odwalla representatives assigned as liaison to health departments.*

EXECUTION

With the company's reputation for making the most healthful, nourishing juices at stake, Odwalla depended on Edelman to develop, hone and communicate the effectiveness of the product recall.

Daily crisis management activities included:

- reviewing all media coverage each day to understand the media play of the issue and communication of Odwalla's position
- creating executive summary kits to update management on developments
- holding daily strategy sessions to plan the day and address problems
- writing press releases daily to update the media on the rapidly developing issue
- conducting daily 'mini' media-training sessions with executives, revising strategic message points on new developments they had to convey that day during interviews
- identifying optimal times for senior management to conduct media interviews

Open communication involved:

- immediately creating a web site to establish an easily accessible location for all communications to journalists as well as information for consumers – the site was set up within 48 hours on Edelman news web, and the site address was published to journalists, web search engines and news groups
- regularly updating the customer relations (800#) script to reflect new developments

Major programme elements were:

- arranging for company chairman to travel to Denver and Seattle to visit families and to meet media
- participating in FDA press conference via telephone when *E. coli* was officially linked to Odwalla; David Kessler, head of FDA, called *E. coli* an 'industry issue'
- expressing company grief when a child in Denver died from *E. coli*
- reintroducing some recalled juices that were reformulated without apple juice
- participating in the creation of the Odwalla Nourishment and Food Safety Advisory Council, consisting of experts in microbiology and nutrition, and company experts

- participating in the rebuttal of some FDA findings in the plant, setting up a press conference for Odwalla's CEO, chairman and Council members to address the issues
- introducing the company decision to use a form of pasteurisation for apple juice
- working with Odwalla to prepare for its presentation to the FDA on mandatory pasteurisation

Trade partners/employees/analysts:

- wrote/compiled materials to communicate all key messages to retail trade partners
- adapted copy from releases and other communications for regular updates posted at Odwalla coolers in stores
- wrote/compiled materials to update Odwalla regional employees on the issue
- conducted telephone training for employees in outer markets who were dealing with media
- conducted conference calls to update the investment community on the issue and company action

Media relations involved:

- developing a tracking system for logging all media requests for information, responding to all media within deadlines with requested information or an interview with the appropriate Odwalla contact – spokeswoman Sydney Fisher, Chairman Greg Steltenpohl or CEO Stephen Williamson
- the Edelman SF team communicated all media requests and especially urgent deadlines to HMB team who secured executives for interviews
- returning more than 200 calls on the first day to media who had left messages overnight on Odwalla's answering service
- maintaining regular contact with approximately 225 broadcast and print reporters, nationally and in local markets
- distributing daily releases via wire services and compiling a database of reporters following the story, for secondary fax distribution of all press releases
- posting to the web site all press releases and background information on *E. coli*, the company, its principles and vision, Q & A, and any other relevant information – the site was updated continuously

EVALUATION

- Communication with consumers was initiated and sustained successfully through media channels, which delivered more than 5000 newspaper/magazine stories, including *The Wall Street Journal, The New York Times, Bloomberg, AP, San Francisco Chronicle, San Francisco Examiner, Denver Post, Rocky Mountain News, Seattle Post-Intelligencer, Seattle Times* and *The Los Angeles Times*, representing approximately 584 million consumer impressions; more than 650 broadcast stories, including national media and all network affiliates and independents in all target markets, reached an estimated 104 million consumers.
- Media coverage was uniformly neutral to positive in tone and factual in content with many media praising Odwalla's quick action, by use of marketing experts' quotes and favourable headlines or editorials.
- More than 3000 calls were received through the 800# in the first week; the usual volume had been 30 calls a week.
- The web site received 19 000 hits in the first 48 hours, and approximately 50 000 by January; Odwalla has expanded its crisis site into a permanent presence on the web.
- An independent AOL survey showed that 86 per cent of on-line respondents supported Odwalla and would return as consumers.
- Other surveys showed 94 per cent of those polled were aware of the *E. coli* outbreak and Odwalla, and 96 per cent of those aware approved of Odwalla's handling of the crisis.
- Unusual praise came from attorneys of families afflicted by the bacteria. In a television interview, one said: 'This company has done everything right and it's important to reward good corporate behaviour'.
- Odwalla was asked by the FDA to make a presentation at December meetings on mandatory pasteurisation.
- Stock price is in the area of $13, from a low of $9 immediately after the crisis. Pre-crisis, it was $19 per share.
- Odwalla retained in excess of 80 per cent of accounts.
- Safeway, Odwalla's largest account, concurred with Odwalla statement that until safety is assured, fresh apple juice should not be consumed. Safeway accepted only pasteurised apple juices and juice blends; many juicers were forced out of store; Odwalla's position was safe.
- All products are currently back on shelves, and new product introductions proceed at a normal rate.

The Pepsi Syringes

Colin Doeg[†]

Pepsi-Cola's handling of a massive scare story was a model of good crisis management. The features included:

- *Using the TV stations and videos to* demonstrate *the safety of the product.*
- *Involving* a credible third party *(the FDA) to convey the 'all clear' after first being seen to thoroughly investigate procedures.*
- *Being driven by an ethos of* genuine concern for customers.
- Employee involvement *throughout.*
- Empowerment, *not organisation charts.*
- *Going on the* offensive *at the right time and in the right way.*
- *Use of* advertising *as well as PR.*
- *A* clearing house *to coordinate messages.*
- *Crisis team* planning *and cooperation before the event.*

It is also another crisis-into-opportunity case study. Pepsi-Cola ended up selling more of its product the week after *the crisis than it had the week* before.

*   *   *

Soft-drinks giant Pepsi-Cola wrote a new chapter in crisis management in June 1993. It led to the company and the US Food and Drug Administration being praised for their handling of the situation by both president Bill Clinton and in the House of Representatives.

Events began to unfold at noon on Thursday, 10 June, when a Seattle television station informed Pepsi's local franchise bottler, Alpac Corporation, that an 82-year-old Tacoma man was claiming to have found a syringe in a can of Diet Pepsi though nothing similar

---

[†] Colin Doeg is a former journalist, a public relations consultant and author of one of the most excellent and comprehensive books ever written on crisis management: *Crisis Management in the Food and Drinks Industry* (Chapman & Hall, 1995) from which this case study is extracted.

is used in any aspect of Pepsi's manufacturing or quality control processes. Initially, Pepsi-Cola judged the matter to be a local issue – standard operating procedure for the company's franchise bottlers and a logical and sensible approach. The local bottler is obviously in the best position to respond to its 'own' local product quality issues.

Alpac's crisis management team and manufacturing staff worked round-the-clock with regulatory officials to investigate the complaint. From the outset, management responded to all press, customer and consumer enquiries with a policy of openness and honesty. Food and Drug Administration (FDA) officials began a thorough examination of the plant, its production records and its personnel. TV crews were allowed to tour the factory to see for themselves how its production and quality assurance processes were such that product contamination or infiltration was virtually impossible.

Yet, within 12 hours, another report of a syringe being found in a can of Diet Pepsi hit the headlines. This led Alpac and the FDA to issue a regional warning to those areas supplied by the plant – Washington State, Oregon, Hawaii, Alaska and Guam. Consumers were advised to inspect all cans of Diet Pepsi for signs of tampering and to pour the contents into a glass or cup before drinking.
Though it was a regional alert, the warning received nationwide attention on network news programmes on Sunday, 13 June, and the issue became the nation's top news story for the next 96 hours.

By the next day, copycat claims were beginning to be made in different parts of the country. Within a few days, they were coming in from 23 states, from Alabama to Wyoming. What had started out as a local matter had exploded into a national issue! Pepsi expanded its core crisis team to manage and respond to the situation. Media reports were widespread, and thousands of enquiries were pouring in from concerned consumers, customers, reporters, employees and regulatory officials. The team provided the facts as Pepsi-Cola communited with these groups, serving as the clearing house for new information as it came in.

The team was 12-strong, and headed by Pepsi president Craig Weatherup. The crisis coordinator was Rebecca Madeira, vice-president of public affairs. She directed the team's actions and coordinated communications to ensure the company spoke with a single voice to all its audiences. The key groups in the team included:

- **Public affairs**   A team of six handled the onslaught of press calls and dealt with hundreds of radio, television and print interviews. A separate team wrote and developed material for the media, including video news releases, audio tapes, press releases, charts and photographs. Six government affairs managers helped to disseminate the latest facts to Pepsi's 400 bottlers.

- **Consumer relations**   Two dozen specialists manned Pepsi's toll-free telephone lines 24 hours a day to allay consumers' fears. They were helped by 40 volunteers from within the company. The tenor of the phone calls also provided a useful indication of public attitudes.
- **Scientific and regulatory affairs**   Technical and product safety experts were the link to the FDA's Office of Criminal Investigation and tracked each syringe complaint.
- **Sales and marketing**   This was the channel through which information was relayed to supermarkets, restaurants, convenience stores and others who sold Pepsi products. Attention to these important groups helped to keep the business running smoothly.
- **Manufacturing**   Experts helped the local FDA investigations and in developing effective explanations of the production and quality control processes for the press and the public.
- **Legal department**   In-house experts coached the crisis team on legal aspects of communications and reporting issues.
- **Communications**   Constantly updated information was channelled through a *communications clearing house*, whose responsibility was to pass it on to Pepsi bottlers, the company's 50 000 employees and hundreds of thousands of customers and consumers.

With this structure in place, the team assessed the situation. Said Rebecca Madeira: 'We had to be absolutely sure this tampering could not possibly have happened in any of our plants. At the same time, we needed to develop a responsible way of talking about the situation before we went public on the issue.'

Therefore, the core team focused on three critical questions:

- Was there a health risk?
- Was there any possibility that syringes could be getting into cans at Pepsi bottling plants?
- Was nationwide tampering occurring?

The FDA took the lead in answering the question about a health risk: the agency determined that the two Seattle needles carried no risk of infection. (Colas are acid products of low pH, both as a result of carbonation and of the phosphoric acid ingredient generally used.)

The agency also exhaustively inspected Pepsi's manufacturing procedures. Every canning line at the plants from which contaminated drinks were alleged to have originated was studied carefully to see if there was any way to infiltrate the process. Consumers making complaints were also interviewed. The result: it was decided the high speed and integrity of the lines ruled out internal tampering. Whatever was turning up in cans of Diet Pepsi had been placed there after they had been opened.

As more cases surfaced across the country, the possibility of sabotage was ruled out. There was no correlation between the complaints, when the cans were made or where they were made. They were produced at different plants, some as much as six months previously, others around six weeks before, and some as recently as six days prior to the complaints being made. For so many cases to turn up in so many different circumstances was illogical.

Both FDA commissioner David Kessler and Pepsi president and CEO Craig Weatherup agreed there was no health risk and that, most probably, there was no relationship between the tampering allegations cropping up right across the country. They also agreed that a recall would not solve the problem. Rebecca Madeira explained: 'We were committed to putting consumer safety first, but clearly a recall would not end the crisis or restore consumer confidence. The only thing that would do that was to discourage any tampering with an opened can . . . in the strongest possible terms.'

Secure in its grasp of the facts and backed by the FDA, Pepsi went on the offensive. Craig Weatherup repeatedly declared: 'A can is the most tamper-proof packaging in the food supply. We are 99.99 per cent certain this didn't happen in Pepsi's plants.' The crisis team set about producing video footage that would clearly show just how safe Pepsi cans really were. The pictures they needed were in the company's bottling plants, where high-tech, high-speed equipment turns each empty can upside down, cleans it with a powerful jet of air or water, inverts it, fills it and closes it – all within nine-tenths of a second and at the rate of 1200 cans a minute!

On the Tuesday afternoon, 15 June, the video footage was beamed by satellite to hundreds of TV stations across the country. It was seen by some 187 million people, breaking all records for such a 'feed'. The total represents more viewers than watch the SuperBowl, America's major sporting event which is equivalent to the Football

Association Cup Final or the Grand National horse race in the UK or the crucial mountain stages of the Tour de France cycle race in Europe.

Pepsi instinctively knew it had to fight videotape with videotape. It did so with four video news releases issued in as many days, reaching some 365 million viewers. By the end of the week Weatherup had appeared in person on a dozen network TV news shows, including the MacNeil/Lehrer newscast, ABC's Nightline and Good Morning America, NBC's Today, CBS's This Morning and CNN's Larry King Live. Several of these programmes are seen on CNN or Sky News in the UK, as well as elsewhere in the world. During the same period, Pepsi spokespeople conducted more than 2000 interviews with newspaper, magazine, TV and radio reporters.

'Our strategy was to reassure the public that this was not a manufacturing crisis', recollected Madeira. 'What was happening with syringes was not occurring inside our plants.'

Probably the most sensational video news release was that made available on Thursday, 17 June. It featured a surveillance tape showing a woman putting a syringe in a can at a convenience store. Shot in a store in Aurora, Colorado, the tape purported to show the woman putting a syringe into an open can of Diet Pepsi while at the checkout counter and later claiming the can had been tampered with. The VNR was seen by an estimated 95 million viewers and helped to turn the tide in favour of Pepsi-Cola. The woman was found to have 16 aliases and a lengthy record for forgery, fraud and theft. Subsequently, she was sentenced to 51 months in prison.

Between June and September, 55 other people were arrested for making false claims and others started to retract their stories.

David Kessler also helped to write the new chapter in crisis management by appearing on some TV programmes with Craig Weatherup and stating at a press conference that not one tampering report had been confirmed by FDA investigations, and that the agency rejected the possibility of nationwide tampering. As far as the author is aware, this is the first time a major regulatory authority has given such a public reassurance. The FDA's involvement gave greatly enhanced credibility to Pepsi-Cola's general stance over the tamperings. Indeed, Rebecca Madeira said that the agency was the company's crisis counsellor, using its vast experience in copycat crimes to help Pepsi. Madeira also made the point that the FDA was valued by the general public as the neutral third party, protecting consumer interests.

On Monday, 21 June, Pepsi-Cola continued its bullish stance. Display advertisements were run in a range of newspapers, from *USA Today* and eleven other nationals to between 300 and 400 regional and local newspapers proclaiming 'Pepsi is pleased to announce . . . nothing'. The adverts emphasised that the stories were a hoax with no evidence to support a single claim and went on to announce special offers to save consumers money all summer long. It ended by thanking 'the millions of you who have stood with us' and declaring: 'Drink all the Diet Pepsi you want'.

In adopting such a positive approach, Pepsi-Cola had a number of factors on its side. The brand was well-established, popular and trusted. Its management was highly professional. The company had long-established links and extensive experience in dealing with its key audiences – the media, consumers, customers, regulatory authorities and employees. Also, Pepsi knew it had to act swiftly and decisively to defend its multi-billion dollar market – especially a few days before the 4 July Independence Day celebrations and holiday period, which was vital to sales. Its 50 000 employees worked to assemble the facts and to allay customer and consumer concerns. Even the FDA came to its support. It had truth on its side and presented its case in such a way that it was perceived to be acting in the best interests of its consumers.

There is much to learn from this case history, no matter how large or modest a company may be. While this was the most serious crisis which Pepsi had had to deal with, the people who dealt with it knew each other well and had worked together successfully on many lesser incidents. They were not a group of strangers meeting for the first time in a highly stressful situation. They had long-established procedures and the necessary resources for handling such incidents. When the problem arose they established the facts quickly and accurately. They set up the structure to deal with the crisis and those involved had clearly defined roles – dealing with the media, consumers, customers, regulatory officials and employees. A clearing house was established for all communications so that the company spoke with a single and unified voice.

At the outset, when the pressures must have been enormous, the core crisis team developed a responsible way of talking about the situation before the company went public on the issue. They provided the media with what they needed to report the crisis – video tape, press releases, photographs, diagrams, constantly updated information, skilled press officers who understood their requirements, and a chief executive officer who was well-prepared and readily available for television appearances and other interviews. The company operated to the media's timetables and provided simple, clear messages. It fought videotape with videotape, being fully aware that television is one of today's top news-making tools and that people believe what they see with their own eyes and hear with their own ears.

Said Rebecca Madeira: 'We concentrated on what consumers care about – the can of Pepsi in their hand, not some kind of assault on Pepsi's national name. We also gave them as many opportunities as we could to let them see real people solving real problems.'

When there is a serious problem no company should ever forget one group of people who will be seriously concerned about the matter – its own employees. If the relationship with them is that of a good employer, the business will find they are an invaluable asset. Pepsi had 50 000 employees on their side. They were kept well-informed. They were good ambassadors for the company. They were also effective communicators to their own family, friends and neighbours because they were well-informed and they too were able to speak with a single 'voice'.

Pepsi had a guiding philosophy or mission statement: 'We will be an outstanding company by exceeding customer expectations through empowered people, guided by shared values'. That operating dictum served the company well, especially when Pepsi was under fire.

Writing about the way the company's vision statement stood the test, Pepsi said:

A crisis means accelerated events, unexpected turns and constant pressure. There is no time to think about what your company stands for. Those values have to be well-entrenched.

Ours were. By instinctually and constantly checking ourselves against what was best for our customers, we constantly made the right choices. Not just management, everyone. Our philosophy lighted our steps in the midst of the storm.

Likewise, the merit of empowered people became readily apparent. When a crisis threatens your very existence, an organisational chart is of limited utility. Employees must be ready, willing and able to accept extraordinary new responsibilities at a moment's notice.

Pepsi's were – and for the simple reason they were used to it. Every day they are expected and encouraged to use their own wits, judgement and initiative to make decisions based on customer needs.

So, in a crisis situation, when employees suddenly found themselves with important, often crucial duties, they did not hesitate. But, rather they responded with singleness of purpose.

Finally, and most important in this crisis, Pepsi's guiding philosophy bound us together and braced our resolve. All 50 000 employees were unified in a sole mission: Do what's right for our customers.

So, at least in this sense, the Pepsi Hoax gave us something very valuable. An appreciation of what this company is all about. A vision isn't worth much if it only works on a clear summer day. The hoax defined the power of teamwork, the energy we get from each other and the pride we share at Pepsi.

The week of the hoax, Pepsi lost approximately $40 million in sales, although the impact varied widely from market to market. In one location a bottler lost thousands of cases in the first day of the scare alone, in other markets business held steady, while in others sales actually went up.

But the dips proved temporary and sales rebounded strongly. One week after the hoax, consumers bought 800 000 more cases of Pepsi products than the week before. American Independence Day, on 4 July, proved to be Pepsi's strongest sales week of the year as millions stocked up for holiday parties. Pepsi had survived the crisis and emerged stronger than ever!

The Aftermath of Multiple Murder

Jonathan Street[†]

The horrific torture and killings of several young people in a Gloucester house made world news when they were discovered. The murderer, Fred West, hanged himself in his prison cell while awaiting trial, leaving his wife and accomplice, Rosemary, to face the music. The author had the extremely difficult task of coordinating the communications of a number of different involved parties at a time of crisis.

The key features of this case study include:

- *the importance of tight coordination of messages*
- *the value of organising a visibly independent inquiry*
- *how myths become facts*
- *the importance of openness and information – including extensive use of video news releases (VNRs)*
- *thinking through what the media will want to know*
- *being helpful to the media – including the provision of no less than five on-site TV studios*

*   *   *

In the autumn of 1995, Rose West was tried on ten counts of murder in Winchester. Her husband Fred had hanged himself in prison the previous January. The events that took place in the notorious 25 Cromwell Street in Gloucester had already been the subject of considerable media coverage. The trial was advertised by some of the tabloids as the trial of the century – an extravagant claim for a century that included Nurenburg – but nonetheless it related to a family whose deeds had shocked the world.

[†] Jonathan Street is managing director of Jonathan Street Public Relations Limited, which has clients mainly in the National Health Service.

A large number of public organisations were involved with the West family, and most of them were members of the local Area Child Protection Committee which had responsibility for children at risk of abuse in the county. When the trial began in November it was expected to last six weeks. Rumour was rife, both about the evidence which the prosecution would be putting before the court, and about Rose West's likely plea. In the event she pleaded 'not guilty' to all the charges.

I was invited to help with the handling of the media interest both during and after the trial. I was commissioned by all the public authorities, including police, social services, education, probation, housing, health and the NSPCC. All these bodies had formed a working party to run the media strategy, and they had already made one major decision: that they should carry out their own inquiry into the relationship between the social services and other public bodies and the West family over 30 years.

The Bridge Consultancy, a well-respected independent child care agency, was given the task. All the bodies agreed to open all their files for the whole period to the Bridge's researchers, whose job it was to track all records of contacts between the family and the authorities and find any failings. This decision was important, firstly because it was the right thing to do. Secondly, it was a brave decision by public bodies who had no knowledge of what it might uncover. And, thirdly, it was excellent public relations in that it reduced calls for a public inquiry at the end of the trial.

But timing was crucial. The organisations originally planned to publish the Bridge Report a week after the trial, on the grounds that the dust would have settled by then and the media would be ready for a sober and expert report giving chapter and verse about the Wests. Of course that was mistaken. The only opportunity we had to publish the Bridge Report was on the day that West was convicted. In the event, despite all the work that was needed to trawl all the records, search for the missing ones and then cross-reference each with another, the report was successfully published on the day the trial ended.

And, predictably, at the press conference at which we placed the Bridge Report in the public domain, there were journalists who had early, incomplete, leaked copies of the draft. Had we not published the full report we would have seen 'exclusive' labels on stories about our 'secret report'.

When I first met the public bodies to discuss the media strategy, my understanding of the story was as uninformed, and as wildly inaccurate, as most of the lay public. I had been told for example, 'as a fact', that social services had fostered children with the Wests while they were murdering their own.

The media strategy working party included chief executives of all the relevant organisations and their in-house PROs. The other major piece of work which was already underway was a detailed chronology of the West story from the 1950s to date, recording all the data that was in the public domain, including their first conviction, and briefing material on everything from child care legislation over the years to the homeless persons policy of Gloucester City Council (another of the myths was that 25 Cromwell Street was an official 'lodging house' for runaways, registered with the Council).

Press officers for Gloucester County Council, whose chief executive chaired the working party, had been dealing with enquiries on the West case since the early 1990s, when an attempt to prosecute Fred and Rose for child abuse fell because the children would not give evidence. By the time of the trial the press office had a formidable backlog of enquiries, some of which had been answered and the majority of which now had to wait until the legal process was complete. But it made our job that much easier because we knew the range of enquiries we would be faced with when the trial was over.

Much of the work of the working party was directed at finding answers to all of those questions during the relatively safe *sub judice* period while the trial proceeded. There were attempts from journalists to get answers during this period, but all were met with the firm line that every question would be answered openly and fully once the trial was over. Many journalists had contacts with West family members and with witnesses – this became an issue of public concern when one witness first denied in court and then admitted she had a contract with a newspaper. From our point of view, knowing that some reporters were close to people at the heart of the story meant inevitably that they knew more than we did about some elements of the story.

TV documentaries were already in production. They had to broadcast on the day of the verdict, and they approached us for interviews beforehand with assurances that no material would be used while the trial was ongoing. We said no – but that spokespeople would be available immediately afterwards.

Although the *sub judice* rules applied, which effectively meant disclosure of information that might be evidence in court could be contempt of court, there were certain questions that we *could* answer, and press officers for the various bodies briefed journalists at length about the work of the Children's Departments which preceded Social Services Departments, about processes for child protection then and now, and other process issues. We also took the opportunity to correct false stories before they became myth. The result was better relations with the host of journalists covering the trial – local, national and international – than would have been the case had we used the *sub judice* rule to reject all inquiries.

The working party met twice a week on average throughout the trial – daily at the end. We had regular reports from the court so that we could examine any new evidence that might result in questions after the trial. As the trial proceeded we developed a question and answer document that attempted to answer every question we might be faced with when the trial was over. That document was edited and refined on an almost daily basis, with every statement rigorously challenged and rechecked.

Throughout the trial we were concerned about the outcome. It was always possible that it might result in a 'not guilty' verdict, or even a mistrial. At one point a panic rumour spread amongst journalists covering the hearing that Rose West was about to change her plea to 'guilty'. She did not.

Our strategy from the start was to hold a joint press conference of all the public bodies as soon as possible after the trial ended. We got agreement from the police to make use of their HQ in Winchester, just up the road from the court. We were concerned that key individuals, such as the Chief Constable of Gloucestershire, might not be able to get to the venue at short notice. After all, no one could tell how long the jury would be out. In the event the trial judge made the logistics easy for us by his management of the closing days, and the jury helped by convicting West just before lunch. We had a social services spokesman on Radio 4 within 10 minutes of the verdict, and we held the press conference within one hour.

In preparing for the press conference we had, of course, media-trained key spokespeople, and we had rehearsed and re-rehearsed all the major issues. We knew that the components of the press story on the day would be:

- Rose West and her crimes
- the reaction of the victims, and
- reaction of witnesses and family

There was sufficient copy in the trial and the aftermath, and the public authorities might play a small part in the coverage. But we wanted to be sure we were there, ready to deal with all the issues. Clearly, social workers, police, education and health staff could well be in the dock of public opinion, and this was our sole opportunity. The media would want to know:

- Should the Wests have been spotted earlier?
- Who was at fault?
- What would happen if another murderous family like the Wests began again today?

We had prepared a video news release including footage of the children's homes, the school that one of the children attended, even the school register showing the entry 'gone to London'. This was widely used that day by broadcasting companies, together with the new stills shots of Fred and Rose West in the police press pack.

We gave the media the Bridge Report and our Q&A document, which we had kept as user-friendly as possible – knowing journalists might have only minutes to read it before the press conference began. We had five separate 'studios' for one-to-one interviews. We wanted the media to interview our spokespeople, not self-appointed 'experts' keen to demonstrate how the public authorities should have behaved. It was our story and we wanted control.

In the end, what did we achieve?

- respect (mainly) from the media for giving them all we could
- a major input into the news coverage of the day
- virtually no interference from government departments
- no need for a Minister to defend what was done
- no major inquiry (except the Bridge Report)

We achieved this because we followed a number of basic principles of good crisis management:

- first, start from the fact that the public has a right to know what happened
- then understand the media's needs and pressures
- plan ahead – but be ready with contingency plans if something goes wrong
- get your facts right. Then check them again . . . and again . . .

- make sure your public statements are relevant – to the public
- work with the media as they are – not as you would like them to be
- if you did well – say so. If you failed – admit it
- remember the human being at the heart of every news story
- if it's your story – see it through

The 'Cot Death Poisonings'

Francis Thomas[†]

The way that Boots handled an unfounded scare story about its cot mattresses is a classic example of protecting long-term goodwill by addressing the perception *and not the* reality. *Features of this case study include:*

- *Isolating the issue within the company and minimising the number of involved parties and decision-makers.*
- *Thorough and rapid staff communications – including 14 000 sales assistants.*
- *Focusing on the public perception and not the facts.*
- *Broadening the crisis to an industry issue.*
- *Avoiding confrontation with the critics.*
- *The value of having an existing network of key contacts.*

*　　*　　*

INTRODUCTION

Nothing is more precious than the life of a baby. How should Britain's most respected healthcare company respond, then, when a popular TV programme says it has evidence that one of the company's products could be linked to sudden infant death syndrome or 'cot death'?

That was the situation facing The Boots Company in November 1994. With less than one week to broadcast, Central TV's *The Cook Report* contacted Boots saying that it planned to run a programme on the cause of cot deaths. Their research had centred on a piece of work by Barry Richardson, a chemist from the Channel Islands.

[†] Francis Thomas is group media relations manager, The Boots Company plc.

214

Richardson's theory was that sudden infant death syndrome (SIDS) was caused by antimony, a fire retardant used on cot mattresses, which reacted with sweat and urine to release a toxic gas, thus killing the baby as it slept.

The researchers said that they had tested mattresses sold by the Boots subsidiary Childrens World, no longer owned by The Boots Company, and found that they contained the second highest levels of antimony fire retardant of any on sale. For this reason they wanted to interview someone from Boots about their research.

BACKGROUND

Barry Richardson had first put forward his theory in 1989. At the time there was considerable media focus on cot deaths and the government's Chief Medical Officer set up an investigation to establish the possible causes of SIDS and to make recommendations. The subsequent Turner Report, published in May 1991 dismissed Richardson's theory.

At around the same time, new legislation was being prepared governing foam-filled furniture. In the late eighties a major fire in the furniture department of a large branch of Woolworth's in Manchester resulted in calls for fire retardants to be applied to furniture containing foam. The Boots Company took the view in the light of the Turner Report and the impending new legislation that fire retardants were both safe and necessary in cot mattresses. As the company has always set out to manufacture its products to a higher than expected standard, demanding targets were set for fire protection. Consequently it came as no surprise to anyone at Boots that *The Cook Report* had found high levels of retardant when it came to do its research.

FIRST CONTACT

Researchers from *The Cook Report* first contacted Boots Childrens World subsidiary on Friday 11 November 1994, just six days before the programme was due to go on air.

Compared to The Boots Company as a whole, Childrens World was tiny in size. Boots at the time had almost 3000 stores, of which just 52 were Childrens World. While the business was run by a senior

Boots executive, the PR team was more junior and less experienced than the parent company's. Fortunately, this did not prevent Childrens World's PR manager Karen Salt from immediately recognising the significance of the inquiry and the potential impact on the reputation of the group as a whole. Karen contacted head office and passed the enquiry onto The Boots Company's corporate affairs department.

The Cook Report was not trying to imply that Boots or Childrens World had acted in anything other than good faith. However, the programme clearly needed a major High Street retailer to appear on the programme. The retailer's reaction to the research would be a major factor in 'setting the tone' of the broadcast.

The Cook Report's reputation as a popular, hard-hitting, investigative programme is well established. The Boots Company had two choices: duck down and hope the attention moved on, or to respond. The first option, while tempting, was always second best. It offered the prospect of the ever-damning voice-over saying 'we contacted Boots for their response but they declined to comment'. While this would have been accurate it always tinges the silent party with suspicion, if not guilt. Passing up the opportunity to state the company's case would also have meant a loss of control. What if another retailer of baby products went on the programme and said something which Boots could not agree with? Could a trade body be relied on to respond quickly enough and keep all the members' interests in balance, given that they would have even less time to prepare? In the minds of Boots' corporate affairs department the only question was the nature of the response.

USING THE PRODUCTION WINDOW

Central TV had given Boots four working days, from the time of initial contact to broadcast, to respond. This 'production window' had to be used to maximum effect.

The first step was to isolate the issue within the company. There is always a danger in such situations that too many people, all with good intentions, want to get involved. Not only does this slow down decision-making in a crisis, it also prevents the normal day-to-day business from functioning properly. As Childrens World (CW) was the only Boots subsidiary selling cot mattresses at the time (Boots The Chemists had ceased the sale of large baby furniture four years earlier) and it had been CW that Cook had contacted, it was decided to manage the issue within that business, pulling in resources from across the group as necessary.

Managing Director Ken Piggott had created a small crisis management team consisting of scientists from Boots The Chemists merchandise technical services (MTS) department, The Boots Company's media relations manager Francis Thomas, and operational staff from within Childrens World. Significantly, Piggott chose not to chair the crisis team himself. He gave that task to his marketing director, Mike Batt. The crisis team would debate the issues and Batt would then make recommendations to the managing director. He would consult senior group management including the director of corporate affairs, Alastair Eperon, only as necessary. This allowed Piggott to focus on decision-making without getting bogged down in debate.

The crisis team met for the first time on Monday 14 November, having spent the weekend getting as much information as possible. Arrangements were in place to 'cover' the normal work of the team which allowed everyone to focus on the task in hand without distraction.

TWO-PRONGED APPROACH

Even before the company's response to *The Cook Report* was debated, the crisis team asked – what do we tell our staff? The company knew that up to 18 million people could be watching the programme on Thursday night and store staff would need to be kept informed so that they could give a consistent message to customers the following day.

Existing systems for communicating with stores were supplemented to ensure that *The Cook Report* would come as no surprise to any front-line staff at Childrens World or Boots The Chemists. This meant briefing some 14 000 sales assistants on how to deal with concerned, if not frightened, parents. But what should the response be?

The crisis team began to split into two camps. The scientists were dismissive of Barry Richardson's work and were able to give detailed explanations of why his theories had been rejected by the government's Chief Medical Officer in the past. From a purely academic point of view, it was almost tedious to see the debate resurfacing. In the other camp was the view that, whether the company liked it or not, a popular and established TV programme was going to run with the story in less than four days. There would be no real chance to hold a scientific debate on the programme, and to attempt to do so would put Boots in a very dim light. The recommendation to the managing director therefore was that the company should manage the perception and not get bogged down in trying to support the scientific debate. This would be taken care of elsewhere.

Ken Piggott accepted the recommendation of his crisis team and took the decision to stop selling cot mattresses with immediate effect. This was not an unusual step as it is standard procedure to suspend products from sale when their safety is called into question. However it gave the company a powerful message in order to respond to *The Cook Report*.

COVERING THE GROUND

The next 24 hours was spent briefing store staff. It was decided that the only reliable information which could be given to customers was the existing advice from the Department of Health. Over 400 000 DoH 'Back to Sleep' leaflets were distributed to Boots The Chemists and Childrens World Stores in preparation for the broadcast. The company would not try to set itself up as an expert on cot deaths, the mattress theory was an industry-wide issue and the company was keen that it should avoid the trap of being seen as the only player.

Merchandise technical services (MTS) continued to look at the scientific implications of Richardson's work. The department also used its contacts to make sure that all trade, professional and regulatory bodies were aware of the company's stance. This gave Boots the advantage of leading the debate and resulted in widespread support for the company's position. Corporate Affairs continued to try and get more detailed information about Central TV's research. Some data was supplied and although it was never comprehensive it was sufficient to take their work seriously.

With 48 hours to go before the broadcast, pre-publicity for the programme was escalating. Questions were being asked in the House of Commons and an Early Day Motion was signed by 17 MPs.

In addition to trade associations and regulatory bodies, it was important to open a dialogue with campaigners and cot death pressure groups such as the Foundation for the Study of Infant Deaths.

The most high profile campaigner for SID research in the UK is the TV journalist and presenter, Anne Diamond. Anne herself lost a son, Sebastian, to cot death and had fronted an earlier government publicity campaign. Francis Thomas contacted Anne direct to tell her about the approach from Cook and the line Boots would be taking. The conversation proved to be timely. The same day Miss Diamond was contacted by Roger Cook and was asked to take part in the programme.

THE INTERVIEW

Having agreed to be interviewed by *The Cook Report*, Boots had to decide who should represent the company and where the meeting should take place. The venue was obvious: not a store but the MTS laboratories where Boots spends £5 million per year to ensure the high quality of its products – a plus point that could be made on camera. Who should be interviewed came down to a choice between Ken Piggott, the MD of Childrens World or the Group's media relations manager, Francis Thomas.

While a female spokesperson would have been the best choice on a subject like this in a crisis there was simply no one close enough to the subject with sufficient media experience. As time did not allow for appropriate training it was decided that Francis Thomas should front the interview.

The Cook Report is made to a very tight schedule, so the only time available to do the recording was 7.30 a.m. on the Wednesday before the Thursday broadcast. As luck would have it, Thomas had had years of early morning local radio experience doing travel reports. This was a bigger stage but the early start was like playing on home ground.

The meeting was never confrontational. Before the recording Cook and Thomas discussed the programme and its aims and what the limited research had managed to uncover. While this took place Cook's cameraman set up in an adjacent laboratory assisted by another member of Boots corporate affairs team. The interview itself was very brief. As anticipated by Boots, the programme needed just one sound bite. Cook did not know what to expect but the company confirmed that as of the previous day it had stopped selling cot mattresses pending detailed findings of the new research which *The Cook Report* claimed to have in its possession.

Following the interview Boots repeated its request for a complete copy of the programme's research and asked if the company could cooperate in any further work. Despite confirming the offer in writing *The Cook Report* never responded.

THE AFTERMATH

Reaction to the interview came faster than Boots had expected. By 10.00 a.m. Central TV had put out a news release saying Boots had stopped selling cot mattresses in response to *The Cook Report*. For the next 48 hours Boots was bombarded with press enquiries from journalists around the world.

Boots, however, was still keen to stress that this was an industry-wide issue, the decision to withdraw the mattresses was a standard safety procedure and, no, Boots was not claiming to be an expert on sudden infant death syndrome. Every caller was given the same response. To avoid the risk of Boots appearing as the 'isolated victim', all other requests for TV and radio interviews were turned down. The Cook interview was already being played on all the ITN bulletins. However, most broadcasters accepted the company's reasons for declining further TV and radio offers.

THE DAY OF THE BROADCAST

All the morning media on the day of the broadcast led with Boots' decision to stop selling cot mattresses; some of the tabloids gave two to three pages of coverage. All the commentators supported Boots' decision citing it as an example of strong leadership. While this gave the company more than a degree of comfort, it also meant that *The Cook Report* would get a very large audience that night.

The Cook Report had set up a helpline to deal with calls after the programme. Boots had also anticipated the need for its own help-lines, one for Boots The Chemists and one for Childrens World. The response was phenomenal. In the first 48 hours after the broadcast Boots received over 2000 calls.

Because the company had no prior knowledge of what else was in the programme, the crisis team reassembled to watch the broadcast. The team was ready to respond to the media, the helpline or other interested parties if required. This did not prove necessary. The interview on the programme and the management of the media had positioned Boots in a favourable light throughout. The task in the days ahead would be to take care of customers as they came into stores, address the logistical issues to find safe antimony-free cot mattresses and monitor official government guidelines.

THE GOVERNMENT RESPONSE

Boots did not have to wait long for a government response. The day after *The Cook Report* the Chief Medical Officer, Dr Kenneth Calman, announced he was setting up a second government enquiry into cot deaths to be headed by Lady Limmerick. This announcement had the press calling Boots again for a reaction. Boots' response was to welcome the announcement, repeating that only a proper government inquiry could give the definitive answer to the likely causes of cot deaths. To draw an exhausting seven days to a close, Boots issued its statement at 7.00 p.m. on Friday closing with the remark that the company would not be making any further comment on cot deaths.

Thirteen months and eleven days after the first *Cook Report* on cot deaths the Limmerick Committee announced its initial findings. In line with a number of other reports, Limmerick dismissed Barry Richardson's theory. The debate as to the cause of cot death continues.

CONCLUSION

The Boots Company never pretended to be an expert on the causes of cot death but found itself at the centre of worldwide media attention. In dealing with what some would describe as a crisis, Boots made some crucial decisions early on and remained consistent. These are summarised below:

- The management of the business and the management of the crisis were separated.
- Clear accountability rested with one person, the managing director of Childrens World, Ken Piggott.
- All necessary resources were made available to the crisis team.
- Internal communications were made as important as external media communications to ensure consistency.

- The company recognised the limited opportunity and chose to address perceptions, not scientific argument.
- Boots used its extensive network of contacts to ensure that all interested parties, trade associations, pressure groups and so on were kept informed of the company's activities throughout.

The Boots Company has a unique position as a retailer and is Britain's best known healthcare company. It enjoys a strong relationship with its customers built on trust. Unexpected and emotive media attention could easily have undermined 120 years of reputation building. However, through careful handling the company turned a potentially damaging situation into one that enhanced its position.

The Eurotunnel Fire

Liz Simpson and John D. Noulton

The fire in the Channel tunnel in November 1996 was one of the most publicised of all crises in which there was no loss of human life.

This chapter documents the frank account of this particularly difficult crisis by Eurotunnel's Public Affairs Director, John D. Noulton, interviewed for this book by author and journalist Liz Simpson. Key features include:

- *The sheer volume of work in a major crisis – more than 1000 calls from the media alone;*
- *The need for a quick version of the crisis plan;*
- *The need to train people to act instinctively and not rely on a manual;*
- *The problems that the emergency services can create when they have control of the communication channels;*
- *The cross-cultural communication problems encountered between subsidiaries, further complicated by their communications with the media.*

*   *   *

LS   Had Eurotunnel ever envisaged a fire happening in the tunnel? And, if so, what sort of training procedures had taken place prior to the tunnel being opened?

JN   Yes, we had and were the first transport company ever to do a safety case – that's to say a thorough-going risk analysis of the whole process. Fires in the tunnel were seen to be the most serious kind of problem we'd have so the system has been designed to cope with that. Our research uncovered that the

223

incidence of fires in stationary vehicles is surprisingly high – you get fires in cars in car parks, for example, with their engines switched off. So we decided that was probably the highest-risk type of event and therefore the system ought to be robust enough to cope with it.

The principal measures we took were directed at saving lives rather than saving the infrastructure, which is why we've got a service tunnel through the middle of the two running tunnels. That's what happened on the night of 18 November. We got all the people out. The big problem was what happened next – the fire continued to burn and it burned for many hours.

LS   Your subsequent news release alluded to 'avoidable delay in executing some of the procedures'. What were the main causes of these?

JN   It was the complexity and clumsiness of some of the procedures. We relied a lot on hi-tech equipment, all of which worked but the speed of decision required of the people in charge of the incident was too much for them. We are talking about a matter of minutes, not hours, here but they could have made a difference in other circumstances so we have completely rejigged everything. You've got to remember that the tunnel is built on what would happen in theory. As a result, the procedures are complex to operate and voluminous.

So what we have had to do is simplify the actions that people have to take, weed out the superfluous stuff and just give them half a dozen things they have to do quickly – they can worry about the rest later on. Secondly, and this is more important, we need to train people to react instinctively rather than have to go to the book to find out what to do. We fell into the trap of planning this on the assumption that we were a railway and therefore old-fashioned railway procedures were the appropriate way to go forward when we should have perhaps looked at the airlines' experience. You don't have time to look up books when you have got an airline incident, you simply have to drill it into people that this is the way they have to behave. I suspect we underestimated the effect of anxiety, pressure, panic from people and now we've completely departed from the old ways and are actually building simulators of the control centre and of the tunnel so that people can be trained under real-life conditions.

LS Having said that fire was going to be the most serious scenario that the tunnel would ever experience, does it surprise you that simulation and that type of training had not been put into effect before the tunnel was opened?

JN I remember in the early days being in wagons full of smoke in order to carry out tests. But we tested the passengers rather the crew. Yet it was the crew that weren't equipped to deal with this incident as well as they might have been. They performed superbly – the train crew got the people out – but it's the little things you learn in these instances that really can trip you up in the future. We are a bilingual company and our crews are bilingual but in a panic situation you tend to lose the ability to speak in the other language with reasonable fluency and so the kind of detail we're now looking at is that simple commands actually have to be drilled into people in both languages rather than just trying to teach them the other language in conversational terms.

LS The internal inquiry and the investigations of the experts, including specialists from outside the company – how soon were these under way?

JN We started our own inquiry the following day while memories were fresh, to go and interview the people involved. The first thing we did was get hold of everybody involved, not just our people, but the drivers as well and question them. Then we downloaded all the software systems. The train has a black box – like on an aircraft – and the control centre records everything that happens, all the data and voice communications were analysed and we had a complete picture straight away of what had happened. We had records, for example, of which fire alarms went off – it was all there, a total picture which was put together only a few days after the incident. Then, as a clear picture began to emerge we set about looking at particular aspects of the incident to see how things could be changed in the future – for example, the way in which we treat fire alarms was looked at in depth and changed.

LS In what way?

JN In a system like this, where you've got fire alarms everywhere of various different kinds, you get spurious alarms all the time because they're set to a certain level of sensitivity and almost anything can set them off. When the tunnel was first opened we had fire alarms going off all the time, so we had this system of confirmed and unconfirmed alarms. If we just had one smoke alarm go off it was treated as an unconfirmed alarm and no immediate action was taken; you became vigilant but you didn't do anything.

In the early days when the tunnel was still full of construction dust it was a wise thing to do. Only if you got two different types of alarm – a smoke alarm and an optical or an ionic – going off did you regard it as a confirmed alarm. This meant that the train actually set off four optical smoke alarms before it became a confirmed fire. It didn't make an awful lot of practical difference on the night but we've come to the conclusion that the moment we get a single alarm we'll regard it as a confirmed alarm and start to configure the tunnel as though it was a real fire.

The most important procedural change is to do with the previous drive-through policy. Every railway in the world as far as we know has a clear policy that when it has a train on fire in a tunnel or on a bridge you get to the other side before stopping the train, and deal with it from the other side. That was always our policy and is still our policy for the Eurostars and the tourist shuttle which are enclosed. With the freight shuttle we've decided that we don't continue with that policy – if we get a confirmed fire we stop the train, get the people out, and then we'll worry about the fire. Again, it's to do with speed of reaction.

LS Let's now look at how media exposure of the fire was handled by Eurotunnel – how quickly was someone from the company on the TV screens or heard on radio giving a comment and what kind of comment was that?

JN Pretty well instantly. It was a variety of people – you've got to understand we're a bi-national company and therefore we had press facilities on both sides so it was initially press officers in Britain and France. Subsequently it was senior managers called in who were on duty – called in for that purpose.

LS How senior were these managers and were they a 'face' of Eurotunnel?

JN Yes, the managing director of Le Shuttle was one of those called in and our chief operations officer – Alain Bertrand in France – was as senior as you could get, bar the chairman.

LS   What sort of messages were they putting across?

JN   They were confirming that there was a fire and that everyone had got out – and that was all right up to then. Having done a media analysis we know that in the first twenty-four hours the coverage we got was quite neutral, so we think we did quite well in very difficult circumstances. Remember that we had two sides, Britain and France, responding to their national and international media. We had something like a thousand telephone calls from the press, there wasn't much opportunity to coordinate the message that was going out – there weren't enough people around to ring up the other side and say 'we have just said this'. But they did a first class job in just handling the messages.

The main problem we had was in estimating the gravity of the incident, because we didn't have our own people in there. The fire brigade were coordinating it and sending us messages. We didn't have a very clear picture of how serious the incident was until some hours later and our mistake that night was to be a bit optimistic about when we might resume our business. I firmly believe that when you're handling a crisis like this you have to set the story – you've got to be authoritative, you've got to be believed. In the days that followed our credibility was damaged because of our over-optimism and the negative slice of media coverage grew in the following days. It wasn't until about the fourth or fifth day that we started to recover credibility and that was what let us down, really.

Eurotunnel is in a unique position – we are very interesting to the media. I've been involved with the media for about eight years and Eurotunnel has been in the newspapers every day. I don't have to get out of bed to get my company's name in the press – in fact, some days I wished I'd stayed in bed – that's a fact of life. We are novel, a lot of people use us – 13 million people last year. We are not all that popular in some quarters so people are ready to knock us down but as I say, they handled it very well. I thought they did a brilliant job but for that streak of optimism and the fact that we had too many spokespeople. We soon put a stop to that and had just two spokesmen.

LS   And who were they?

JN   Me and my colleague in France, Dominique Maire. I did all the media handling. If the media wanted to talk to the chairman they spoke to him and we coordinated that but no-one else was permitted to talk to the press by general direction of the chairman, with the exception of wheeling out somebody who's an expert on something to do with a technical question. But it was very tightly controlled from then on in a way that we hadn't managed to do in the second forty-eight hours of this incident.

LS Given that there had been this immense exposure for Eurotunnel in the media, had you not considered some form of crisis management techniques in terms of training people in how to handle the media prior to this event?

JN It was all planned and practised – all written down prior to this incident.

LS But you still had so many people all giving uncoordinated messages?

JN Yes. There was a number of reasons for that. Firstly, we had physical arrangements for entertaining the press and dealing with them all planned and these worked fine. We had always assumed that in the event of an incident there would be massive interest and we would need to draft in extra people to deal with the issue.

None of the people we put up made a bad job of it but I think that we had one example involving one of the broadsheets whose journalists asked somebody in the London office, in the Folkestone office, at Calais and in the Paris office the same question. They got 90 per cent the same answer but with the other 10 per cent were able to spin it into confusion. I guess that's something we have taken away from this – you need much tighter control of what messages you're putting out than we had actually foreseen. The formal statements we'd issued were fine because they were in both languages; they were pored over to make sure they were accurate but just by the inflection of someone's voice you can give a slightly different message.

Remember we've got a variety of audiences we are talking to ... we are talking to the investors, we are talking to our customers, and with the customer who wants to know whether his ticket for next week is going to be all right. You don't say to him, no you've had it: you sort of keep him jollying along. To our staff – who were destroyed by this – you have got to cheer them up a bit, motivate them – to our safety regulators you've got to put across a certain message that everything worked okay. I guess the subtlety of these different messages can get lost when you have got this avalanche of questions constantly coming in.

LS One of the examples used as the best way of handling a crisis was what Mike Bishop did after the British Midland air crash. . .

JN . . . he's my idol. . . .

LS . . . which is go straight out there, admit that he didn't know what was going on but reassure people he was there to find out and they appear not to have unduly suffered from that. How do you feel Eurotunnel could learn from something like that and how would you have liked it to be handled ideally?

JN Well I think we did learn from him and I think we did an awful lot of that. We did come clean about it, we said what had happened and admitted that we made mistakes and we were going to put it right. I think where we are different from Michael Bishop is that we have got a lot of enemies. We were born in controversy and there are some politically motivated people out there who've got an axe to grind and access to the media. Bishop didn't have that, he had immediate media sympathy whereas we didn't.

LS Having said that, people died in the British Midland crash. . . you had the advantage that nobody died in your incident. To have handled that so well and to get that sympathy when there were fatalities is quite phenomenal, isn't it?

JN Yes. I think that you go back to an even worse disaster, the *Herald of Free Enterprise*. Initially they handled it badly but once they had got to grips with it they got a lot of sympathy and I don't think it's necessarily the gravity of the incident that influences how well you come out of it. You can get a bad image from doing something quite innocuous – remember the Hoover fiasco and the free flights – nobody was hurt or injured by that but that was a PR disaster. I think with us we are a bit of an Aunt Sally.

LS If you could take yourself back to the night in question, how would you handle that scenario again in an ideal situation?

JN I would have used a lot less optimism in the pronouncements. We had another fire two years ago, prior to this one – the back end of 1994, on possibly the most unpropitious day that you could imagine, the day we were awaiting the operating certificate for our tourist shuttle. Prior to that we had been running the shuttle with invited customers – our shareholders and others – as a kind of introductory service to demonstrate that it was safe.

During loading of one of these shuttles a car caught fire, still in the platform area. We immediately sealed off the wagon, got everybody out and most people didn't even know there was a car on fire. We decided to take the initiative with the press and issued a statement that there had been this fire, all contained, end of problem – everything worked. Because the train was on the surface there was much greater certainty about information. Even so, we did take a bit of a chance saying that it was all over.

That story was dead – totally dead – within three hours and I was able to say at the end of it 'well, it's come at a particularly unfortunate day because we were expecting our operating certificate today – clearly there will be a pause while the safety people look to see how we handled it, to see how it's dealt with. But assuming they give us the tick you can be sure that everything's all right.' Everybody yawned and went away – the story didn't even get into the next day's press.

LS Do you not think it's because it was on the platform as opposed to in the tunnel?

JN No, I think it was the way we handled the information. Because that day, when we were waiting for the operating certificate, it could have been a huge disaster story and ruined Eurotunnel.

LS So what made the difference?

JN I think the difference was wholly in the way we handled the message. We didn't handle the fire any more cleverly than we had that particular night.

LS If we do go back to the November 1996 fire, how do you feel you could have better handled the coordination with the fire brigade?

JN   That is a particular problem with us. We are required – and want anyway – to have our own permanent first-line response team on site. So we have two fire stations – one on either side – that are paid for by us. These people are fire brigade personnel under contract to us. When there's a big fire we call in a second-line response team drawn from fire brigades outside. They are under the control of the fire brigades, not under our control, and at that point the first-line response teams meld back into the second-line response team and come under the management of the control of the fire brigade. So there's a kind of muddled management line we haven't got right yet. Secondly, of course they are bi-national, so they are two camps, not one.

There's not a single first-line response team under managerial control of Eurotunnel which is one of the problems we are currently addressing. One solution – and I don't know if we'll ever get there – is that we have our own single, in-house fire brigade under single control which would do all the first-line response things. Then, when the second-line response team came in it would liaise but then get out the way and let the firemen get on with it. That's the way I think it should go.

LS   And the good news. . .?

JN   We've carried out polls of our customers and they remain satisfied with our safety. Some 85 per cent of them have confidence in the system and 80 per cent of them prefer us to the ferries.

Crisis Checklists

1 PREPARATION

- **What** crises could hit us?
- Who are the **audiences**?
- How do we **communicate** with them?
- What are the **messages**?
- Who will form the **crisis team**?
- What are the **resources and facilities**?
- Are the crisis team and spokespeople **trained**?
- Do we know how to handle **stress?**
- What **crisis manual** do we need?
- Does it **work**?
- Have we built **bridges** with our audiences?

2 AUDIENCES

Here are some headings for most types of crisis audience; you will need to break them down further to suit your particular company and operations. For example, 'regulatory bodies' can include the Rivers Authority, the Health and Safety Executive, your own industry's regulatory bodies, the Environmental Health Department – and so on.

And there may be other audiences not listed who are relevant to your organisation. Have a 'brainstorm' session to identify them.

- **Media** — national   . . . press, general and specialist
                        . . . TV
                        . . . radio
              local   . . . press, general and industrial
                        . . . TV
                        . . . radio
              trade and/or professional media
- **Official** — government . . . relevant department(s)
                        . . . MPs (especially local)
                        . . . MEPs
              authorities . . . regulatory bodies
                        . . . local councils

- **Support**   . . . police
                       . . . fire
                       . . . hospital
                       . . . ambulance

Remember that the support services have their own PR teams, who are often very professional – and who may also have a vested interest in deflecting publicity which may be unfavourable to them.

- **Corporate** – employees
  – group: head office; parent company etc.
  – trade unions
  – lawyers
  – insurers
  – shareholders, investing institutions and City
- **Business** – customers
  – competitors
  – suppliers
  – trade and professional associations
- **Other** – relatives
  – local community
  – environmental and pressure groups

The 'general public' is also an audience, but it can usually only be reached via your communications with other target audiences (for example the media).

3 THE CRISIS ROOM

Some big companies have dedicated crisis centres with every conceivable resource. For most companies this is an unrealistic investment but you should at least establish *something*. The more you have in place the easier it is to get on with managing the crisis without constant distractions about inadequate phone lines, people not knowing where to go, looking for something to record the radio news in five minutes' time – and so on. Some ideas:

- venue: conference room? nearby hotel? dedicated facilities
- alternative venue (in case of for example, fire, explosion)
- controlled entry
- adequate room and furniture for the crisis team and others

- whiteboard/flip charts (and pens that work)
- a number of telephones, including at least one with an ex-directory outgoing line
- hotline facility
- mobile communicators and cellphones
- fax, E-mail and Internet
- TV and radio monitoring equipment (plus, for example, Reuters)
- TV/radio 'studio' facilities – to rehearse interviews
- ISDN line for videoconferencing and transmitting video; footage and interviews
- videoconferencing
- stationery
- access to mass mailing
- a means of logging all actions
- services (press/broadcast monitoring: printing, distribution, etc.)
- if feasible, a means of recording telephone conversations
- refreshments
- nearby or on-site sleeping facilities
- a separate and nearby venue for hosting the press.

4 INDIVIDUAL KIT

What kit is available to individual members of the crisis team – especially, for example, press officers out in the field? Some suggestions:

- crisis manual and background briefs
- relevant 'phone numbers
- press list
- mobile telephone
- mobile communicator
- pager
- phonecards
- stationery
- tape recorder/dictater, plus tapes
- radio
- pocket TV
- portable alarm clock
- spare batteries

- laptop PC
- cash
- credit cards

And a big briefcase!

5   BACKGROUND BRIEFS

Subjects for pre-prepared briefing notes for the media and other audiences include:

- company details: size, products, operations, history, financial figures, numbers employed and so on
- manufacturing processes and/or operating methods
- product details
- chemicals and/or materials – what they are, what they do, why they are used, etc.
- safety and quality: track record, investment, how the company achieves high standards
- location: plant history and details
- anything else relevant to your company?

Produce them in such a way that a busy journalist can quickly assimilate the important information (for example, one page bullet-point summaries).

Is it feasible to produce camera-ready artwork – of, for example, processes, organisation charts and so on – in other words, something to help fill their pages graphically with your own material?

6   STAFF INSTRUCTION FOR MEDIA CALLS

All staff should receive regular reminders of what to do if they receive a call from the press and they are not authorised or trained to handle it. The key points are:

- Don't give any details – not even your name. Don't be drawn into conversation.
- Assure the journalist that you will pass the enquiry on at once to an informed spokesperson who will call them back at once.

- Establish – who is calling?
  - job or title?
  - which publication or programme?
  - phone number?
  - what do they want to know?
- Pass the enquiry and details on immediately to an authorised person on the list (which is attached to this instruction). Check up with that person to ensure that they have indeed contacted the journalist.
- Be polite at all times.

Try if possible to back the instruction with direct briefing or training.

7 CRISIS MANUAL

Try not to produce a manual in isolation; stand-alone instruction books seldom work. Your crisis manual should be a supporting document to the meetings, brainstorming, crisis-awareness training and simulations. Every organisation will have different requirements. The following is an example of the contents of a typical manual:

- *Introduction*: brief description of what is expected of team members in a crisis; corporate philosophy; how to use the manual.
- *Procedures*: brief summary of company's crisis procedures.
- *Crisis team*: names; titles; brief descriptions of their responsibilities; day and 24-hour phone numbers of team and services (legal, PR and so on); details of stand-ins if on holiday or ill.
- *Audiences*: list of audiences and how to contact them; addresses and telephone numbers. Emergency numbers for, for example, regulatory bodies, employee communications, lawyers, MPs etc.
- *Messages*: reminder list of the types of messages to communicate in a crisis.
- *Resources*: location of crisis room and so on. What resources there are, where they are kept and how to use them. Instructions in manual or in crisis room on how to operate fax and communicators, how to activate the freephone helpline etc.
- *Media*: reminder checklists on handling media and preparing for and succeeding with interviews.
- *Background briefs*: copies of the briefing notes on company, products, processes and so on. Useful technical data.

- *Useful addresses and numbers*: for example press monitoring service; caterers.
- *Other*: any other useful and important information, for example list of frequencies of radio programmes for tuning in and recording in a hurry.

8   HANDLING THE CRISIS

Here is a list of the key ingredients:

- holding action and holding statement
- assemble and isolate crisis team
- assess the situation (see strategy checklist)
- decide on the strategy
- identify the audiences
- decide on the messages
- prepare and effect a plan
- brief relevant people
- centralise information
- uderstand your audiences
- give information
- give reassurance
- resist combat
- be flexible
- think long-term

9   CRISIS STRATEGY

These are the questions to ask yourselves when assessing the crisis and formulating your strategic approach:

- *What is the crisis?*   What precisely has happened? Do we all have the same understanding of the situation?
- *Is there a more fundamental problem?*   Could this be the tip of an iceberg? Could this incident call into question the reputation of the whole company; the group; the industry? Does it call our safety standards into question? Could this become a broader issue? And so on.

- *Is there more to come?* Are there likely to be more of these explosions; product tamperings, etc.
- *What is the worst case?* Prepare for the worst case scenario.
- *What are the audiences likely to make of it?* Step outside the crisis and imagine what it is like looking in from the outside – for the worried local community; the staff who are only just learning what's happened; the other audiences – especially the media? What would you make of it if you were in their position? Can you ask them? Have you thought, for example, of sounding out one or two journalists to see if they regard it as a minor story or if the editor is holding the front page?
- *What are the likely time scales?* First: How long before the various media – daily, weekly, trade, TV, radio – start reporting the story? Is our holding statement all they will have to publish or do we have a little time to develop a more detailed brief for them? And by when do we need to have established communication with the employees; the regulatory bodies; group headquarters; the insurers?

  Second: how long is the crisis likely to run – the initial burst and then all the follow-ups; litigation; clean-up campaign; dealing with pressure groups and so on?
- *What is actually at stake?* If the worst comes to the worst, what will we actually lose? How loyal are our suppliers, our customers, our shareholders – and will they stay with us in bad times? How long are people's memories? Are we panicking unnecessarily? But don't let a positive answer to this question be an excuse for inaction.
- *Can we involve any allies?* Would our messages come better and more credibly, for example, from our trade association? An independent research department? If the MP praised us last month for being a good member of the community is he or she prepared to say it again now? The HSE gave us a clean bill of health recently – can we persuade them to put their heads above the parapet on our behalf?
- *Who else is involved?* Another party to the accident? Slack regulatory bodies? Suppliers? An extortionist? Vandals? This could affect your strategy. It might be that if you're the first to speak you will automatically be seen as the culprit. Or you may have an opportunity to focus your anger – and that of the public – on some other 'culprit'.

- *Can the crisis be contained?* In a broad sense: how can our actions help to contain the speculation and publicity as quickly as possible and stop the crisis running out of control? In a narrow sense: can the crisis be identified with a single plant, a subsidiary or a product? If you only refer to, say, the geographical name of the plant and give all spokespeople a title relating only to the subsidiary, you can sometimes keep the name of the parent company and/or its other products out of the picture – or at least reduce the damage.

10   MESSAGES

Consider communicating some or all of these core messages in a crisis:

- Details: as much information about the incident as possible.
- Human face: 'We care' – sympathy, concern, understanding; maybe regret; possibly even 'Sorry'.
- Reassurance: no further danger; not harmful; what to do if worried; one in a million; and so on.
- What we are doing about it: especially a thorough (independent) investigation.
- Track record: and the good your company/product does.
- Further information: when and where further information will be available. Numbers for information hotline or helpline.
- Background briefs: details of products, processes, chemicals, company and so on.

Wherever possible give details and practical examples. If you simply say 'Our safety standards are among the highest in the industry' it lacks credibility. But if you describe how often the HSE team examines the plant in minute detail; how much you invest in safety; how many people; some examples of what they do to ensure safety – then people will start to believe you.

This principle applies to all messages (for example, reassurance; track record) where your own side of things is not going to be taken for granted.

Index